(handwritten) To Andrew,
September 2019

Are We There Yet?

THE DIGITAL TRANSFORMATION
OF GOVERNMENT AND THE
PUBLIC SECTOR IN AUSTRALIA

Martin Stewart-Weeks
Simon Cooper

LONGUEVILLE
MEDIA

LONGUEVILLE

MEDIA

First published 2019
for Martin Stewart-Weeks and Simon Cooper
by
Longueville Media Pty Ltd
PO Box 205 Haberfield NSW 2045 Australia
www.longmedia.com.au
info@longmedia.com.au
T. +61 410 519 685

Editing by Siobhan Gallagher, Longueville Media
Cover design by Nina Nielsen, Logueville Media
Printed and bound in Australia.

First published in 2019.

Print ISBN: 978-0-6485107-3-4
eBook ISBN: 978-0-6485107-6-5

So much has been written about the nature of digital transformation over the years that the phrase has started to lose all meaning. No wonder people get confused about it. No wonder so many organisations fail to understand it, and ultimately fail to make it happen.

It's time to cut through the waffle and set it out clearly: digital transformation is the act of radically changing how your organisation works, so that it can survive and thrive in the internet era.

Mike Bracken,
former head of the UK's Government Digital Service

'...a valuable and very timely addition to Australian thinking and practice about digital transformation in government and the public sector from two "reflective practitioners" with a lively and relevant mix of theory, strategy, and practical operational experience...'

– Dr Sarah Pearson

Chief Innovation Officer and Chief Scientist, Australian Department of Foreign Affairs and Trade

'I've read a lot about the potential impact of digital technology on public services – how it can enhance productivity, improve citizen service, and require new workplace skills. But this is the first book to persuade me that the power of digital, properly conceived, really can transform the nature of democratic governance.'

– Professor Peter Shergold AC

Chancellor, Western Sydney University, and former Secretary, Department of Prime Minister and Cabinet

'In decades to come, governments will be digital to their core, providing enormous benefits for everyone. Stewart-Weeks and Cooper have used this book to open our eyes to the opportunity and challenges of the transformation ahead. Far from being daunted, we should be excited by the vision that they paint.'

– Robert Hillard

Chief Strategy & Innovation Officer, Deloitte and author of *Information-Driven Business: How to Manage Data* and *Information for Maximum Advantage*

'This is an unusually thoughtful and wide-ranging book on a subject that's too often treated with shrill hype or hysterical fear. It rightly acknowledges just how revolutionary digital technologies can be. But it's also clear that part of their value is to help governments change in ways they should be doing anyway: becoming more open, responsive and problem-solving, and throwing away the stiff hierarchical cultures that long ago lost whatever justifications they may once have had.'

– **Dr Geoff Mulgan**
CEO, National Endowment for Science, Technology and the Arts (Nesta), former head of Strategy, UK Cabinet Office and author of *Big Mind: How Collective Intelligence Can Change Our World* and *Good and Bad Power: The Ideals and Betrayals of Government*

'*Are We There Yet?* lucidly diagnoses how digital technologies, including artificial intelligence and big data, are transforming the role of the public servant and the project of governance itself. In this timely provocation, Stewart-Weeks and Cooper describe the important shift from power to problem-solving and explain how to harness digital transformation to make government work better for all of us.'

– **Beth Noveck**
Author of *Wiki Government*, former Deputy Chief Technology Officer in the Obama White House, Professor in Technology, Culture & Society, New York University and Chief Innovation Officer for New Jersey

Contents

Chapter 2   65
A Changing World

List of Figures

Foreword

Professor Peter Shergold AC

I find it easy to get excited about the convergence of technologies that presage a "fourth industrial revolution". Equally, I find it hard not to become discouraged by the apparent decline of trust in the institutions of democratic governance. And I become increasingly and publicly frustrated by the fact that those two social forces cannot be brought together, the first helping to address the second.

Why is it, I have wondered, that billions of people can stay connected through pervasive mobile devices, access vast amounts of newly created data, be assisted by capable machines and robotic process automation, and yet find it ever harder to talk to each other about how to find solutions to the wicked problems of human existence?[1]

A digital communications technology that seems ideally suited to the creation of more civil and harmonious public discourse and has the potential to allow many more citizens to participate in decision-making, too often seems to hinder rather than help. The instancy of social media too often generates the "fake news" and creates tribal groupings that can easily give rise to populism, hate and authoritarianism.

That's why I was pleased to read this unusual book.

It's a book about the digital transformation of government that isn't primarily about digital transformation. It's a book which is willing to address the bigger questions.

It's written by two reflective practitioners whose perspectives and experience are different but complementary. It's a brief history of a story in which half of the plot – perhaps the most interesting half – is generally missing.

The book starts the exploration of the digital transformation project not with technology but with an exploration of government's underlying "theory of the business". It examines some of the big trends and shifts in politics, economics and society which form the context, and create the conditions, for the work of transformation itself.

It's a distinctively Australian story, but its significance can only be understood in a global context of change and innovation. It's a story that in many important ways has no end and is changing almost as fast as the narrative itself. It's a tale fuelled primarily by technology's intense and hectic metabolism.

The book suggests that digital transformation is altering the way government and the public sector develop policy, impose regulation and design and deliver services. The technology is changing both the work of the public sector and the way the public sector works. It has the capacity to measurably lift levels of integrity and legitimacy in the role, purpose and function of government and the public sector.

On the face of it, you could argue there isn't a need for a book like this. After all, there is plenty of evidence that jurisdictions around the world, not the least in Australia, are already busy working on digital transformation agendas of more or less scale, scope and significance. For example:

- the emerging work that is being done on artificial intelligence and machine learning in government
- the proliferation work of "digital transformation" labs, groups and offices including Australia's Digital Transformation Agency (DTA)
- the bold changes to the structure and performance of government following the recent state election in New South Wales (NSW), that places digital at the heart of a whole-of-government customer service strategy
- the daily litany of breathless stories I receive in my emails and text messages reporting the latest and greatest implementation of some very clever new digital capability for better services and improved quality of public life.

So why this book and why now?

The first reason is that although there is plenty being written and said about digital transformation, there is a need for a consolidation of what we're learning, what we've achieved and how we might energise and direct the next phase.

Frankly, there is presently a wide gulf between rhetoric and reality: there's an awful lot of talking but too little walking.

A second reason is the view that the story of digital transformation in Australia, and globally, is missing half the plot. And therein lies a profound problem.

For the last 20 or 30 years, we've construed digital transformation largely in instrumentalist and transactional terms.

The watchwords have been cost, speed and convenience. The message has focused on making the traditional practices and processes of public administration easier to navigate, a little less clunky and confusing for the users of services and, often as a central motivation, making government much cheaper. I worry that the digital government agenda has been overly influenced by the desire to save money and time, with only a cursory genuflection to how it can improve "consumer directed care", "cross-sectoral collaboration", "citizen engagement" and "public value".

Too often, the impression has been that the digital piece has been happening in isolation, invariably tech-led by high-powered digital teams being clever and busy in their organisational enclaves. Meanwhile the business of government carries on with incremental improvement around the edges.

Much less time and effort has been spent figuring out how digital shapes some of the core assumptions about the context, mission and capabilities that support a "theory of the business" for democratic governance.

The time is well overdue for a major rethink about those presuppositions. Many are being severely tested and, often, found wanting in the digital and connected world. There are big questions emerging about the role and purpose of government in the digital age that need to be tackled.

Even more significant is the failure properly to frame the transformation venture. The manner in which digital technology is talked about simply isn't keeping up with its gradual shift from the margins to the mainstream of public administration and government.

It is true that the digital agenda is moving from the exotic periphery to the serious centre of public administration. That means it's hard to undertake a serious role in the public service, or to pretend to a public work career of any substance, without a pretty good working knowledge of digital tools, platforms and practices.

But the problem is that many government executives find themselves being asked to make a transformation when its contours and potential are poorly understood.

This book is an attempt to fill that gap for those working in and with the public sector.

The authors hope to use those same tools and platforms they describe in the book to engage in something of a "permanent beta" approach to their work. They intend to invite others to join the process of testing, changing and then testing again many of the framework's assumptions and implications in the light of experience.

As questions emerge about the best way to prosecute the digital transformation of government at national, state and local level, as the work of the independent review of the Australian public service comes to its conclusions; and as new governments take their place in Canberra and Sydney, this book is timely.

It invites anyone interested in how Australia can improve the quality and impact of its public work to think boldly about what the digital transformation of democratic governance could mean for our shared ambitions for prosperity, sustainability and inclusion. It encourages all of us to think big.

Professor Peter Shergold AC
Former Secretary, Department of Prime Minister & Cabinet
Chair, NSW Public Service Commission Advisory Board
Chancellor, Western Sydney University

About the Authors

MARTIN STEWART-WEEKS is an independent advisor, writer, and facilitator who works at the intersection of public sector policy and management, technology, and innovation. He has held roles as a Ministerial chief of staff and policy advisor, worked in the Commonwealth and NSW public service, led the Asia-Pacific team in the global public sector practice of Cisco's strategy and innovation group, and helped to design and implement public sector strategy and social impact programs for Deloitte and PwC.

He is a regular writer, speaker, and blogger (http://www.publicpurpose.com.au/) on digital government, policy reform, and public sector management. In 2014 he published a book, co-authored with former Australian Finance Minister Lindsay Tanner, *Changing Shape: Institutions for a digital era*. Martin holds advisory roles for the NSW and Australian Governments and is also on the Board of The Australian Centre for Social Innovation and the Centre for Policy Development.

From 2016, Martin has chaired the Digital Government Advisory Panel (DGAP) for the former NSW Department of Finance, Services and Innovation. He is also chair of the Expert Advisory Group for the federal government's Welfare Payments Infrastructure Transformation Program (WPIT) which is being implemented by the former Department of Human Services (now Services Australia).

Follow him on Twitter @martinsw.

SIMON COOPER is a Director who specialises in the digital transformation of government and customer service strategy for a Big Four consultancy. Since moving to Australia, he has advised and delivered digital transformation with over 20 government agencies and departments across the country. He has also worked with a number of Australian companies.

Previously he spent a decade as a public servant, including as a Head of Digital and Data in the Home Office, in a Ministerial Strategy Unit, and as a

Regional Operational Assistant Director covering visa and immigration operations in Europe, North Africa and the Middle East in the UK. Simon holds an MBA with distinction from Cass Business School at the City University of London, where he specialised in digital change in government. Awards received include a scholarship for his MBA and an Innovation Prize from the Cabinet Secretary.

Follow him on Twitter @simoncooper74.

The authors in a Sydney café, April 2019, Simon Cooper (L)
and Martin Stewart-Weeks

Acknowledgements

We are both grateful to the following friends, colleagues, and public service leaders who shared their expertise, quotes, and time to comment, collaborate, and critique our work, including:

Martin Hoffman, Greg Wells, Pia Andrews, Robert Hillard, Paul Shetler, Jordan Hatch, the Hon. Ed Husic MP, the Hon. Victor Dominello MP, Peter Alexander, Leisa Reichelt, Adrian Turner, Professor Didar Zowghi, Tom Burton, Peter Shergold, Geoff Mulgan, Beth Noveck, Sarah Pearson, James Riley, Giles Nunis, Jithma Beneragama, Jessie Callaghan, Jennifer Cochrane, Madison Shaw, and Emma Gawen.

We are grateful to the following authors for permission to use their quotes and work as well as the inspiration and learning from their publications:

Mike Bracken, Tom Loosemore, Marianna Mazzucato, Jamie Susskind, Hila Mehr, Harvard Business Publishing on behalf of Peter Drucker, William Eggers, John Hagel, Hilary Cottam, Professor Thomas W. Malone, Stewart Brand, the New South Wales Government, the Government of Western Australia, the UK's Government Digital Service (GDS), the Digital 9 Nations, the Cluetrain Manifesto authors, the Copenhagen Letter authors, David Eaves, Ben McGuire, Richard Pope, and Geoff Mulgan.

Simon is hugely grateful for the support and patience of his wife, Melinda. Much of this book was researched and written whilst their young kids were asleep, so he is grateful for children who sleep! Simon is also thankful for the encouragement and support from his Deloitte colleagues for this independent project, including Allan Mills, Robert Overend, Ellen Derrick, Ursula Brennan, John O'Mahony and Jason Hutchinson. His father, Edwin, and sister, Laura, back in the UK, and his mother-in-law, Christine, up in North Queensland provided continued encouragement from afar. In addition, a big thank you to Nicola Alcorn, who first suggested to Simon that he find an opportunity to work with Martin.

Martin would like to thank the many leaders and practitioners active in the public space, inside and outside the public sector itself, from whom he has learned so much over many years, particularly recently and in the development of this book: Peter Shergold, Gary Sturgess, Simon Willis, Geoff Mulgan, Charlie Leadbeater, Tom Bentley, Beth Noveck, Sarah Pearson, Rod Glover, Chris Vein, Andrew Cappie-Wood, David Halpern, Nicholas Gruen, Stefan Czerniawski, Ben Gales, Dominic Campbell, William Murphy, and Marianna Mazzucato. He would also like to thank Dr Jeni Whalan for her insight and wisdom, and her patience and forbearance while this book was being written.

Finally, for every public servant who has advocated for the needs of citizens, been inspired by the promise of digital transformation, and who have got on and delivered rather than just talking about doing so, we hope that this book encourages more of your colleagues to be like you.

Disclaimer

It is traditional in a venture of this sort to acknowledge that, while we are grateful for all of the advice and feedback we've received, we remain responsible for any errors or omissions. We're happy to accept that, of course. But in the spirit of the book and its embrace of a thoroughly digital mindset, with its predisposition to test and share widely and early as a way to improve and learn, we might put that disclaimer more positively.

We acknowledge there will be errors and omissions, and there are inevitably places where we need to refine our arguments. But we're happy to release our work now in the certain knowledge that there are others out there with whose expertise and insight we would like to join, if they have the time and interest.

The fact that there will be errors and omissions is not necessarily a bad thing. The end of the project is the beginning of the next phase of debate and learning.

Our Manifesto:
What we Believe

This book is a call to action for a new 'national mission' for the digital transformation of government and the public sector in Australia, building on what has been done, but at a scale and speed and intensity that matches its national significance for trust, legitimacy, and inclusive prosperity.

The book argues that digital transformation's progress across the public sector has stalled. It is a story missing half its plot, and quite possibly the most interesting part.

Digital transformation should not just be about cost and convenience, although it is certainly about both. It should not just be about improving the customer and citizen experience of dealing with government, although it has to be centrally about that.

As well as these important business-as-usual improvements to the way we govern, the way we do policy, and the way we design and deliver services, digital transformation should also be an opportunity to think about what business as unusual might look like.

The book is an invitation to see digital transformation as a chance to rethink the assumptions we make about the context, mission, and capabilities of the public sector, or, as we explain it, of public work in all its variety and complexity.

Below, we set out 20 propositions that outline a bold vision to refocus and accelerate the digital transformation of government and the public service in Australia.

The propositions reflect what we believe. In the rest of the book, we explain where the propositions came from, the leaders in this space we tested them with, and why we think they are important. In the final chapter, we explain their significance and implications, and present some specific initiatives that could supercharge this transformation agenda.

This work would engage policy makers and those at the centre of government with practitioners already active on the different edges of the public sector and/or public work.

A new theory of the business for governing and the work of the public sector (chapter 1)

1. Progress with digital transformation in government and the public sector in Australia has stalled, jeopardising its full promise and potential. Australia's progress to this point suggests that while we've often hit the target in some of the digitally based transactional and operational improvements to the way we deliver, we are in danger of missing the point. Far from keeping up, we are falling behind. We risk failing to meet the stated ambition to become a top-three digital government, compared to our global peers.

2. We need to shift our focus from technology modernisation to meeting citizen (customer) expectations of the performance of government in a digital age. The prize is the restoration of trust and legitimacy in government and the ability to harness the power and creativity of the public sector for inclusive prosperity.

3. We define digital transformation as a way of seeing and rethinking the entire business of governing, government, and the work of the public service, including to better serve citizens and customers, in a democratic society and across all levels of government. It is a lens through which to reconsider the nature of that work, its enduring foundations, and its disruption in a very different and rapidly changing (digital) world.

4. The 'theory of the business' for governing and public work is changing. At the heart of the new theory of the business for digitally transformed public work is a mission that is less concerned with the accumulation and management of public power and authority and more concerned with the assembly of collective intelligence to collaboratively solve problems. That is a hugely exciting prospect for public servants. The point of digital transformation is to help the public sector discover, embed, and then

live that new theory. Unless it's cast in that light, digital transformation progress will remain stalled.

A changing world (chapter 2)

5. Digital transformation only makes sense if it also helps to make sense of the intersection of a changing world with changing technology, the changing role and purpose of government, and the changing work of the public sector. This should include, but go beyond, making service, policy, and regulation as simple, fast, and convenient as they can and need to be.

6. Australia can't afford to 'wait and see' what happens in the rest of the world. It needs to use digital transformation to urgently rethink the underlying theory of the business – aligning changing assumptions about context, mission, and capabilities – for success in the digital global economy, for a stronger and more accountable democracy, and to dramatically improve the effectiveness of government and public work in Australia. Nothing less should be expected from a public sector that aspires to global leadership.

Digital technology: Current and future tools, and methods & Digital Central Units (chapter 3)

7. No longer should people need to spend their spare time working out how to complete transactions using complicated and disconnected government websites, filling in long forms, or waiting on hold. Citizens expect to experience the same quality of interactions in their dealings with government as they do in other parts of their digital lives. The technology, funding, and delivery methods are available so that services can be joined up, responsive, and experience-focused around citizen needs and expectations. These include simplicity and convenience, flexibility, renewal, and a proper concern for privacy and safety. Where it is happening, it needs to accelerate and scale with urgency. Where it isn't, it should be.

8. The digital transformation of government is not just about technology. It is relevant for every public servant from the department-based policy

makers to people working on the front line. Of course, the technology has to be done exceptionally well, and that is often more complex and demanding than we sometimes assume. But its real value is the way in which it offers the opportunity to rethink the way we govern and do public work, including the opportunity to develop new operating models (assumptions, beliefs, values, and behaviours). If it's not doing that, it's probably not transforming.

9. Digital transformation is no longer the preserve of the digital or tech teams or 'Digital Central Units', vital though they remain to the transformation project. Nor is it sufficient to rely on a few visionary and energetic mandarins prepared to invest some of their personal political and institutional capital to drive a few pockets of great performance that occasionally hit the 'delight' button.

10. Opportunities from the use of new technologies such as artificial intelligence (AI) in the public service needs to be embraced. Realising these opportunities as well as confronting the risks, and the impact on work and employment of AI requires significant attention and Australia needs dedicated (new) institutions to do this to keep up with our peers such as the UK and US. This includes moving towards responsive and personalised services enabling government to help citizens, e.g., telling them where they are entitled to rebates or savings. There should also be a focus on how these can lead to more fulfilling public service jobs and be used to drive clever but fair and truly accountable new ways to solve problems.

11. Making more data open and investing in public servants' capabilities to analyse and interact with data is essential to fulfil the potential of using it to create better services and to solve problems. This must be combined with an instinct for open and legible government and a high degree of ethics, privacy and accountability.

12. The security of data and transactions is at the heart of the relationships between citizens, businesses and government. Cybersecurity has to become a more central and strategic consideration for public service leaders. Appropriate levels of security and privacy controls across every service

transaction and relationship in digital government are the basic stakes to play effectively in the transformation process. It's not just a concern for technology leaders and specialists nor a 'tick box' compliance function.

13. Australia's investment in, and curation of, the necessary public digital infrastructure that will enable and amplify the process of digital transformation will have to be increasingly national, integrated and shared. Done properly this will require billions of dollars of investment and new government machinery to make this happen. This will be a major national endeavour, as significant and visible as public physical infrastructure, such as roads and airports, is to the development of Australia.

14. The public service of the future will make much greater use of platform models and the creation of the infrastructure and enabling tools which should be common and shared across different levels of government and, often, with the corporate and non-government sectors too.

Changing the work of the public sector and the way the public sector works (chapter 4)

15. The Council of Australian Governments and every level of government in Australia need to dedicate time and resources to renovating the model of government services to fit the digital era. The work of government and the public sector, and the way governments and the public sector work, are both changing. This is due in large measure to the impact of digital tools, methods and culture that are also a central part of the emergence of the new public work.

16. There is a strong link between the perception of, and experience by, citizens of government's competence and capability in their service transactions and their willingness to invest deeper levels of trust in government itself. Failing to understand the contribution of competence in basic service transactions to trust and confidence risks eroding both.

17. We should not underestimate the considerable effort and resources required to do good transformation work that changes things and sticks.

Effective digital government transformation of government and the work of the public sector needs to focus on:

- Deeply ingraining that customer outcomes which benefit citizens, communities, and businesses as the focus of performance indicators and transformation matter most, not activities and outputs.
- Remuneration, status and performance management systems that should change to focus on the number of customers served or transactions overseen and move away from previous symbols of power such as the number of people they are in 'command' of or budget size.
- Delivering new value at a faster pace with a 'trial-test-learn' mindset without over-planning or taking an overly purist design approach but with the appropriate levels of consultation, risk management, and consideration.
- Creating whole-of-government platforms that enable consistent experiences and can easily be scaled to respond to rising demand with little additional cost. Examples include websites, payment, and identity platforms. Such a platform approach stops departments' (and potentially state and federal governments') wasteful investments in building multiple versions of the same capability.
- Public servants should, at least once a year, spend in-depth time with the citizens, businesses, institutions, and communities with which they interact to develop better empathy so that policy and decision-making bears some resemblance to the contours of people's lives, their experience of government interactions, and expectations.
- Much more transparency about performance and impact by using publicly available customer service performance dashboards which show the quality of services provided in real time (including prominently in government buildings) and open collaboration and development of (non-security-sensitive) projects.
- Adopting service standards as long as they are pragmatically applied, are not digital-specific, and are focused on meeting customer (citizen) needs.
- Changing funding models to help improve the speed and flexibility with which services and expertise can be procured for projects that include rapid, agile learning and experimentation at one end of a

spectrum and long-term, multi-jurisdictional, shared infrastructure projects at the other.

18. The practice of leadership in the public sector should demonstrate the same collaborative, open, human-centred and 'platform' characteristics that increasingly define the public sector in a digital age. Public leaders need to create and hold spaces in their organisations that allow creativity, innovation and agility to flourish, including the need to develop new measures of performance against which to evaluate their teams.

19. Public service learning and capability programs require a massive overhaul to reflect the need to dramatically re-skill the workforce while blending these with enduring skills of good public work. Tens of thousands of current public servants will rapidly need to learn new skills, such as human-centred design, storytelling, and digital ways of working focused on adaptability, transdisciplinary, and self-organising collaboration, working in the open and driving speed to value. Learning methods such as bite-sized modules on accessible, shared platforms, on-the-job coaching, public service academies, and training courses, as well as through schools, TAFE, and universities, all need to be updated, leveraging the best of global resources and used across Australia. Individual public servants will also share some of the responsibility for developing their own skills.

20. Public servants will need help to become more comfortable with sensible risk and intelligent failure associated with problem solving and delivering new value at a faster pace with a 'trial-test-learn' mindset. New ways are needed to reinforce this shift through different rewards built into performance management systems.

Respect and ambition

For those in government and the public sector, it can sometimes seem as if technologists have a poor understanding of the complexities and nuances with which all public work is constrained. That can come across as a mixture of arrogance and disrespect, as if the proponents of digital transformation, or any of the earlier waves of technology's role in government, disregard the essential nature of a representative system of democratic government.

Ministers and citizens can't be ignored (no matter how frustrating that might be) in favour of technocratic and, these days, more automated and 'intelligent' systems that risk undermining deeply held notions of political and institutional accountability.

We hope we've made it clear from our approach and by virtue of the different paths we have both taken through our engagement with government over many years that we are certainly not advocating some kind of new digital politics. In fact, we think the transformation agenda we're proposing, and the call to action around the manifesto we're issuing with this book, represent an act of deep respect for the complexity and contests of good government and the complexity of public work.

But showing respect doesn't mean a diminished ambition for the transformation agenda around the uses and values of digital thinking and practice. We'd argue it is because both us have learned to respect the work of government that we believe that anything less than the fullest and highest ambition for real and deep digital transformation would itself stand as an act of disrespect.

What we would like you to do

The book is associated with the website www.arewethereyetdigital.com where we intend to continue the conversation. In particular, we're keen to obtain advice about ways in which this manifesto could be improved and, importantly, how its intentions might be translated into practical decisions and achievable pieces of work.

Introduction

Australia has been on the road to digital transformation in government and the public service for the last 25 years or more. So, after a quarter of a century of determined effort, investment, and reform, can we declare victory?

And if we can't yet reach for the satisfaction of 'mission accomplished', can we at least claim that we're getting close? Or are we still stuck with institutions, services, methods, and cultures that remain stubbornly impervious to any kind of change, much less something we could legitimately label as transformation?

Why are politicians announcing the ambition for Australia to be in the top three digital governments in the world[2] as the Australian Senate claims that 'digital transformation is beset by soaring rhetoric and vague aspirations'?[3]

So, are we there yet?

The simple answer is no.

But as optimistic realists and, drawing on a great deal of experience as practitioners, advisers, and analysts, we share a conviction that Australia can get 'there', if not always as fast, then certainly as convincingly as any other jurisdiction.

Which begs the question – where, exactly, is 'there'?

We might speculate that it is at least a place where digital transformation is the process and the power for change but isn't the point, a place where digital tools, platforms, and shared infrastructure, together with the associated cultures of open, collaborative working, fuel rapid mutual learning and better judgement for policymaking and decisions that earn legitimacy and ensure trust, respect, and relevance.

It might be a place where the search for better responses to problems and opportunities is shared, engaging, and accountable, and where public services shape themselves around what people and communities need.

It could be a place where digital transformation enables the public service to be (re)focused on the sustained, persistent and successful solving of complex public problems rather than its internal obsessions with the accumulation and exercise of public power and authority.

It's impossible to understand the Australian story of the digital transformation of government, both where it is now and especially where it could be into the future, without understanding the larger context of economic, social, political, and technology change, and the associated opportunities and risks, from which it emerges and to which it is, in large measure, a response.

The real question is why we're not there yet and what we can do about it. There's an even more basic question too – why should we care? What are some of the practical implications that people in government, and the community more broadly, might notice?

We think the story boils down to trust and relevance, the only currencies of good government. And stocks and flows of both are at low levels, dangerously low some argue.

So, the real test of digital transformation is not more apps or clever ways to use AI and blockchain – although it's likely to feature all of that and a lot more besides. It ought to be about where and how the time, effort, and money we are investing in digital transformation make a material difference to the way government works in a changed and changing world.

To jump ahead a little, faster and more convenient transactions comprise only half the answer, and quite possibly an important but least interesting half.

The wider debate: some points of connection

There's no shortage of writing and research about different aspects of the digital transformation story, both in government and more widely. Some of that work has been engaged in by the authors. However, the purpose here is not to attempt a more academic or comprehensive review process of that work.

That work includes several books and extended studies of everything from e-government through to more contemporary treatments of the current and emerging trends in digital government. It also includes a steady stream of articles and studies, ranging from the academic to the practice-based reflections of current public servants and a range of thinkers and advisors.[4]

The work, for example, of people like Mike Bracken, Tom Loosemore, and Richard Pope has been picked up, and they are referenced later in this book. There's a lot of work emerging from academics and writers, like Helen Margetts and William D. Eggers too, some of which has been particularly influential in marking the territory and research of successive waves of eGovernment, Government 2.0, and digital government.

Beth Noveck's writing and research, especially in leading The Governance Lab at the Tandon Engineering School of New York University (NYU), have been especially influential in the development of one of the author's (Martin's) own thinking and work in digital government.

The point of these references is to set this work, from the start, in the context of what is clearly a larger conversation about how digital technology impacts the work and performance of government and the public sector.

It also gives us the chance to reinforce a few themes that these writers, thinkers, and practitioners have consistently manifested in their work, and which will emerge in different ways throughout this book.

One theme is the seriousness of the digital agenda as a force for deep change and potential transformation in every aspect of governing and the work of the public sector – policy making, regulatory reform, service design and delivery, democratic engagement, and citizen participation.

Another is the willingness to search for the true significance of all of this digital and tech change, not only in things like speed, efficiency, productivity, and convenience but also in the bedrock currencies of good government, including trust, power, accountability, and legitimacy.

What seems to link these and others interested in treating the digital agenda with the seriousness it deserves is that they discern in its contours and disruptive demands powerful forces for deep change. In these examples, the real story is not the first-round effects of more use of digital and related technologies but the deeper and longer-lasting impact on the underlying assumptions that drive institutional behaviour and performance.

In our terms, much of this work is characterised as instinctively drawn to awkward questions about the underlying theory of the business for governing which digital transformation tests, and to which it also offers some responses.

A third theme of this work is the different ways in which the writers and researchers combine a proper concern with the pragmatic impact of these changes on the operating realities of governing and the public sector with a curiosity about their deeper structural and strategic, sometimes philosophical implications.

Indeed, what connects them is an assumption that these concerns are not mutually exclusive.

Quite the opposite.

The digital transformation agenda elides the practical and the philosophical, holding in a tight and natural embrace deep questions about government's role, purpose, and relevance, and equally searching questions about intensely practical things, like organising structures, the search for skills and talent, leadership, the day-to-day engagement with people as users of services and as citizens, and how to measure and reward performance.

If we've taken anything from these influential writers, it is this need to avoid splitting the digital transformation story in government into simplistic pieces. The point is how all of the pieces – transactional, relational, operational, structural, philosophical, and strategic – interact and shape some big questions and, we hope, offer some useful answers to the persistent dilemmas of good government and effective public work.

Our perspectives

This book takes a timely and distinctly Australian look at a global phenomenon – how digital technologies, and their associated tools, platforms, and cultures, are changing the business of governing and the design and delivery of policy and public services.

A unique and contemporary analysis, written by two 'reflective practitioners'[5] with over 40 years' combined global experience in policy, public-sector management, and digital strategy, and with input from policy and digital leaders, thinkers, and practitioners from around the world, this book offers a fresh perspective on:

- Why we are experiencing difficulties and frustrations on the road to 'real' digital transformation in government and the public service
- What we can do to get 'there' with more speed and confidence.

This book was born out of caffeine-fuelled conversations where we discovered a shared interest for using digital technology and culture to make public services better, and an equally shared frustration that the speed of digital transformation in Australia seemed to be slower than we were seeing and hearing about in other countries.

So, rather than admire the problem and complain, we decided we'd write down how to get there. We want to spark a debate and discussion.

We drew on Martin's more than 30 years in and around policy and government at the national and state levels in Australia, as well as his time at Cisco and helping to shape the emerging field of social innovation, and on Simon's recent experiences in Sydney, Canberra, and London working with governments both as a public servant and as a consultant. Martin was also keen to write a follow-up to his book *Changing Shape: Institutions for a Digital Age,* co-authored with former Australian Finance Minister Lindsay Tanner in 2014.[6]

After discussing our concept for a book with government, digital leaders, and start-up owners, we recognised a demand from public-sector leaders, workers, and advisers for some guidance to inform their thinking and actions in Australia and beyond.

Paradoxes

The question about how well Australia is doing in the digital transformation of government begs other questions – digital transformation for what? What's the point of the exercise? And how do the answers to that question provide a frame within which to assess progress and performance to date and, more importantly, future possibilities and pitfalls?

Take an example drawn from work that Martin is currently involved with in one of the largest programs of technology infrastructure, the Welfare Payments Infrastructure Transformation program, or WPIT for short.[7]

The federal government's investment of $1.7 billion in a 'transformed' welfare payments infrastructure,[8] for example, should be about a lot more than quicker, more accurate, and responsive welfare payments. A worthy ambition, for sure, but why shouldn't it also be about new digital and technology capabilities driving a bigger set of changes about the design of the welfare system itself? And, in turn, a chance to pose and answer some big questions about the nature of the welfare and human services system in Australia in a changing world, and how we want it to interact with people and communities seeking support, dignity, and the ability to make choices in their lives?[9]

The point, surely, is not simply efficiency, speed, and convenience. Shouldn't the point also be to harness the tools and culture of digital to a larger ambition to recast policy and redesign completely by changing the relevant enabling and delivery institutions and practices?

In many ways, the WPIT story, as with many of the big programs of digital change in Australia, is an example of a phenomenon that is also appearing in the commercial sector.

As a recent survey of corporate sector Chief Digital Officers notes, '[O]nce a digital transformation plan has been formulated, it needs to be implemented, and many companies realize that this process will involve much more than they initially thought'.[10]

In particular, the realisation is growing that as well as introducing new technologies, 'legacy systems need to be revamped, internal processes changed, and employees persuaded to adapt to new ways of working – all of which cuts across a company's organisational silos'.[11] It's a useful reminder that the frame we advocate is replicated in different conditions in the business world, with the same implication that digital transformation is much bigger than the technology frame into which it has been constrained for too long.

That bigger picture is largely a story of the way profound changes in technology, economics, politics, and society have fed off each other to create a world whose defining characteristics are speed, intensity, and connectedness.

In many ways, expectations of government, despite often mind-boggling changes, remain much the same: to be fair, open, ethical, competent, accountable – and completely different, all at the same time. Expectations about how government should work and behave have been blown up by our encounters in other parts of our lives – how we shop, and travel, and learn, and entertain ourselves, and connect with friends and family – with new obsessions about the quality of the experience (as opposed to the specifications of the product or service), customer service, personalisation, responsiveness and choice, and, by and large, openness and transparency.

Another big piece of the story involves the new, exciting, but unsettling rules being written about the relationship between people and machines.

The impact of technology on human endeavour has been around pretty much since we worked out fire and the wheel. This time, though, it feels different. What we're witnessing in this phase of intelligent machines and the new algorithmic destinies to which we seem bound but which we barely understand, much less control, is a new fusion of human capability and machine intelligence. Digital determinism, appealing and appalling by turns but on a trajectory that is apparently implacable, is turning out to be a new motive force in human affairs.

Partly for that reason, but driven by larger issues of trust and accountability, a new struggle for legibility – the ability for people to be able not just to see what's going on but to 'read' and understand what's happening in business, government, politics, and the community – is reshaping many of the assumptions and limits of the trust underlying aspects of culture, commerce, government, and politics. New, largely digital assumptions are being baked into the way we conceive of and use power, knowledge, and accountability to make the world more democratic, as well as fairer and less unequal.

Powerful new opportunities are dramatically exploited by a few emerging 'platform' giants – think Amazon, Google, Apple, Facebook, and Microsoft – which are replacing them with even greater reach and control. At the same time, opportunities for influence and action are opening up as people learn the new rules of agency and interaction in the digital economy. But barriers, too, are emerging, of access, participation, and influence. We refer later in the book to the work of Shoshana Zuboff, particularly on 'surveillance capitalism', which picks up this theme with unsettling implications.

We can see the good and the bad of this new world, and often find ourselves strung out between extremes of hope about the emerging break-up of old sources of economic, political, and cultural power and the fear and anxiety about where the new rules and assumptions of digital power and influence might take us.

Just as, for example, we're all learning to be gobsmacked on a daily basis by the magical potential of AI, a few notable and influential voices – the late Stephen Hawking, Bill Gates, Elon Musk, Toby Walsh in Australia, and many others – offer dire warnings with increasing anxiety about the existential threat to people and the planet of the unconstrained development of machines we won't be able to control.

Where in this storm do ethics, human choices, notions of public purpose, and the common good feature? How do projects that need predictability and consistency escape the risk of political interference which can undermine the potential to realise the full public value of the investments that are being made?

It's a confusing period, marked by uneasy and contradictory evidence that the world is becoming at the same time more open and more closed, more competitive and empowering, and less hospitable to new and smaller players.

This provides the basis for a fairer and more equal distribution of resources and authority, and at the same time closing access to both through new and apparently inexorable concentrations of power and influence.

The point about these confusing signals of a new digital world order is that government is both a major player in, and a victim of, the consequent process of deep and rapid restructuring. That's a suitably ambiguous place from which to find the requisite energy and motivation to lead and shape many of these ideas and possibilities.

So, the big question about how well digital transformation in Australia is progressing might be framed not so much as a simple calibration of speed and performance – are we doing enough, are we going fast enough, are we actually transforming anything? – but a more nuanced assessment of how digital transformation is part of a larger choreography of change in which governments are part victim, part agent.

To the extent that digital transformation changes pretty much every dimension of the way governing and government works, those trying to prosecute the case for digital don't spend enough time understanding those dynamics. This is a classic case of a change process proceeding without enough time spent considering deeply, and being respectful of, its context and conditions.

Designers understand context and conditions. There is no point, a good designer would argue, getting the design of the chair right without also understanding the room in which it will be used. If you don't know or care much about the nature of the room and how its dynamics will impact how the chair will work – what is the room for, what kind of work or activity goes on there, involving what kinds of people, when, how...? – the chair is likely to be functional at best, but mostly just more or less decorative.

The UK Government is blunt. 'It is too often the case that citizens feel that they live at the convenience of the state: that the government acts not as a servant but as master'.[12] We can't help but think that Australia is behind the curve without demonstrating the kind of action-backed ambition of 'We [UK Government] will transform the relationship between citizens and the state – putting more power in the hands of citizens and being more responsive to their needs'.[13]

Financially this makes sense too. In 2015, Deloitte Access Economics reported that whilst 811 million of all Australian government transactions each year are now online, 40% were still completed face to face, by telephone, and by post.[14] Politically, it is recognised that $17.9 billion in savings are to be had if 80% of high-volume transactions become digital.[15] So, why is it taking so long to get there?

Our thesis

The digital transformation project for government – the term we use to describe the sum of the efforts of digital change across government and the public sector – is going more slowly than it should, and failing to deliver its full transformational dividend, because we are only telling half the story. We think that we are not 'there' yet in the digital transformation journey in Australia, because we have settled for a view of 'there' that is too limited.

The best way to frame the challenge is within a digital transformation 'diamond' of four big changes (see figure 01), each of which contributes to and helps shape the new public work, and to which we have dedicated a chapter in this book:

- **Changes in the role and purpose of government** as new questions about public work and public value test the purpose and practice of many public institutions seeking new sources of relevance and legitimacy that define their role and animate their work; a new 'theory of business' is emerging around successfully solving complex public problems rather than accumulating power and authority.
- **Changes in the world** and the big social, economic, and political shifts of power, risk, and vulnerability that fashion the risks and opportunities governments grapple with and seek to control.
- **Changes in technology**, infused with a new relationship between people and machines, and in which the big questions of who's in charge of whom, or what, and to what end all seem to be back up in the air and threatening to land in some awkward places and patterns.
- **Changes in the work of the public sector**, whose patterns and rhythms are being disrupted and whose search for requisite talent, leadership, and structural relevance is only just beginning.

Figure 01: Digital transformation 'diamond' of four big changes

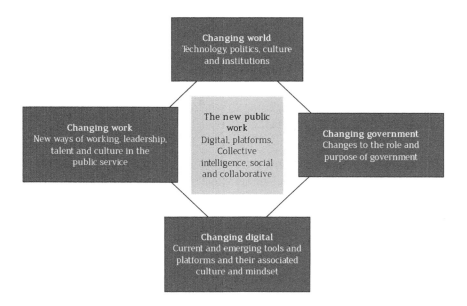

Are we there yet?
The digital transformation "diamond"

Changing world
Technology, politics, culture and institutions

The new public work
Digital, platforms, Collective intelligence, social and collaborative

Changing work
New ways of working, leadership, talent and culture in the public service

Changing government
Changes to the role and purpose of government

Changing digital
Current and emerging tools and platforms and their associated culture and mindset

At the heart of the 'diamond' is the emergence of something we describe as the 'new public work'. This is a way working that tackles complex policy, design, and execution capabilities by combining new forms and practices of public leadership, digital platforms and tools, collective intelligence, and an instinct for 'open and legible' to tackle big opportunities and risks that impact the lives we live in common.

Within the interaction of these four big sets of change will emerge the real test for digital transformation. What does it have to offer us by way of new modes and methods of working that are remotely fit for purpose, where 'purpose' is defined by the interaction of big changes in each of the four points of the diamond? How is digital transformation impacting and being impacted by each, and, increasingly, their interaction? And is it even sensible to think that governments themselves are in any shape to evolve the architecture by which these interlocking changes hang together in some semblance of purpose and order?

Digital transformation will have its most profound effect, and will realise its promise beyond its intermittent successes, when it successfully navigates the connections between these four points of the diamond.

Digital transformation will be 'there' when its mindset and capabilities mobilise the new public work so that people thrive and human possibility expands for everyone in a world changing with unspeakable intensity and speed.

It's hard to be precise about the practical implications for Australia's comparative performance on digital transformation of some of the concerns we've raised in this book.

Our best guess, based on our own experience and the insights of others we've spoken with, suggests that we might be about four or five years behind some of the leading countries. Assuming those countries, like Singapore, Estonia, the UK, and Denmark, for example, don't stop improving, we can assume that, without a big effort by Australia, the gap will continue to widen. And that carries implications on many levels, including economic growth, innovation, productivity, and service quality.

Using this book

We believe that the signs are good, given the resources, context, and motivation we see in government. This fertile ground for change counters the extremes of unhelpful hype and over-optimism at one extreme and, at the other, the pessimism touted by some commentators and former public servants.

We characterise ourselves as optimistic realists, critical, clear-eyed, but ultimately convinced that the task is not only necessary and inevitable but well worth the effort.

We want this book to be used to inform a wider and less siloed debate about digital transformation of government in Australia (and beyond), including influencing the decision makers in government and the public servants grappling with these issues.

A significant review of the Australian Public Service[16] was announced as we researched and wrote this book. We know some of the themes and arguments presented here are featuring in the review's thinking. We're hopeful its results will amplify their influence and accelerate their impact on a 'fit for the future' public service.

There are a few things you need to understand about this book and which make it a little different to many of the books and other writing about these topics.

First, the book is part philosophy, part strategic analysis, and part practical guide to the tools and methods of digital technology and their operational implications for public agencies. We have deliberately covered the story we think needs to be told about digital transformation from all angles, and often from angles that we have not seen in much of the available writing and analysis.

So, if you are more interested in the strategic and philosophical context for digital transformation, and the contours of its 'big picture' context and conditions, you will be most interested in chapters 1 and 2 and in the exploration of the changing work and working styles of the public sector in chapter 4.

If you are more interested in the technologies themselves, and in getting your head around the current and emerging suite of digital and data capabilities, you will focus more on chapter 3.

Whichever dimension of the discussion you are interested in – and we hope, like us, you are interested in both and their interaction, opening up a debate which is too often limited by its technology dimension – you will want to see how we conclude our analysis with a 'manifesto' of beliefs and practical initiatives that we think will advance the cause of deep, sustained, and positive digital transformation. Chapter 5 sets out our view of what 'there' might look like and how we could drive more forcefully towards its potential.

Given the way it's been written, and our different tracks to arrive at our shared interest in the digital transformation project, the book reflects our distinct but complementary voices. You will notice some difference in style and approach across the different elements of the book. You will see that we draw on a number of UK examples in particular, which is a consequence of our experience, their progress, and the availability of information to reference. What you shouldn't notice, though, is any distinction between us in the commitment to, and daily engagement with, the work of digital transformation and how it might be amplified and accelerated in Australia.

Finally, although it's possible to take the digital transformation discussion deep into the architecture of Australia's system of government, politics, and democracy, we don't take the discussion in that direction, at least not in any depth or detail.

We both understand, work daily with, and are vigorous supporters of our democratic structures and culture. We accept the important distinctions between political leadership and accountability for large questions of national interest and direction, and the leadership and management work of the public sector supporting the government of the day. We're certainly not advocating some kind of digital enhanced technocracy in which a layer of unaccountable experts, aided and abetted by new digital technologies, becomes dominant in the wider democratic conversation.

Our focus, in the end, is on the work and culture of the public sector and the business of governing within those broad parameters. Our audience is primarily public servants and those engaged in public work inside and outside its formal institutional boundaries at federal, state, and local governments in Australia as well as around the world. We hope that politicians and citizens generally will find what we have to say both interesting and a little challenging.

Definitions

This book takes a predominantly national view of digital transformation of government and the public sector in Australia. It touches on the work and achievements at a State and Territory level, but its focus and proposals (our manifesto) for the future take a national approach.

We concentrate on the digital transformation of government and of the public sector. The public sector refers to any activity or agency funded or run by government. It includes, but goes beyond, the departments and agencies established to service and support the operations and activities of government, which is generally described as the public service. There are legislative, funding, and operational distinctions between the inner public service and the wider public sector, which carry important implications.

Although these are important distinctions in public administration theory and practice, for the purposes of this work we have used the term 'public sector' to refer broadly to organisations and work owned or run by government, either to provide services to people and communities or to support the administration of government itself. And our definition of digital transformation emphasises the importance of exploring the full implications of its value and potential – transactional, cultural, and institutional. Digital transformation is a way of seeing and rethinking the entire business of governing, government, and the work of the public service to better serve citizens and customers in a democratic society and across all levels of government. It is a lens through which to reconsider the nature of that work, its enduring foundations, and its necessary disruption in a very different and rapidly changing world. In the end, the definition of digital transformation in government isn't as important as getting a sense of what it might look like if it were happening in the way we suggest it isn't happening yet. If we're not 'there' yet, what might we expect to see as signs of having arrived?

The two definitions of digital transformation we've engaged in our thinking each imply at least some of the attributes of 'there'. Mike Bracken's definition, for example, claims that 'digital transformation is the act of radically changing how your organisation works, so that it can survive and thrive in the internet era'.[17]

We've added our own: 'Digital transformation is a way of seeing and rethinking the entire business of governing, government, and the work of the public service, and to better serve citizens and customers in a democratic society and across all levels of government'.

Like the Bracken definition, we don't think anything is digitally transformed unless and until an organisation, or in the case of the public sector, an entire institution, asks big and uncomfortable questions about the nature of its work and, as a consequence, is open to the possibility that many of the underlying assumptions on which that work is based need to be challenged and replaced.

The patterns of organising and doing business are likely to be more like Uber and Spotify and Amazon, and perhaps the kind of changes to its basic travel and retail business that older companies like Qantas and Woolworths[18] push. That doesn't mean, though, that running government and working in the public sector is the same as running Netflix or Uber.

But it does suggest that unless there are signs that some radical change is going on, impacting basic ways in which the enterprise, public, private or civic, engages with those it serves, it is unlikely that there is much transformation happening either.

Perhaps in the government space it's more like the near total shift to digital that has been driven for some years in Denmark or, on a much smaller scale, but potentially with big changes for a key sector, the platform model of a venture like HireUp.[19] There, a combination of digital technology and human-centred design has seen a new way emerging of linking people with disabilities with those who can offer them care and support in ways that reinforce the power and authority of those people with disabilities.

The other dimension of the transformation story in government and the public sector reflects a close relationship between the competence with which people see government operating in the design and delivery of basic services and the degree to which they are prepared, based on that competence, to invest their wider sense of the work and value of government with trust and legitimacy.

So, an important dimension of 'there' will be signs that governments in Australia recognise that the way services are designed and accessed by citizens, and bigger questions about government's role and purpose, are intimately connected.

Our argument in this book is not that governments can either adopt a relatively narrow definition of digital transformation and focus only on improving the transactions that people and governments experience or deeply rethink their underlying 'theory of the business'. Our argument suggests that transformation won't get us 'there' unless both of those ambitions – transactional competence and the emergence of a new theory of the business – are given equal weight.

Note where we have used the term 'citizen', this extends to users or customers of government services.

In the spirit of the notion of 'minimum viable products' that we advocate in the book, we're sure there are some errors and deficiencies that need to be worked on. In some ways, the book isn't quite ready to go out into the world. Which means, of course, that this is exactly the time it should go out so the world can help to make it better.

You can reach us at author@arewethereyetdigital.com or via the website www.arewethereyetdigital.com.

Chapter 1

A New Theory of the Business:
A Framework for Digital Transformation
in Government and the Public Sector

The 'theory of the business',[20] a way of thinking about the underlying assumptions of any organisation or institution in any sector, for governing and the work of the public sector has shifted from 'the accumulation and exercise of public power and authority' to 'the sustained, persistent and successful solving of complex public problems'. Lining up culture, structure, and capability with this emerging theory of the business is the key to combining relevance and competence to rebuild trust, legitimacy, and inclusive prosperity.

The point and purpose of digital transformation is to help the public sector discover, embed, and then live that new theory. Unless it is cast in that light, the digital transformation project – the term we use to describe the sum of the efforts of digital change across government and the public sector – will remain incomplete and ultimately fail to deliver its full potential value.

The argument

Those are big claims and this chapter explores them in more detail. It explains what we mean by 'theory of the business' in this context. And it examines the implications for the public sector and the digital transformation project in Australia.

Traditionally, and certainly up until recently, the performance of the public sector as we have come to know it in Australia, and in many other western industrialised countries, has reflected an implicit mission, which in turn has been fuelled by an underlying theory of its business, to accumulate and carefully manage public power and authority. It has been largely a hierarchical, closed, and elite endeavour in the relatively settled context of predictable issues and steadily emerging problems, and, for the most part, incremental solutions.

But while making policy and shaping public services has always been its work, often the point of the exercise has felt, especially for those outside the formal institutions of governing and public work, as if the art and practice of public power has been an end in itself. Hence the rise of a 'mandarin' class of top bureaucrats serving essentially as high priests curating power as the currency in which their power was measured and their relevance admired.

Solving problems was part of the job, of course, and sometimes pretty knotty problems at that – think the birth of the National Health Services or the establishment of public pension systems and the post-war institution building in Australia under the stewardship of 'Nugget' Coombs and the 'seven dwarves'.[21] Big pieces of work like the introduction of Medicare, the general sales test (GST), and the evolution of our big systems of public health and education would be other obvious examples.

By and large though, this was an era in which powerful public servants worked in relatively settled times to design and deliver public services and institutions of public governance to and for the people, who largely were grateful and happily ignorant of, and not really interested in, their arcane, often apparently rather dull and slightly mysterious work.

But conditions have changed and, as the world has become more tangled in complex or 'wicked' problems that demand new strategies and approaches, the power versus problem-solving equation has been flipped. And with it, the search for a new theory of the business has become urgent. Digital transformation is part of the reason and a significant part of the solution.

In the new equation, power and authority are much more obviously in the service of a new type of search for solutions – more open, connected, rapid, and accountable – to increasingly tangled and complex problems. The shift to a more experimental and prototyping model of working can be experienced as a threat to lobbyists and others who have been used to being in command of many of the points of influence and engagement in the system.

The surrounding political, technological, economic, and cultural contexts have become volatile and unpredictable. Respect for formal and institutional expertise is eroding. Deference is contingent, reluctant, or withheld altogether. Services and solutions are meant to be designed with and by the people they are supposed to help or impact.

The nature of power is changing from largely top-down, institutional, and hierarchical to bottom-up, distributed, and networked.[22] Power has dispersed and become diffuse, often accumulating in different, unexpected places. Technology companies, 'flash' crowds, and movements convened and activated on social media like Twitter or on Facebook shift opinion and close off or open up potential solutions with unnerving speed and intensity.

Accountability mechanisms that were once satisfied with the minimal formal transparency of an unread annual report are now hostage to a deep, if inchoate instinct for legibility. People strain to 'read' what is going on inside institutions, most of which have lost their veneer of unspoken trust and respect. This is through a mix of their own misconduct or arrogance or simply as a function of the big shifts in culture, social expectations, and technology to which they have been too slow to respond.

It would be hard to go past the Hayne Royal Commission into Australia's financial and superannuation system[23] in 2019 as a better and certainly topical example of this ungainly and contested ballet of institutional shape shifting, or, for that matter, the emerging Royal Commissions into the state of Australia's aged care and disability services sectors.[24]

Many of our big institutions, including the institutions and processes of public governance and the public sector, have proven to be inept in this process or have 'gone missing' altogether.

It's a very different game, we would argue, a game whose predominant purpose has shifted from the accumulation and exercise of public power to the sustained, persistent and successful solving of complex public problems.

Governing and the public sector confront a very different game, whose predominant purpose has shifted from the accumulation and exercise of public power to the sustained, persistent, and successful solving of complex public problems – we might also add, in quite different patterns of power, authority, and accountability with and by people and the communities they are designed to serve, and to whom they should always be accountable. And in that shift are buried tectonic shifts in culture, structure, systems, and skills that are reshaping governing and the public sector.

The work of governing and the public sector are in a difficult and awkward transition from one old and increasingly irrelevant theory of the business – the alignment of an institution's assumptions about context, mission, and capabilities, and how each of those sets of assumptions make sense to each other and to the world outside – to a new one whose dimensions and solutions remain unclear.

Digital transformation, as both chief cause and core remedy, is, or ought to be, at the heart of those shifts.

Does it have anything useful to say about, and contribute to, the pragmatic, philosophical, technical, and institutional search for the answers to these big questions? Or is it happy to remain firmly stuck in the useful but limited task of adding some speed and convenience to a way of doing government and public services that is fast running out of steam?

We think we are not 'there' yet in the digital transformation journey in Australia because we've settled for a view of 'there' that is too limited. Digital transformation should be deliberately stepping into the battle for a new theory of the business for governing and the public sector.

Too many of its proponents, many of whom remain hostage to the important but limited technology obsessions that are part of the transformation, are either not interested or not aware of this larger canvas, which itself is changing as a function of the work they are doing.

And we're not alone.

This tough call on the quality of the digital transformation program in the UK's NHS (National Health Service) reinforces the point. 'Sadly', it concludes, looking at the £4.2 billion ($7.6 billion) IT strategy for the NHS, that far from being a digital transformation program, 'it is clear this is predominantly a technology modernisation programme that has very little, if anything (despite the money and effort), to do with understanding and preparing for government's place in the digital economy'.[25]

And what that might look like if there were a concerted effort to redefine government's purpose of the digital era, might be 'to maximise the potential benefits to citizens [and] work much harder on interoperability to connect the market with the data, and regulate accordingly'.[26]

But we need to back up a little.

In this chapter, we:

- Explain the concept of the 'theory of the business'.[27]
- Apply the theory of the business framework to government and the public sector, looking more closely at the way in which current assumptions about context, mission, and capabilities are out of step with reality and with each other.
- Explore why those who are concerned to advance the digital transformation agenda in government need to concern themselves more purposefully with the search for a new theory of the business, especially at a time when the public service as an institution is strung out uncomfortably between the perils of a deep decline in institutional confidence and practice and the (largely digital) promise of a new combination of respect, recognition, and relevance from which it might forge its new purpose.

The problem – and this is completely typical of the conditions in which the search for a new theory of the business becomes not just urgent but unavoidable – is that the imperative for some dramatic and creative institutional rethinking and redesign comes at a time when it appears the public service itself, a dangerously low ebb of morale and capability, is least well positioned to do this hard, testing work.[28]

There's a risk that the way we have set out our argument in this book, and especially the focus on the importance of evolving a new theory of the business, sets up a binary choice between the current forms of digital transformation and the deeper, more structural approach we advocate.

The real choice is less stark, much messier and perhaps more interesting.

Digital transformation, especially across an institution as complex as the public sector and, more broadly, of government itself, is necessarily a process of transition, not of sudden and miraculous change. As in any transition from one set of institutional settings to another, the process is gradual and cumulative.

In most cases, the dynamic is similar as systems move from where they are now (horizon 1 on a trajectory down and out) to where they know they need to be. But what happens inevitably is that pockets of the new are incubated by innovators and entrepreneurs in business, government, and civil society in the midst of the old.[29]

Some of the work of designing and testing a new theory of the business for government is already happening in disconnected pockets of inspiration and energy.

We need to keep looking closely at the work that is already underway in the digital transformation process and not, as might be implied by some of the challenges we have set here, to dismiss it as falling short of the bar we have set. More usefully, we need to discern whether its impact reinforces an old way of working or is a vanguard attempt to imagine and build a new way.

Current models and investments in digital transformation and the deeper and more disruptive challenge of imagining a new theory of the business are not simple and necessary opposites. They are connected; the question is how, and with what long-term implications for those who work in, and are served by, government and the public sector.

Theory of the business: a quick review

In 1994, Peter Drucker published an influential article in the *Harvard Business Review*.[30] The article outlined a simple argument: organisational and institutional success is a function of the alignment between the assumptions people make about context, mission, and capabilities and the reality of the world in which they operate.

Context + Mission + Capabilities = Theory of the business

Do the assumptions about context, mission, and capabilities on which the organisation or institution relies as the rationale for its work still fit the external conditions? Are they internally aligned and are they mutually consistent?

Drucker argued that not only do those three sets of assumptions have to match reality, but they also each must make sense in the context of the others. In other words, they must be internally coherent as well as externally aligned.

If these assumptions line up with each other and with reality (in this case, reality is simply what is happening outside the organisation), success tends to follow.

But where internal coherence starts to fracture and assumptions and reality drift apart, which usually happens in a reinforcing cycle of frustration and eventually despair, things will inevitably go badly.

Once this starts to happen, Drucker suggests, there is little point in looking for solutions in better performance, harder work, changed incentives, or smarter strategy. None of them will help.

And the reason is that the symptoms of declining performance – or, as Drucker puts it, what happens in an organisation when they seem to be doing everything right, but things are still going wrong – signal the need for a different answer.

What is likely happening, he suggests, is that the assumptions on which the organisation has based its sense of purpose, context, and capability are out of date. They don't fit the world in which it is working. The symptoms of frustration and existential angst should prompt a harder and deeper interrogation of the current assumptions in all three domains and the need to find some new ones that fit better.

This is how Drucker makes his point:

'The root cause of nearly every one of these crises is not that things are being done poorly. It is not even that the wrong things are being done. Indeed, in most cases, the right things are being done – but fruitlessly. What accounts for this apparent paradox? The assumptions on which the organization has been built and is being run no longer fit reality. These are the assumptions that shape any organization's behaviour, dictate its decisions about what to do and what not to do, and define what the organization considers meaningful results.'

And this is how he defines the three domains between which there needs to be a robust alignment:

'The assumptions about environment [context] define what an organization is paid for. The assumptions about mission define what an organization considers to be meaningful results; in other words, they point to how it envisions itself making a difference in the economy and in the society at large. Finally, the assumptions about core competencies define where an organization must excel in order to maintain leadership.'

We think the public service sector faces exactly the same challenge – to rethink the assumptions about mission and purpose, about context and conditions, and about capabilities and skills. And we think, like Drucker, that much of the current anxiety and demoralisation that is often noticed in public-sector cultures around the world, and certainly in Australia, are not a function of poor work or lack of capability.[31]

They are symptoms of a deeper malaise, one which speaks directly to a 'theory of the business' for governing and the public sector that is out of date and in urgent need of a change. And a new 'theory of the business' has to be thoroughly and deeply digital.

As for what you should do about it, Drucker has three suggestions:

- *Systematic abandonment* – according to this demanding doctrine, organisations should regularly look across the full sweep of their structures, systems, and practices and ask, 'If we weren't already doing this, would do it now?' And they should be prepared, if the answer is no, to start again or abandon it altogether.
- *Look outside* – the most important test of a theory of the business is the degree to which its assumptions about context, mission, and capabilities fit the world as it is, as opposed to the world as you think it is, or, worse, as you thought it was when you formed the earlier theory of the business and which you assume is still the case. And the only way to know that is to keep looking outwards, tracking any signs of shifting attitudes, behaviour, and capabilities 'out there' that could render irrelevant what is happening 'in here'.
- *Preventive care* – partly linked to the habit of looking out, the notion of preventive care simply suggests that it's always better to prevent than cure when it comes to adjusting the theory of any business; to make the small changes and constant improvements and updates necessary to keep the assumptions aligned and up to date.[32]

Theory of the business in government: then

The Drucker frame is powerful.

But he didn't advocate simple or simplistic answers. In fact, his exhortation was that the best way to avoid the risks of being trapped in the wrong theory of the business is to combine deep, curious, and demanding analysis with hard work.

What happens when we apply the theory of the business framework to government and the public service?

It's likely that the sketch we've outlined here won't be correct in every element. Its analysis will be contested. But we're trying to illustrate the point. Digital transformation of government is about something more profound than adding some speed and convenience to the way we do government now. It is forcing, and responding to, a more profound set of questions about whether the assumptions on which we've based the way we structure, provision, and conduct the business of government and the public sector are still useful and valid.

Our view is that they are not and that those who are involved in the endeavour of digital transformation should have something to say about how these new tools, platforms, and mindsets can help to evolve a new and more useful theory of the business.

We think the current theory of the business for government (see figure 02) formed in the period after the Second World War and drawing on inherited 19th century traditions of power and accountability in public governance and the public sector could be sketched out along these lines.

Figure 02: Theory of the business for government then

Theory of the business for government THEN

Context – predictable, slow, high trust in institutions, a settled order, time for decisions.

Mission – first, the orderly accumulation and management of public power and authority and second, solving problems.

Capabilities – scarce expertise; policy skills; managing power and authority; conservative and incremental; designing and delivering public service to and for people (the welfare state); understanding and responding to the changing needs and values of the communities served; accountable to the Government, parliament and people; simple, linear and hierarchical accountability.

- Settled
- Hierarchical
- Predictable
- Elite
- Closed
- Old trust – institutional, upwards
- From the centre
- Deference

Context: settled and predictable

If we look back over the past 70 years or so, the context within which government and the public sector worked was relatively settled and predictable. That doesn't mean there weren't the usual supply of 'black swan' moments (think the oil shocks of the early 1970s) of unexpected and unlooked for changes and intervention that demand relatively rapid responses.[33]

But the overwhelming sense was of an era in which external conditions were easier to predict and respond to; there was a familiar and relatively stable process of dealing with issues and getting decisions and policy made, and there was time to deal with issues as they arose.

Mission: the management of public power and authority

In that context, the mission of the public sector was predominantly the orderly accumulation, management, and use of public power and authority. There was a sense in which the chief concern of those inside the system was its preservation and endurance.

This reality is implicit in these observations by the co-founder of the UK's Government Digital Service (GDS), which was one of the first Digital Central Units tasked with driving digital transformation across government, which we explain in chapter 3. Tom Loosemore has noted that 'it's an unfortunate reality that most government departments in most countries see themselves as units of power to be wielded, or control to be protected. They are always very keen to operate in their own interests, and very reluctant to operate in the interests of other departments. It's all very 'us and them'.[34]

To some extent, it's because mandates, budgets, and the governing political structure reinforce this behaviour. As Mike Bracken, the GDS's first leader, said in a recent interview: 'Whitehall isn't built to share, it's built on straight lines and silos'.[35]

Later in the same essay, in part of a larger collection of thoughts about the progress of digital transformation, Loosemore points out that '[T]hey're starting to understand that it doesn't just mean new technologies and new user-centred services. It also means a lot of new ways of working (new for government, at least) and new ways of governing. More leaders are thinking about funding teams, not projects, about working iteratively, and about shifting away from rigid hierarchies towards networks of multi-disciplinary teams.[36]

That was the best way to ensure government and the public sector could do its work in policy and regulation and services, even if in many cases those services were developed 'to and for' people with little room to accommodate too much variation in the interests, needs, and circumstances of those at the receiving end.

Rhythms of work, hierarchies of control, expertise, influence and power, and relationships with citizens and communities followed well-established patterns.

Capabilities: control, policy, and services to and for people and communities

In that context and with that mission, the capabilities in the public sector tended to privilege relatively narrow and specialist expertise, the skills of top-down policymaking, good administrative process and practice, and the ability to understand, nurture, and extend power and authority. The assumption was that you'd get a lot further on the ability to fashion elegant memos and play crafty political games at the centre than you would in the messy business of delivery and frontline service out on the edge.

Technology skills and capabilities were relatively basic, except in some of the more specialist areas of policy like defence, science, and different aspects of research and development. Consultation and 'conversation' skills to manage the relationship with citizens and communities were rudimentary or non-existent. People outside of government were usually informed, not asked or invited to participate.

In his original essay, Drucker makes the point that the elements of the theory of the business – context, mission, and capabilities – have to make sense in the face of the reality. And they have to make sense to and with each other.

In our case, these features of a more traditional theory of the business of the government certainly made sense for the world in which government operated and, to some extent, still does. They each made sense in the context of the other elements, with which they made up a coherent and plausible set of assumptions about what government was for, how it should do its work, and what mix of skills and expertise it needed to get that work done.

The watchwords for the current theory of the business for government and the public sector include: settled, predictable, hierarchical, elite, relatively closed, a reliance on high levels of institutional 'upwards' trust, a focus on the centre of the system for power and authority, and a level of deference and at least implicit respect.

Theory of the business in government: now

There isn't a definitive new theory of the business for government and the public sector right now; it is still forming.

In fact, this feeling of transition and the uncertainty that pervades some dimension of the daily lived experience of so many public servants, is a defining characteristic of the context in which digital transformation has arrived and has, to some extent, caused.

We think it might be one of the underlying reasons, for example, that in his 2018 conversations with public servants around the country as National President of the Institute of Public Administration Australia, former Secretary of the Department of the Prime Minister & Cabinet Peter Shergold reported a 'deeply uncertain public service,' increasingly unclear about 'how it is perceived by the governments it serves, how it is perceived by outsiders, and how it perceives itself.'[37]

If we were to take a stab at sketching the elements as least from which a new theory reflecting a new set of realistic and well-aligned assumptions is being formed, it would look something like this. See figure 03 for the new theory of government now.

Context: speed, intensity, and connection

The obvious change in the context over the past 20 years or so has been the deep disruption of the digital revolution. Its primary impact has been the speed and intensity with which change happens, and to which policy and other responses need to be formed and deployed.

There are, of course, other sources of disruption and dislocation that have impacted the rate and direction of transformative change. Decades of outsourcing, often masquerading as commissioning but largely driven by a desire to cut costs or fulfil an ideological commitment to 'smaller' government, hasn't helped. Layers of service design changes and so-called reforms, often introduced in accreting layers of disconnected change, have added unnecessary complexity to the reform task.

The drive to cut budgets, and therefore to miss out on the necessary investments of time and money that deliver longer-term benefits, has added to the context in which patient, strategic reform and redesign haven't been allowed, much less permitted to flourish.

And the service environment has shifted too, as new rules and eligibility requirements accumulate on top of old ones and new expectations for speed and convenience, often driven by the availability of cheaper and more efficient digital channels, shift the standards against which service quality and experience are tested and measured.

As well, deference has died; we have become ambivalent about expertise (we want it, we want to rely on it, but have become gun shy about where it comes from and which experts we should trust). Many of our institutions of public governance, including the public sector, are suffering from different kinds of crises of confidence.

The trust game has changed completely,[38] no longer simply a 'vertical' business of trusting and respecting those further up the hierarchies of power and authority but increasingly a 'horizontal' process of trusting peers and networks.

Figure 03: Theory of the business for government now

Theory of the business for government NOW

Context – deep digital disruption; speed and intensity; the "death of deference"; ambivalence about expertise; the decline of institutional confidence; a new equation of trust; the smartest person in the room is the room

Mission – first, activating dispersed collective intelligence to solve complex problems and, second, the curation and judicious use of public power and authority

Capabilities – thriving in the new work order (flexible, distributed, open); from transparency to legibility as the basis for accountability; collaboration and communication; designing and delivering public services with and by the people whose use them (i.e. shifting from government needs to user needs); speed and scale.

- Experimental
- Volatile and unpredictable
- Distributed
- Open
- Collective
- New trust (peers, networks, outwards)
- From the edge
- Legibility

And all the while, driven by the dominant characteristic of the age – connectedness – the policy agenda has become crowded with a tangle of complex problems to which many of the inherited instincts and practices of policy and governance seem poorly matched.

For many outside of government, the perception is that the harder governments try to tackle these difficult problems drawing on the current theory of the business, the worse those problems seem to get.

Mission: solving problems

The new mission of the public sector is problem solving, not the orderly accumulation and management of public power and authority.

That might sound odd given that governments have been in the problem-solving business for a long time and public power and authority clearly still matter.

The point, though, is that whereas the previous theory of the business was grounded in an assumption that the mission of the public sector was the orderly management of public power, which could be used solve problems in a particular way, in the new theory of the business those assumptions are turning around.

The assumption, more and more, is that the value of the public sector derives from its ability to solve problems for people and communities. But the problems are becoming more 'wicked', more connected each to the other and harder to solve using many of the tools, methods, and institutional practices of the past.

It also includes understanding and responding to the changing needs and values of the communities with which it engages, and a public sector that remain accountable to the government, to parliament and to the people it serves.

As the context for government and the public sector has changed, failure to recognise the need to shift their mission will fuel frustration and anger.

Capabilities: assembling intelligence for policy and services with and by people and communities

The watchwords for this emerging theory of the business could include:

Experimental, volatile and unpredictable, distributed, open, collective, new models of trust (peers, networks, outwards), from the edge, an obsession with legibility.

If problem solving in a context of speed, intensity and complex connectedness is the mission of the public sector, relying on traditional skills of policymaking and hierarchical deference to elite expertise wielded largely from the centre of government is not going to work. (Note that we cover capabilities in detail in chapter 4.)

Connecting or assembling more dispersed and complex networks of expertise and knowledge, including the expertise of service users, citizens and front-line staff will become the dominant way of working.[39] There is a premium on experimenting and testing ideas rapidly and then adjusting, calling on the ideas and expertise of a much wider array of people and interests than in the past, not the least being the experiential knowledge of citizens, customers, and front-line staff. That will have the added effect of undermining the impact of those who currently lay claim, through traditional forms of lobbying and 'insider trading', to some of the commanding heights of policy influence and political priority setting.

The skills of design, of data analysis (including especially the policy, technical and ethical skills to render the mantras of 'open government' and 'open data' both meaningful and practical) and of effective collaboration and convening will be in demand.[40]

A better way to communicate and engage with citizens and communities will have to respond to the decline of trust and ambivalence about the sources and impact of expertise by finding better ways to make the work of government and the public sector more legible.

Agencies are being asked to confront new demands for speed and scale. And there is a continuing push to replace a focus on government needs (the producer) with client or customer needs (the consumer) as the organising principle for service and policy design and delivery. It turns out that the rhetoric of 'citizen-centric' is much easier to repeat and include in a strategic plan or statement of values than it is to turn into subversive but liberating practice.

Those who lead and work in the public sector will need to become more adept at helping those outside government 'read' what is happening, why, and to what effect. That's a skill in itself and demands different bundles of courage, empathy, and emotional intelligence, a confidence with greater openness in the conduct of government.

If we're right about the direction of travel in which the theory of the business is moving for government and the public sector, it holds some practical implications for the work of the public service and public servants themselves.

It's an interesting speculation that the proliferating 'ombudsman'-type roles across different domains of public work reflects an old theory of the business that pays insufficient attention to the need for problem solving as a direct and more important part of the work of the public sector.

As a final reflection, it's worth recalling that in Drucker's original article, one of the examples he draws on to illustrate what is at stake if an organisation fails to renovate its theory of the business is IBM's failure to react quickly enough at the beginning of the laptop revolution.

It is tempting to see some parallels between IBM's failure to see the significance of a world shifting from large, cumbersome but still powerful mainframe computing to highly distributed and increasingly powerful individual computing on laptops and the need for a similar shift in thinking by governments away from large-scale and centralised command and control solutions and practices to smaller and more place- and people-responsive models of care, service, and support.

What's digital transformation got to do with it?

In a word, everything.

But not in the way we might expect if we stick to the largely transactional and process nature of much of focus that largely serves as the digital transformation story up to now.

The time is right for a new theory of government, because the current way of working isn't working.

The Australian Senate set out a 'litany of failures' following an inquiry into digital services in 2018, including the sale of Medicare card numbers on the dark web, repeated crashes of the ATO website, halting the start of online schools' 'NAPLAN' (National Assessment Program – Literacy and Numeracy) testing, and the abandonment of an apprenticeship platform, as well as the limited delivery – to date – of the DTA[41] – more on that later.

The reasons, including systematic problems, contractual issues with suppliers, the shortage of skills, senior leaders moving on, split accountability, and often managing to requirements and plans rather than user needs, are well documented in audit and parliamentary reports in Australia (and also in global comparators like the UK).

People are starting to ask why this is the case, including the former Shadow Minister for the Digital Economy and the Shadow Minister for Human Services, the Hon. Ed Husic MP, who has raised the profile of so-called government waste of taxpayers' money and has called for a different approach to delivery.[42] This includes government taking on (or back) more of the direct responsibility for digital delivery, which is in line with our argument here.

A bigger picture

The piece we're missing, or at least substantially under-estimating, is the extent to which digital is changing everything about the way we conceive of and conduct the business of the public sector and government. And it is doing that at a more profound level than we are factoring into our discussions about what we should expect digital to deliver.

What do we mean?

Well, according to Jamie Susskind's tough-minded analysis, for example, digital tools and the underlying shifts in the ownership and deployment of the technology platforms from which they arose and which they rely on, are rewriting the rules about democracy, freedom, power, and legitimacy.[43]

The premise of his book *Future Politics* is that 'relentless advances in science and technology are set to transform the way we live together, with consequences for politics that are profound and frightening in equal measure.' Ominously, he argues that 'we are not yet ready – intellectually, philosophically or morally – for the world we are creating'.[44]

The analysis is grounded in the observation that 'those who control these technologies will increasingly control the rest of us.' And what that means, in practical terms, is profound:

> 'They'll have power, meaning they'll have a stable and wide-ranging capacity to get us to do things of significance that we wouldn't otherwise do. Increasingly, they'll set the limits of our liberty, decreeing what may be done and what is forbidden. They'll determine the future of democracy, causing it to flourish or decay. And their algorithms will decide vital questions of social justice, allocating social goods and sorting us into hierarchies of status and esteem.'[45]

In an interview about the book, Susskind explains why this wave of deep digital disruption will be different to those that have come before.

Digital technologies, he explains, have a threefold effect on power.

Firstly, they constrain us when we use them, through the rules contained in their code. He points out that as more and more of our important freedoms are exercised through technology (freedom of speech via online platforms, freedom of movement through driverless vehicles, and so on, each with their own rules and limits), we become 'rule-takers, constrained by digital technology.'[46]

Secondly, he argues that the way these technologies scrutinise us, through the gathering of data, is itself a form of power.

For the first time in history, 'almost everything about our lives can be captured, processed, and stored'. And there is a simple rule emerging – the more data governments and tech firms hold about us, the more easily they can influence us. As well, 'the mere act of data-gathering functions as a deterrent to certain types of behaviour – if we know we're being watched, we're more likely to discipline ourselves.'[47]

And thirdly, these pervasive and unaccountable technologies 'control our perception of the world.' – We rely on these technologies to gather and filter information. So, which slice of reality we are presented with will determine our political priorities, and what goes on the agenda of public priorities and issues to tackle.

The underlying problem, which he uncovers in some depth in the book, is that our attitudes to technology need to change. We can't just be consumers or assume we're engaged in a simple commercial transaction. He advocates that we 'apply the same scrutiny and scepticism to the new technologies of power that we have always brought to powerful politicians.' Why? Because technology affects us not just as consumers but as citizens. In the twenty-first century, '[T]he digital is political.'[48]

The answer, he writes, is to develop a new intellectual framework 'that can help us to think clearly and critically about the political consequences of digital innovation.' In particular, because these are technologies that fundamentally impact the two central elements in political life – communication and information – they strike at the heart of the three things on which Susskind claims political order is based – coordination, cooperation, and control:

'It's impossible to organize collective life without at least one of the three. And none of them is possible without some system for exchanging information, whether among ordinary people or between ruler and ruled.'[49]

In other words, Susskind is arguing a kind of 'stop laughing, this is serious' line that provokes us to consider whether we comprehend the seriousness of what is happening.

In our frame, Susskind reinforces the need for the digital transformation project in government to engage a much deeper complexity, including its implications well beyond the ability to speed up a few transactions.

His analysis is also a powerful rendition, even though he doesn't invoke the Drucker frame, of some of the unravelling assumptions about the fit between how we govern and do public work, and the changing world around us, that is an inevitable part of the search for a new theory of the business.

He accepts that, while the state and big tech firms that control digital technologies will increasingly determine questions of freedom, democracy, and social justice, in each of those areas there is potential for gains and for disaster.

For example, benefits such as job and credit card applications will increasingly be determined by algorithms. He explains that if you get those algorithms right, they can be fair and unbiased and non-discriminatory, and can enhance and create opportunity for people. But if you get them wrong, 'they can be bigoted and blind to, or reflective of, injustices that already exist – by blocking out particular social groups inadvertently or deliberately.'[50]

The digital transformation conversation is 'the major political debate of our lifetime' because it is about 'the extent to which our lives should be governed by powerful digital systems – and on what terms.'[51]

If Susskind's thesis is confronting and offers a powerful illustration of the kind of complexity and seriousness with which the digital transformation project should be prosecuted, Shoshana Zuboff ramps up the stakes even higher. Her book looking at the rise of what she describes as 'surveillance capitalism', carries the subtitle, 'The Fight for a Human Future at the New Frontier of Power', which hints at its scope and implications.

For her, the digital realm is overtaking and redefining everything familiar 'even before we have had a chance to ponder and decide'. She accepts that 'we celebrate the networked world for the many ways in which it enriches our capabilities and prospects'. The problem is that it has 'birthed whole new territories of anxiety, danger, and violence as the sense of a predictable future slips away.'[52]

The book is uncompromising on those few, large technology companies who have pioneered, and are profiting immensely from, the rise of this 'rogue' form of capitalism, based on collecting and then selling, often without our consent, the 'behavioural surplus' we generate in the form of the data about ourselves in our increasingly comprehensive digital lives.[53]

For Zuboff, we need to ditch the illusion that 'the networked form has some kind of indigenous moral content, that being "connected" is somehow intrinsically pro-social, innately inclusive, or naturally tending toward the democratization of knowledge.'[54]

It hasn't worked out that way. Far from ushering in new forms of distributed and accountable power and authority, it appears to have concentrated that power, and therefore disturbing capacities for control and manipulation, in fewer and fewer hands.

By analogy, she suggests that 'just as industrial civilization flourished at the expense of nature and now threatens to cost us the Earth, an information civilization shaped by surveillance capitalism and its new "instrumentarian power" will thrive at the expense of human nature and will threaten to cost us our humanity.'[55] Its expression in a 'ubiquitous sensate, networked, computational infrastructure' she describes as the 'Big Other' elided to a 'novel and deeply antidemocratic vision of society and social relations.'[56]

Zuboff aspires to something much more positive, what she terms a 'third modernity', 'in which a genuine inversion and its social compact are institutionalised as principles of a new rational digital capitalism aligned with a society of individuals and supported by democratic institutions.'[57]

We don't have the space or time here to explore in depth the rich and unsettling analysis that emerges from the work of writers like Jamie Susskind and Shoshana Zuboff. They both raise the huge concerns and powerful opportunities in which the digital transformation project, unstoppable as it now seems, comes wrapped.

But it reinforces the need for the discussion about the significance and direction of digital transformation in government and the public sector to connect into the deeper and often contested dimensions of what is happening in the changing external world.

The point is also to reinforce the observation, which we've sketched in this opening chapter, that these big structural and institutional shifts offer more evidence that our view about the mission, context, and capabilities on which our current theory of the business for governing and the work of the public sector are based are drifting apart.

Another take on the same kind of reframing that both Susskind and Zuboff offer is the recent analysis by Jamie Bartlett of the contest, as he frames it, between the 'people' and 'tech'.

It's a blunt and pessimistic analysis. 'In the coming few years', he announces, 'either tech will destroy democracy and the social order as we know it, or politics will stamp its authority over the digital world.'[58]

What he means by tech includes social media platforms, data, mobile technology, and AI, all terms that we explain in chapter 3. A familiar litany, but a list that contains technologies to which, Bartlett argues, we have ceded too many of the fundamental components of a functional political system – control, parliamentary sovereignty, economic equality, civic society, and an informed citizenry.

These two 'grand systems' – technology and democracy – are 'locked in a bitter conflict.' They are the product of quite different rules and principles. The outcome of the contest will determine the extent to which what Bartlett identifies as the six pillars of a functioning democracy – 'active citizens, a shared culture, free elections, stakeholder equality, a competitive economy and an independent civil society and trust in authority' – cannot just function but flourish.[59]

His thesis is simple. We need to avoid what he describes as a 'moral singularity', the point at which we delegate 'substantial moral and political reasoning to machines'. By contrast, the imperative is to make sure that politics and democracy assert their authority over the technology.[60]

The odds are not good.

Rehearsing the same trends of predictable agglomerating technology and commercial power to a very few large companies, which is the point at which the technology evolution has reached, Bartlett points out that 'whenever there is such concentration of economic strength, there is usually a corrosion of politics, because wealthy and powerful people will always wish to maintain and increase their power.'[61]

The thesis and its ramifications explore more extensive and troubling territory than we need to follow here. But it's the same insight as we drew from the work of Susskind and Zuboff, that the digital transformation project invites more substantial inquiry and analysis than it often seems to get, especially in its work impacting government and the public sector.

These insights carry big implications for the way governments respond through policy and regulation to the way in which digital is now so marbled into the fabric of society and the economy. And those responses have a lot riding on them, not the least because of the impact on the flow of trust and legitimacy through our democracy and its institutions and practices.

Mike Bracken, the former leader of the UK's GDS, has spoken in blunt terms about the challenge of following the digital transformation impulse deeply in the architecture of the public sector.

The problem is that, as public administrators, 'we need to work differently and more collaboratively in a system that is not set up to do that.' Disturbingly, Bracken recounted that, when he started in government from his role as the digital lead for transforming The Guardian, 'Whitehall was described ... as a warring band of tribal bureaucrats held together by a common pension scheme, and there is something in that.'[62]

His answer, and the answer manifest in the work of the GDS under his leadership, is implied in this query: 'Are we going to back a centre of government that works for all of government and is not departmentally aligned to a single issue? Or are we going to try to use a civil service system that is tremendously resilient but works in silos, to try to effect digital transformation.' He concludes, 'The jury is out, but that's the real question.'[63]

Another part of the solution, which GDS and other Digital Central Units, including Australia (more on those in chapter 3), have copied in various ways, is to shift towards a 'platform' view of government. It can't work any longer for different agencies to build platforms for different parts of their work – payments, identity management, procurement – with no reference to the use of those platforms by others outside their agency.

Bracken's reflection that he had hoped 'the system would have had more capacity for institutional reform than it has' is balanced by a warning that is a lesson for every institution in every sector: '[T]he internet always wins. Government is no different. We ignore that at our peril.'[64]

It is a journey that encounters battles that have to be constantly re-fought. As Ministers and permanent secretaries change (in the UK civil service context), '[Y]ou have to win these arguments over again. Just because you've won them once doesn't mean you've won them permanently, especially in a system that will roll back to what it knows.'[65]

This tendency to 'roll back', if you stop pushing, points to a deeper challenge. Without institutional reform (by which we assume he means structure, culture and underlying assumptions, along the lines of the 'theory of the business' framework we are using here), then you are 'destined to repeat the failures of the past.'[66]

Others, like Richard Pope who worked with Bracken and with the GDS in its various early stages, grapple with similar conundrums at the heart of the digital transformation project. Pope's work, especially on government as a platform, which we will look at in more detail in chapter 3, grapples with issues of design, technology, and culture from whose collision new methods to organise and execute the work of government is emerging.[67]

What does it mean in practice?

So far, so good, but for some perhaps, too theoretical and conceptual.

It is a measure of the digital transformation conversation in Australia and elsewhere as it applies to government and the public sector that, for many, this chapter might be construed as a bit of an indulgence. And it does sometimes feel that the digital dimension of our discussion in government and the public sector remains stuck in an intellectual and theoretical frame that is thinner and less nourishing than it should be. (There are some notable exceptions and we'll come to them in a moment.)

Let's be clear, again, that this isn't a claim that the immediate and practical work of service improvement and adopting new digital tools and platforms in government that address the more immediate transactional needs isn't important and valuable. It is. It's one inescapable part of the transformation process.

But it isn't enough.

Accepting the bigger challenge of evolving a new theory of the business is essential to create a context in which the more immediate and pressing daily work of digital change make sense. It is the only way in which we can properly understand the real significance of the work that is being done and often under-valued or misunderstood.

But this discussion is not just theoretical.

There are plenty of examples from the real world of governing and the work of the public sector in Australia, and around the world, that betray some powerful signs of an emerging new theory of the business. And we should recognise them for what they are and add to their momentum and spread.

For example, what does it mean when the CEO of the NHS (Simon Stevens) in the UK starts to talk about his business as a social movement?[68] What is happening when this quintessentially 'old theory of the business' public institution, almost classically defined by its instinct for centralised, top-down, one-size-fits all uniformity of services basically offered 'to and for' people, appropriates the language of movements and networks? Why does Simon Stevens think it's necessary to invent a new theory of his huge, iconic but troubled public sector business?

Still in the UK, the Chief Economist of the Bank of England, Andy Haldane, engaged in an unusual program of 'town hall' meetings and conversation with people and communities across the UK to try and explain how the Bank worked and why its work was significant.

In an interview with the *Financial Times*,[69] Haldane said, 'I have been thinking about how far the Bank of England has so far climbed the citizen engagement ladder. Truth be told, I suspect for the first 300 years of its life, the Bank of England scarcely had its foot on the first rung.' He went on to explain that 'it saw little need even to inform the wider public about the economy and policy. Trust among the public was anonymised, institutionalised and given. When tempted to step up a rung, the Bank quickly contracted an acute form of vertigo.'

In the same interview, he explained that things are changing. The bank is making a big effort 'to simplify and demystify its words' and to 'challenge its ideas and thinking'. The bank's staff blog, *Bank Underground*, is one example of such challenge. Last year, it recorded its millionth hit. The Bank of England running a blog recording over a million hits stands as a powerful example of an institution coming to terms with a digital transformation process cutting deeply into the tough membrane of its own theory of the business.

Something interesting is clearly going on when a 300-year-old institution feels compelled to wander the countryside trying to explain itself better to people it has assiduously ignored for most of that time.

The same ethic is manifest in many different domains.

In the area of child protection, for example, after too many years of too many royal commissions and reviews (over 50 in the last few years) spending billions of dollars for what seems to have been too little in the way of real change, different approaches are being trialled. The work of projects like Logan Together, ChildStory in NSW, and the work of the award-winning Family by Family program from The Australian Centre for Social Innovation are just three examples.[70]

In the world of international development aid, the work the Innovation Xchange in the Department of Foreign Affairs and Trade, led by Sarah Pearson as the Department's first Chief Innovation Officer and Chief Scientist, is doing to one of Australia's most venerable, some might argue impenetrably conservative and traditional, institutions of public governance reflects a similar process of theory reinvention that Simon Stevens is leading in the NHS.[71]

The Xchange is using a mix of human-centred design tools and techniques and innovation challenge models to flush out not just entrepreneurial skills and inventiveness from the donor community but innate creativity and problem-solving capabilities in the countries to which the aid is being directed.

There are more examples: the use of predictive analytics in New York to become faster and more confident about pre-empting fires in poorly maintained and high-risk buildings;[72] the inversion of a traditional regulatory policy process of top-down research, drafting, and limited consultation in the arcane but, it turns out, vital area of providing access to public and private land for commercial and recreational apiarists in NSW to be replaced by a process of ethnographic observation and intense focus on the user experience of regulation.[73] Something more basic like the transition away from manual checking at border controls in airports and ports, or the use of digital licensing for cars and car registration. Some of the experiments with open banking[74] offer another example of an industry using digital transformation to explore big issues of purpose and role.

What all of these examples speak to are government agencies in different ways feeling their way into experiments with different theories of their various businesses. Assumptions about the work and mission of government, about the context in which that mission is lived and delivered, and, especially, assumptions about the skills and capabilities necessary to discharge that changing mission in a changing context are all resulting in new work and new ways of working.

A new theory of the business for government and the public sector

There's nothing simple or straightforward about the hard work we need to do, digital transformation and all, to rethink the theory of the business for government and the public sector in Australia.

Adding to the complexity is the realisation that the digital transformation work for government is different to that of the private sector, especially as government has a role both as a direct player in the use of new digital capabilities and as a regulator, and often as a platform provider that impacts the way others outside of government engage with and use those same digital tools and capabilities.

Before we conclude, there are a few other ideas we think are foundational to the new theory's evolution, however it finally works out.

Rediscovering the value of 'public'

Jane Jacobs' work to tell the story of the life and death of cities, including especially her adopted home of New York City, reminds us of two attributes that are entwined in the search for a new theory of the business for government and the public sector.

One is the value and virtue of 'public' itself.

Jacobs' struggle with the power of the formal structures of city planning, led at that time in the 1950s by Robert Moses, developer and New York City Parks Commissioner, was in part a sustained effort to reassert a sense of public that emanated not from the institutions and practice of public power – basically the top-down dictates of Moses and his big plans for urban regeneration and growth – but from the more complex, less visible but still powerful bottom-up interactions of people in and between their communities.[75]

The other closely associated attribute was the discovery of the spontaneous order in much of our social life in cities, an order which city planners and engineers often mistake for messy or even chaotic hanging around or simply ignore altogether. 'The point of city sidewalks,' Jacobs explained, 'is precisely that they are public.'[76] And the job they do contains any number of deep assumptions about the way a city is supposed to work – its theory of the business, if you like:

'Under the seeming disorder of the old city, wherever the old city is working successfully, is a marvelous order for maintaining the safety of the streets and the freedom of the city. It is a complex order. Its essence is intricacy of sidewalk use, bringing with it a constant succession of eyes.'[77]

She goes on to say:

'This order is all composed of movement and change ... not to a simple-minded precision dance with everyone kicking up at the same time ... but to an intricate ballet in which the individual dancers and ensembles all have distinctive parts which miraculously reinforce each other and compose an orderly whole.'[78]

She finishes with this classic observation: 'The ballet of the good city sidewalk never repeats itself from place to place, and in any one place is always replete with new improvisations.'[79] We can note the larger implications for a rethink of the theory of the business for the role and identity of the public sector in the first place.

One of those implications speaks to the way in which the sector, and those who work in it, conceive of their role and work. Perhaps in recent years there has been too much emphasis placed on the role of the public service as the 'delivery arm' of Ministers and the government (which of course, at one level, it is) and not enough on its enduring institutional obligations for stewardship and the quality of public work beyond the term or interests of any particular government or governing party or parties.

The work of evolving a new theory of the business for the public sector must include some discussion of its role as a servant of three legitimate masters: the government of the day, the Parliament as a representation of the will of the people, and the people themselves.

Public purpose and public value

In December 2018, Professor Mariana Mazzucato came to Australia as part of a rising global movement, fuelled in large measure by her writing, research, and teaching, which is rethinking the role of government and the public sector in terms of mission-driven innovation, inclusive growth, and public value.

What her work reminds us is that at the heart of the new theory of the business for the public sector is a new theory of public purpose and public value. And that conversation is fired by the evidence about how the public sector, at its best, has purposed its authority and power for creative and courageous investments in problem solving, often fired by bold and breakthrough innovation.

Professor Mazzucato's work forensically rediscovers 'the entrepreneurial state'[80] and explains why bold public imagination and public values are at the heart of capitalism's reinvention. More recently, she has peeled back years of received economic theory to reclaim a theory of value hijacked by an ideology of entrepreneurial ascendancy that has mistaken 'takers' for 'makers' in the broader economy and, in the process, dangerously diminished the role of government and the business of the public sector.

She notes, for example, that breakthroughs like the Internet itself, Global Positioning System (GPS), touch-screen display, and Siri voice-activated personal assistance all emerged from radical public investments that embraced extreme uncertainty. They did not come about due to the presence of venture capitalists or 'garage tinkerers'. It was, Mazzucato argues, the very 'visible hand of the State' that made these innovations happen, which would not have come about 'had we waited for the 'market' and business to do it alone – or government to simply stand aside and provide the basics.'

Later in the same analysis, Mazzucato argues that the public sector has been the lead player in the 'knowledge economy' too – an economy driven by technological change and knowledge production and diffusion.

She points out that, from the development of aviation, nuclear energy, computers, the Internet, biotechnology, and, more recently, green technology, '[I]t is, and has been, the State – not the private sector – that has kick-started and developed the engine of growth, because of its willingness to take risks in areas where the private sector has been too risk averse.'

Her conclusion, that 'in a political environment where the policy frontiers of the State are now being deliberately rolled back, the contributions of the State need to be understood more than ever,' offers another take on how a larger project to rethink government's theory of the business frames its digital transformation.

In an important insight for our analysis, the observation that 'the creation of value is collective' suggests that, as part of the new theory of the business, rather than being mere 'regulators' of health care or digital innovation, 'as co-creators of that care and digital transformation, policymakers would have a more justifiable right to make sure that the benefits are accessible to all.'[81]

Some early markers

Starting a book about digital transformation in government with a chapter expounding the need for a new theory of the business for governing and the work of the public sector reinforces the point that the digital transformation project is important enough to be taken seriously.

This is not a distraction to the main game. Quite the opposite. We think that, in many ways, these ideas and trends *are* the main game.

We don't think it's possible to engage the full potential and implications of the digital transformation story in government without mobilising a new theory of the business for governing and for the work of the public sector.

The assumptions about mission, context, and capabilities, on which current models and methods of government and public sector work rest, have been eroding for some time and, in some cases, have become obsolete. In many important ways, they have drifted apart, which is just as bad as losing sight of them altogether. Some of them have been obscured by decades of reform and more or less ideologically driven policy and operational change.

We need to think again and work out the best way to line them up for contemporary and emerging conditions (or trends, as we explain in the next chapter). It is from its contributions to that fundamental work that digital transformation ultimately derives its significance and value.

We'll look at some of these in more detail in chapter 4 on changing the work of the public sector and the way the public sector works. But we're already witnessing a series of shifts of practice which are strong markers of the new theory of the business journey.

Power and authority structures and cultures are shifting from relatively centralised, elite, and closed to relatively open, shared, and devolved. It's one of the reasons that many of the more profound shifts of shape and culture for government and the public sector heralded by deep digital change are so stoutly resisted by some whose contemporary positions of power and control reflect conditions that digital transformation erodes. This shift seems both implacable and necessary.

Accountability is shifting from more or less up-and-down, steep vertical hierarchies that link together positional power and status to more or less down-and-out networks that privilege authentic engagement with people and communities. Our models of oversight and audit, ranging from annual reports to Senate Estimates committees to the work of the various Auditors-General around the country tend still to be firmly fixed on the former and have difficulty offering much insight into the tools, practice and consequences of the latter.

The problem is that the most promising emerging attempts to tackle the complex public challenges we want to fix evince accountability patterns that are consistent with this trend, which leave those mired in an older theory of the business perplexed and sometimes hostile. The problem is promising new ways to tackle entrenched public problems, reflecting new forms of working, and new patterns of accountability often encounter debilitating efforts to hold them to old forms of account.

In a related trend, our notions of accountability are still largely dominated by the pursuit of transparency instead of an obsession with legibility. In the old theory of the business, a relatively closed, centralised, and elite conduct of public power and authority offered a minimum level of intermittent and highly formalised, bare minimum visibility about what it was doing and how it conducted itself.

This was reflective of a world of relatively high public trust and almost supine deference.

Now, the demand is not just for transparency but for legibility. People don't just want to see; they need to 'read' and understand. And they often need to ask much deeper and more persistent questions, not just about what has happened and been done in their name but why. Legibility fuels legitimacy which, in turn, mobilises trust. That's a whole new dynamic of power somewhere close to the heart of the new theory of the business.

This is very much about the shift that others have noticed from 'old power', which sees it as currency to be spent (closed, inaccessible, and leader-driven) to a 'new power' which is more like a current that is 'open, participatory, and peer-driven ... it uploads, and it distributes. Like water or electricity, it's most forceful when it surges.'[82]

The conversation between government and citizens is changing from episodic, structured, and largely controlled by government to one that is more persistent, less structured, and largely controlled from the bottom, by people and communities. Elections and a few flyers from your local MP aren't enough to satisfy the demand for an exchange about democracy and public purpose that is more open, consistent, and less confected. Not that everyone wants to talk about, and to, government all the time – they don't. We're all busy. But when it comes to the sense of a more authentic manifestation of the democratic deal which increasingly people feel isn't working for them, we want something more.[83]

The way the public sector solves problems is gradually moving from a structured, linear, and largely government-controlled process to one that is more experimental, engaging, and fuelled by new and more distributed sources of expertise, experience, and knowledge.

Ways of working in the public sector are changing (painfully slowly at times, it must be said) to become less rigid and constrained by structure and hierarchy and more flexible and collaborative. These shifts impact the sequencing of work, its pace, and the methods used, and they challenge entrenched assumptions and practices of authority and control.

They are also testing well-established patterns of where work is done and the physical arrangements and conditions that are most conducive to the mix of research, engagement, deliberation, and analysis that go into good policy and decision-making.

Gradually, workplaces and work styles are building in degrees of flex and adaptability which are still relatively new to the more settled patterns of work and leadership in the public sector.

How to find and nurture the right mix of talent inside the public sector, and to then blend that talent with skills and expertise outside the public sector, is becoming more complex and demanding. The talent game in the public sector is changing in a number of ways. The range and mix of talent is changing. It's still important to find and grow talent in traditional areas like research, analysis, policy, advising, administration, and technical expertise.

But new skills are emerging, including design, data analysis, collaboration, and convening, 'campaigning' (or what perhaps the Organisation for Economic Co-operation and Development (OECD) might include in 'insurgency')[84] and coalition building in support of complex, long-term policy solutions and rising levels of comfort and confidence with digital tools, platforms, and culture. And how talent is treated in the public sector is coming under renewed scrutiny, with a premium on more effective ways to motivate talent and create and hold the spaces in which it can perform at its best.

Finally, the rhythms of discernment and judgement for policy development and decision making are becoming shorter and more fragmented, requiring new ways to use collective intelligence and collaboration. In a world which has become 'too big to know' and in which 'the smartest person in the room is the room',[85] the way policy is developed, and decisions get made is changing. It's neither possible nor helpful to retain earlier notions of analysis and judgement largely internal and exclusive to the public sector, with perhaps occasional bursts of 'consultation' or external expert advising.

Knowledge, insight, experience, and analysis are increasingly functions of dispersed and sometimes unexpected networks of people and organisations with important parts of the policy puzzle to contribute. Faster and more reliable ways of finding and connecting them into the policy and decision-making process is at a premium.

This is the focus of work at GovLab in the US, whose goal is to 'strengthen the ability of institutions – including but not limited to governments – and people to work more openly, collaboratively, effectively and legitimately to make better decisions and solve public problems.' The lab's research assumes that increased availability and use of data and 'new ways to leverage the capacity, intelligence, and expertise of people in the problem-solving process, combined with new advances in technology and science' can have a deep impact on the way we govern and take decisions for the public good.[86]

As a final observation, we can speculate that earlier and continuing experiments with the 'open government' agenda, especially as it has been joined to the digital government project, have also foundered on the failure to match the priorities for reform with a deeper discussion about the implied shift in the assumptions about government's mission, context, and capabilities.

It's another domain in which a bigger discussion about the theory of the business for governing and the public sector might unlock more of the intended benefits of a reform agenda, in this case around the adoption of an open government philosophy, than focusing only on the immediate reforms themselves.

Three important messages

There are three messages to take away from this chapter:

1. To explore its full potential, we need to connect the digital transformation project to a larger context and a bigger task – the search for a new theory of the business for governing and the work of the public sector – which it is partly causing, and to which is a big part of the answer.

2. The analysis points to some of the markers of an emerging, digitally infused new theory of the business. The transition from an old to a new theory is underway, which is both exciting and unsettling, especially as a new theory remains a work in progress.

3. The chapter has also sketched some dimensions of the larger context, including the implications of digital transformation for big questions about power, democracy, and accountability, the value and significance of the public realm, and the importance of an active, creative and risk-taking public sector.

Chapter 2

A Changing World

The point about the digital transformation of government is that digital transformation isn't the point.

The point is, or should be, what's happening to government and governing and the structures and values of public work. All of them are being tested like never before for the competence, relevance, and trust from which they derive their value and legitimacy. Digital transformation is the solution to a set of structural, institutional, and operational opportunities and risks it has largely caused and certainly intensified.

Understanding the trajectory of the digital transformation project in Australia means putting the discussion into that larger context.[87] If you don't, the danger is that 'transformation' may hit the target but miss the point.

In this, as in many other domains, Australia can't afford to 'wait and see' what happens in the rest of the world when it comes to the digital transformation of the way we govern and prosecute our public work.

This should be a time to urgently rethink the underlying theory of the business – aligning changing assumptions about context, mission, and capabilities – for success in the digital global economy and for a stronger and more accountable democracy. The pace and intensity of digital transformation around the world offers a country like Australia a compelling invitation to keep up and stay connected to its leading edge.

But because of our size and relative economic and technology weight in the world, the temptation is to sit back and monitor developments, in areas like AI and data, for example, and then to 'fast follow' when action becomes unavoidable. That would be a disappointing outcome.

In the first chapter, we argued that this way of looking at digital transformation in government should remind us that digital transformation is fuelling the transition from an old to a new but still unformed and unclear theory of the business. In the new conditions of a society and economy themselves being transformed (or disrupted), for good and for bad, by digital, how does the business of governing and the work of the public sector realign assumptions about context, mission, and capabilities?

In this chapter, we take that framing further and sketch some trends and developments in society and the economy, governance and democracy, and work and technology.

We present here a summary of these trends. Our purpose is not to interrogate any of these trends in depth. There are some references and detail we have not included. We have provided links to the original studies so you can delve deeper – if you have time and interest. The focus of this chapter is to summarise a lot of detail from the studies and reports we analysed to sketch of the larger canvas of emerging and anticipated change that creates part of the context in which digital transformation is taking place and against which its quality and impact should be weighed.

This brief review hammers home the observation that at least some part of getting 'there' in the digital transformation project in government is a function of conceiving of its significance in a much larger canvas of change and transition. 'There' is partly defined by evidence that digital transformation offers some new ways to confront the implications of each of these trends as well as the consequence of their interaction.

The context and purpose of transformation

The persistent failure, in what has become something of a dialogue of the deaf between the digital disruptors and those being digitally disrupted in government and the public service, to construe what is happening in these larger strategic terms is one of the reasons our progress here in Australia is patchy – occasionally brilliant, often frustrating.

We have to understand better what digital transformation means for policymaking, legislation, and regulation, for the way decisions are made about public investment, for the design and delivery of services, for the evolution of new relationships of communication, influence and accountability with citizens and communities, for government's role as both 'platform' and 'player', and, finally, for the changing nature of public work and public workers. We'll deal with many of those issues in more depth in chapter 4 when we look at the way the work of the public sector is changing and, therefore, why the way the public sector works also has to change.

For the most part, the discussion in Australia about digital transformation in and across government is obsessed with the digital part.

Those who drive much of the discussion understand the digital piece, and its sometimes overhyped technology innovation and invention, but they understand much less about the world they are trying to transform.

On the other side, those who understand the world of governing, of policymaking, and of settled, sometimes scratchy and awkward public institutions and processes know little about digital and technology. Too often, the default is a kind of mutual suspicion, even hostility, or accusations of 'stubborn resistance', or 'digital for digital's sake'.

Like two fractious and occasionally warring tribes, the digital part and the government part don't really understand each other all that well. Occasionally they try and connect, but often it seems as if they are talking with great animation and insight to themselves and past each other.

Periodically, bits of the conversation do join up and dialogue breaks out. Seemingly random acts of mutual understanding turn into shared ambition, common cause, and purposeful action. Stuff happens, impressive stuff sometimes, that joins the enduring instincts and ambitions of public work with intelligent, empathetic, and creative digital design and execution. Intimations of transformation greatness are glimpsed when we stop simply doing digital and start to be digital.

But too often, digital transformation in and of government is an extended exercise in distracting and expensive frustration. Those leading and doing public work can't make themselves understood as they try and explain the excruciating complexity and nuance of their work, drenched with the ambiguities and contradictions of politics and the head-banging clash of values and interests.

Meanwhile, the 'digitalists' can't understand why the compelling and irresistible logic of their insights and inventions can't more easily and rapidly be absorbed into the weird fabric into which they are trying to weave their magic.

Instead, they find themselves too often being stoutly resisted by a mix of ignorance and intransigence, dusted sometimes with complacency or arrogance, or a bit of both.

Too often, the discussion about Australia's progress in its ambitions for digital transformation of government drifts from a grounding sense of purpose and context. Pretty much forever and in all domains, the transformative consequences of technology are inextricably linked to the shifting purpose and conduct of the business they are disrupting. Technology causes problems to which it turns out to be largely the solution and, in a well-worn insight known as Amara's law, we've learned that we tend to overestimate the short-term impact of technology transformation and wildly underestimate its long-term structural consequences.[88]

It's no different in government.

In fact, it's an effect whose paradoxical implications in the public domain are amplified many times over.

Rising expectations: trust and ethics

Somewhere in the mix of these big changes, a new equation of trust is being written. Wherever they are at work, these patterns of transformation weave great possibilities for better service, convenience, productivity, and empowerment, and they can do the same in and for government.

Another big piece of the story is the new rules being written about the relationship between people and machines.

A new struggle for legibility is reshaping many of the assumptions about trust underlying aspects of culture, commerce, government, and politics. New, largely digital assumptions about transparency and the capacity to mobilise support or criticism, for example, are being baked into the way we conceive of and use power, knowledge, and accountability to make the world more democratic, in the broadest sense, as well as fairer and less unequal.

Powerful new opportunities to break up old sources of economic, political, and cultural power are being wrought just when the new digital rules are being dramatically exploited by a few emerging platform giants – think Amazon, Google, Netflix, Apple, Facebook and Microsoft – to replace them with even greater reach and apparently unaccountable control. At the same time, opportunities for influence and action are opening up as people exercise agency by mastering the routines of digital campaigning. But barriers to access, participation, and influence are emerging.

The good and the bad of this new world are often strung out between extremes of hope and possibility on the one hand and, on the other, fear and anxiety about where these new rules might be taking us.

Government is both a major player in, and a victim of, these gyrations of deep change and rapid restructuring.

So, the big question about how well digital transformation in Australia is progressing might be framed not so much as a simple calibration of speed and performance – whether we are doing enough, going fast enough – but a more nuanced assessment of how well digital transformation of government is contributing to its larger purpose.

For now at least, that purpose might simply be construed as helping people, communities, and society at large to shape and influence these big economic, social, cultural, and political transitions, and, beyond that, helping to maximise our collective chances of engaging this new world with a distinctively Australian mix of energy, inventiveness, and practical humanity.[89]

Setting the stage

In 2016, Klaus Schwab, the executive director and founder of the World Economic forum (WEF), wrote a short essay introducing the concept of the 'fourth industrial revolution'. He opened with this assessment:

'We stand on the brink of a technological revolution that will fundamentally alter the way we live, work, and relate to one another. In its scale, scope, and complexity, the transformation will be unlike anything humankind has experienced before.'[90]

He went on to say:

'We do not yet know just how it will unfold, but one thing is clear: the response to it must be integrated and comprehensive, involving all stakeholders of the global polity, from the public and private sectors to academia and civil society'.[91]

Schwab introduced a concept – the fourth industrial revolution – to frame many big shifts and trends already underway and which have become even more significant. He also signalled in that introduction some essential features of a response, including especially from governments and the public realm, to which we will return.

Understanding how those trends create the conditions in which the purpose and business of government are being tested and redefined is the right place to start in any effort to assess the digital transformation journey for government and the public sector in Australia.

The point is that judgements about how well we are tracking in our efforts across Australia to digitally transform government must be measured against their contribution to helping government and the public sector respond to these larger trends.

Global trends

The condition-shifting trends we have picked here reflect a range of inputs, including the study of a number of recent Australian and global 'megatrend' analyses, the work of the WEF itself through its global risks reports from 2017 and 2018, and our own reading, research, and engagement with public servants.

We've listed in the appendix the megatrend studies, including the recent work from the Commonwealth Scientific and Industrial Research Organisation (CSIRO), on which this chapter is based so that those who have the time and interest can dig a little deeper.

Here we present a summary of the trends defining a larger stage on which the changing role and work of government is playing out, and therefore the stage on which the digital transformation project itself is playing out. We then explore some of the implications for government and for digital transformation in Australia.

This analysis explains what we mean by the first of the four points of the 'digital diamond' – a changing world.

We group the trends under three headings – society and the economy, governance and democracy, and work and technology.

Society and the economy

1. Equality and inequality
2. The reinvention of market capitalism
3. The fourth industrial revolution (4IR)

4. Identity, inclusiveness, affiliation, and community
5. Sustainability, resource limits, and climate change
6. Demography is destiny

Governance and democracy

7. Collective intelligence
8. Lots of pieces, no puzzle
9. Rediscovering the possibilities of 'public'
10. Shifting patterns of global power and influence
11. Who can you trust, and the future of democracy

Work and technology

12. Deep digital disruption
13. The new work order

There may be a fourteenth trend that underpins all of these, and that is the changing expectations of citizens themselves.

Expectations about how government should work and behave have been changed by our encounters with digital in other parts of our lives as customers – how we shop and travel and learn and entertain ourselves and connect with friends and family around Australia and across the world. New obsessions about the quality of experience (as opposed to the quality of product or service), about authentic customer service, including personalisation, responsiveness, and choice, and, by and large, openness and transparency are the hallmarks against which we judge digital satisfaction.

We look briefly at each of these 13 trends and draw out their significance, individually and together, for the story of digital transformation of government. At the end of the chapter, we explain how these trends set the context for the future trajectory of digital transformation.

Society and the economy

1.   Equality and inequality

Intersecting conversations about equality and inequality have become the defining political feature of our age.

Fired especially by the global financial crisis of 2008, and picking up the fierce debate that has raged about the extent to which economic inequality in particular has reached tipping point proportions of instability and risk, the search for new settings for fairness and equality has become a policy obsession.

The obvious domain within which these debates now rage is economics and the growing anxiety about the dystopian spread of inequality in wealth and income. Much of the evidence, and the underlying statistical analysis, are becoming very familiar.

In Australia, over the 25 years to 2010, real wages increased by 50% on average, but by 14% for those in the bottom 10% of the income distribution, compared to 72% for those in the top 10 per cent.

Between 2004 and 2011, the average wealth for Australians in the top 20% of the distribution increased by 28%, while for those in the bottom 20% of the wealth distribution, it increased by 3%.[92]

In its analysis of global inequality, the OECD points out that income inequality in OECD countries is at its highest level for the past half century.[93] The average income of the richest 10% of the population is about nine times that of the poorest 10% across the OECD, up from seven times 25 years ago.

The same analysis, which also includes studies of inequality in health, education, wellbeing, and gender for example, notes that across the developed countries of the OECD, the average Gini coefficient[94] of disposable household income reached 0.318 in 2014, compared to 0.315 in 2010. This is the highest value on record since the mid-1980s.

In its work on inequality, Oxfam calculates that the world's eight richest men control more wealth than half the world's population (about 3.6 billion people).[95] Quoting a Credit Suisse analysis, in Australia the top 1% own over 20% of the total wealth and more wealth than the bottom 70% of the population combined.[96]

Despite the pyrotechnic quality of some of these statistics, the equality and inequality conversation is not without contest.

Thomas Piketty's work,[97] as perhaps the leading example of the analysis of the new divergence of wealth and income, is debated vigorously by other economists.[98] Similarly, there are plenty of analyses that remind us that inequality between nations is actually reducing while inequality within nations seems to be getting steadily worse.

By some measures, the world has never been richer, healthier, more productive, or safer than it is right now, an analysis whose evidence base often seems to bump up against the lived experience, and certainly the sentiments, of those whose lives don't seem to reflect the same optimism.

Stephen Pinker's book, which has also drawn some criticism, sets out some evidence to suggest that enlightenment values based on reason, intellect, and science and a couple of hundred years of sustained public, private, and civil society investment and hard work have delivered some pretty impressive results.[99]

But the inequality meme goes deeper than economics. Its real impact is the claim that its persistence and deterioration deny access to opportunity and the chance to shift some of the social and economic conditions that perpetuate diminished horizons and failing hope.

The social media-infused campaigns for changes in sexual conduct and relationships, including those at work (think #MeToo and the Harvey Weinstein effect),[100] is a powerful example of the instinct for equality and fairness at work. So, too, was the 2018 marriage equality debate and plebiscite in Australia, culminating in an unexpectedly robust engagement with a process, messy and protracted though it ended up, whose narrative was equality and fairness. So are increasing commitments for gender equality, including for equal pay and representation in senior roles.

Look, too, at the discussions around equal contributions to parenting in families and the surrounding dialogue about work-life balance, especially as people adjust to new patterns and rhythms of work in the 'new work order' of highly contingent or so-called 'gig' working.

In different ways, these are big conversations that engage social, cultural, and economic structures whose capacity to deny people a fair and reasonable chance to change their lives and improve their prospects is as undeniable as the stubborn resistance any of these factors put up to any number of policy efforts to change them.

2. *The reinvention of market capitalism*

The reinvention of market capitalism is driven by two insights.

One is equality and inequality. Markets and some forms of capitalism are certainly still capable of remarkable feats of invention and distribution of opportunity and access to wealth.

But the evidence suggests that making those opportunities available is only part of the job. Limiting disparities of wealth and outcome, which threaten to erode underlying social compacts and give rise to the kind of populist resentment we have come to at least acknowledge so well since the election of President Donald Trump in 2016 and Britain voting to exit the European Union ('Brexit') is another part of the job.

The other, related insight speaks to the growing realisation that there needs to be a new settlement between markets, capitalism, and the state, not only to chase legitimate concerns of equity and fairness but also to improve the rate and quality of capitalism's capability for innovation and wealth creation. Capitalism, goes the mantra, needs to be saved from itself.

New conversations are emerging about the importance of inclusive growth and the way in which markets and governments have to make common and much more equal cause in pursuit of a few 'mission-led' changes in policy, funding, and practice.[101]

In most cases, these are campaigns in pursuit of a few very big shifts in sustainability, climate change, and adaptability, in health and social care, in education and skills, and in infrastructure. The crisis of capitalism might be summarised in these three concerns:

- An unacceptable and unsustainable level of inequality in the accumulation and distribution of assets (wealth), income, and, as a result, economic influence
- A growing concern about the ability to mobilise the necessary mix of policy, expertise, and money at a speed and intensity necessary to take advantage of rapid changes in knowledge, technology, and economic opportunity to create new sources of innovation-fuelled competitive advantage
- Perhaps slightly oddly, a realisation that the demands of competitive economic policy and performance require new levels of collaboration and integration within and across sectors and industries which some traditional models of capitalism seem ill-equipped to deliver

These big shifts in policy and business reflect similarly shifting debates about the surrounding context of globalisation.

We seem to be in the middle of a fierce debate about the extent to which globalisation, at least in some of its manifestations, helps or hinders the ambition for sustainable and inclusive prosperity.

Globalisation in its more recent forms – open borders, more open and freer trade, more porous boundaries for expertise and talent – is credited with massive shifts in global economic wellbeing. This is a story told in impressive figures about the rate at which poverty has declined and an increasingly wealthy middle class has emerged in countries like India, China, parts of South America, and now Africa. [102]

But globalisation's progress has been marred by the consequences of some of the dramatic shifts in economic activity which has seen jobs decline and grow unevenly in different parts of the world.

As a result, new anxieties about economic security fuel combinations of populism, nationalism, and protectionism, the rise of 'nativism', marked usually by rising intolerance to immigration, refugees, and unfamiliar 'others' as policymaking, and political cultures threaten to turn inwards.

3. *The fourth industrial revolution*

According to the WEF, the first industrial revolution was about steam and water, the second was about the introduction of electricity to enable the mass production of things, while the third is characterised by the Internet, digitising everything, and mass communications through technologies. Now we are entering the fourth industrial revolution, which is about blurring the real world with the technological world.[103]

The features of this revolution that make it both powerful and tricky include the speed, intensity, and interdependence of the main elements from which it forges its influence and impact.

This is how Klaus Schwab described that effect in 2016:

'Now a Fourth Industrial Revolution is building on the Third, the digital revolution that has been occurring since the middle of the last century. It is characterized by a fusion of technologies that is blurring the lines between the physical, digital, and biological spheres.'[104]

He went on to say:

'The possibilities of billions of people connected by mobile devices, with unprecedented processing power, storage capacity, and access to knowledge, are unlimited. And these possibilities will be multiplied by emerging technology breakthroughs in fields such as AI, robotics, the Internet of Things, autonomous vehicles, 3-D printing, nanotechnology, biotechnology, materials science, energy storage, and quantum computing.'[105]

The WEF analysis goes on to nominate four chief effects of this cascading fusion of technology, invention, and cultural change – new customer expectations for services and products that break some of the old trade-offs between cost, convenience, safety and speed, product enhancements (think Alexa, Siri, Cortana and Google Home voice assistants), collaborative innovation, and organisational form.

The Australian opportunity from the digital economy, which is fast becoming the actual economy, has been mapped in a 2018 report that estimated the opportunity for Australia to engage and navigate this economic landscape at over $300 billion within a decade. But the good news comes with a warning:

'...as a mid-sized market, it is critical that Australia defines its own path to success at digital innovation, rather than attempting to emulate the breadth of Silicon Valley or the scale of China. Australia is most likely to succeed if it focusses on producing new digital products and services for industries in which it already has a global competitive advantage – thanks to its natural resources endowment, strong institutions, diverse and highly skilled workforce, and existing infrastructure and customer base.'[106]

One of the eight areas nominated in the report for Australia to focus on, which includes things like precision healthcare, digital agriculture, and cyber-physical security, is 'proactive government':

'Low institutional trust, rising civil expectations, accelerated decision cycles and greater strategic uncertainty are forcing organisations to become more responsive and evidence-based. The increased availability of data, combined with greater analytic capabilities, has the potential to increase the effectiveness of policy and decision-making and reduce expenditure.'[107]

There are two dimensions of the fourth industrial revolution, or 4IR, that are especially relevant for our story.

One is the challenge to infuse the transformative potential of the 4IR with a human purpose so that its benefits mix individual advancement and opportunity with a proper regard for the public or common good.

According to an analysis from Nesta, an innovation foundation in the UK, while the potential inherent in the 4IR is, well, revolutionary in the best sense (prosperity, productivity, the baking of a larger cake which we can all share), it comes with pitfalls too.

4IR risks widen the divide between vanguards and the rest, accelerating job destruction ahead of job creation, and introducing potentially serious threats to personal privacy and cybersecurity.

Industrial revolutions are, generally speaking, good things, although their benefits are never unalloyed. The first one 'probably did more to benefit humanity than any other event in history (certainly as measured by its effects on life expectancy, income, and freedom)'.[108]

One of the risks is that many of the technologies on which 4IR relies, and which it is busy spreading and amplifying, have emanated from the military, and have a focus on productivity, efficiency in a naturally and fiercely contested and competitive realm. One recent Australian commentary suggested that we're already in the group of a new 'digital industrial complex' which threatens to be as insidious and tough to control as its military predecessor.[109]

Making the revolution 'good' will engage four 'fundamental shifts' in its conception, development, governance, and application:

- A clearer focus on ends and purposes, privileging health, social care, labour market reform, integrating refugees into their new societies, mobility, and education and less focused on warfare, advertising, and the search for commercial edge.
- A deliberate widening of the range and mix of voices and values in the means and participation of shaping the revolution's direction and destiny. The conversation needs to open up to millions of entrepreneurs, innovators, makers, and citizens.
- The revolution needs to be humanised, reinforcing our disposition to 'cure, care and relate' as well as being more open and cautious about its ability to amplify some of the darker dimensions – aggression, addiction, compulsion – of our shared human heritage.

- And finally, the revolution needs 'complementary innovations' in regulation, institutional form, and practice and across broader social spaces like the way we use data for common and shared knowledge.[110]

The second challenge emerging from the 4IR is recasting the purpose and conduct of innovation – public, private, and social – and, in that process, rethinking the contribution of government and the public realm.

One of the unintended consequences for the public sector of an economy and a wider society in which structures and work become more fragmented across a larger number of smaller players is the challenge to secure the necessary level of trust as the basis for people's interactions. That means that public servants need a good level of technical competence and the ability to deal with people inside the sector and the interactions with those working in these more fragmented structures.

The speed and focus of innovation are shifting from discovering new products, processes, and services, especially in the wake of successive waves of the digital revolution, to the tougher challenge of innovating whole new business models.

The ground rules of so many sectors are being tested as incumbent businesses find themselves outflanked by newer players anxious to demonstrate not so much that they can beat the older players but that they are inventing new ground on which to play in the first place.

Decisions in 2017 by the Lowy family to sell down their share of the Westfield Empire and Rupert Murdoch's decision to sell Fox have both been characterised as 'writing on the wall' moments.[111] These decisions were driven by new power contesting the assumptions and habits of old power. In both cases, the timing seems to have had less to do with short-term economic and business conditions and more to do with a pre-emptive strike in the face of undisputed shifts in the dynamics and structure of the retail and entertainment industries. Better to sell and leave the business – and make some money on the way out – than be innovated out of existence.

Deloitte's John Hagel, perched at the Centre for the Edge, has researched deeply the business model implications for substructures of whole sectors as the predominantly digitally driven 'big shift' re-writes the rules of engagement.

Those rules include a shift from knowledge stocks to knowledge flows, from explicit to tacit knowledge and from transactions to relationships. The big implication of the big shift is the transition from an underlying model of what Hagel describes as 'scalable efficiency' to 'scalable learning'.[112]

The premise of a successful business model is not how efficient you can be or become – which is essentially a static and transactional calculation – but how quickly you can learn – which is essentially a networked and relational calculation.

In fact, Hagel goes further and argues that learning collectively across not just the organisation but across whole business ecosystems has become the new definition of efficiency.

Business model or 'institutional' efficiency is now at a premium:

'It is from these innovations, which are hardest to pull off because they force organisations to dig deeply into the assumptions and cultural structure that has served them well to this point, that the largest payoffs can be expected – 'redefining the rationale for institutions and developing new relationship architectures within and across institutions to break existing performance trade-offs and expand the realm of what is possible.'[113]

That dynamic is having two impacts on government and therefore on the context for digital transformation.

One is that government and the public sector are not immune from this increasingly intense search for new business models, if you define business model as that set of assumptions about the way organisations work, about the people they serve, about the way they achieve viability, about the products and services customers expect, and the larger economic, technological, and cultural conditions to which they have to respond.

Secondly, these 'big shift' trends beg some fundamental questions about the role and purpose of government and the state.

For example, traditional notions of last-resort intervention to fix up market failure and avoiding the risk of 'crowding out' the investment, creativity, and animal spirits of the private sector are being questioned.

The concept of an 'entrepreneurial state' is gathering momentum in the light of substantial evidence of the state's unique capacity to harness substantial long-term and often highly speculative capital to pursue both 'for its own sake' blue sky research, or more specifically directed 'mission'-led innovation for big social and public purposes.

We touched earlier on Mariana Mazzucato's *The Entrepreneurial State* which argues the case, positing a creative and intelligently selective approach to 'pick the willing' rather than 'pick winners' as the basis for big societal 'missions' whose realisation carries the promise of big payoffs in terms of growth, inclusion, and sustainability.

Mazzucato argues that we have to understand the State as 'neither a "meddler" nor a simple "facilitator" of economic growth.' Rather, she suggests, 'it is a key partner of the private sector – and often a more daring one, willing to take the risks that business won't.' Further, the State 'cannot and should not bow down easily to interest groups who approach it to seek handouts, rents and unnecessary privileges like tax cuts.'[114]

For our purposes here, this line of argument brings big implications for the work and culture of government and the public sector:

> 'The State's ability to push and direct is dependent on the kind of talent and expertise it is able to attract. And the irony is that the latter is more of a problem in countries where the State takes a back seat, only "administering" and not leading with dynamic vision. Unless we challenge the numerous "myths" of economic development and abandon conventional views of the State's role in it, we cannot hope to address the structural challenges of the twenty-first century nor produce the technological and organizational change we need for long-term sustainable and equitable growth.'[115]

These are useful reminders of the mix and scale of this revolution's implications for government, policy, and the public sector. To make an obvious point we make again later, digital doesn't transform anything until we can get a handle on the extent to which its tools, platforms, culture, and practices give us some genuinely new and better ways to tackle the kinds of dilemmas that emerge from these changes.

4. Identity, inclusiveness, affiliation, and community

One of the big tests for any government is how to engage citizens and communities in conversations about complex choices for policy and economic and social development, especially where those choices demand difficult trade-offs in an environment where issues of identity and belonging seem to be fracturing.

How people nurture identity and affiliation in a world where the opportunity to belong has changed over a long period, driven often by new forms of communication and connection that transcend traditional boundaries of family and local community, is both an opportunity and a risk.[116] It's particularly an issue for Australia's indigenous communities.

There are almost limitless ways for people now to identify and build a sense of solidarity with others who share their interests and values, even if they are physically dispersed. But the easier that has become, the more difficult it seems to be to forge the kind of robust connection and mutual engagement between governments and communities so essential to the prosecution of hard decisions and difficult choices.

All sorts of issues flow from the way people identify themselves and with others around them – a sense of fairness and equity, a feeling of connection and mutual obligation to those with whom they share spaces and places in common, and the willingness to forge and be bound by a sense of the greater or common good.

5. *Sustainability, resource limits, and climate change*

All of the megatrend studies we looked at for this book put a cluster of issues around climate, resources, and sustainability, often with a focus on energy cost and sustainability, at the heart of their predictions for the future.

Although the politics of climate change and adaptation remain contested, the need to tackle the big policy challenges in climate, resource security, including especially land, water and energy, food and agriculture, population and urban human settlement, is becoming more insistent and more accepted. And there is some evidence that a consensus about the need for action is forming across boundaries of politics and ideology.

This is how the Commonwealth and Scientific Industrial Research Organisation (CSIRO), in their 'more from less' megatrend report, explains the dilemma:

'The earth has limited supplies of natural mineral, energy, water and food resources essential for human survival and maintaining lifestyles. Data are revealing many of these resources are being depleted at often alarming rates.'[117]

At the same time population and economic growth are creating new pressures and demands. The expectation is that companies, governments, and communities will discover new ways to ensure quality of life for current and future generations within the confines of the natural world's limited natural resources.

Science, technology, business processes, government policy, lifestyle patterns, and cultural norms are all, individually and together, in the increasingly complex and urgent mix.

For many, this cluster of issues is less of a trend or condition for the future as it is a way of framing the other trends and conditions. From this perspective, all of the work of government and the public sector, digitally transformed or not, is conditioned by the overriding obligation to respond and adapt to climate change.

The implications ripple out through the entire policy landscape, including the design and management of cities, agriculture and food production and distribution, the provision of sustainable and affordable sources of energy for business, industry and domestic consumption, the impact on foreign and defence policy through issues such as climate-induced disruptions to the flow and quantum of refugees and displaced people, and new sources of governance responsibility in the private sector for risk mitigation and management for businesses large and small.[118]

In some ways, one of the most fundamental tests of the value and impact of the digital transformation project across government and the public sector will be the extent to which it fuels shifts in the use of data, the application of knowledge, and the use of new capabilities for communication and collaboration that feed into climate and resource management policy.

6. *Demography is destiny*

Broadly, the west (and Japan) is getting older while the east and 'south', especially countries like India and many in the Middle East, are getting younger or are at least harvesting the mixed consequences of a youth 'bulge'.

Either way, it's rare to find a serious study of the future that doesn't play with some variation on the theme that, more or less, demography is destiny.

According to the UN, the current world population of 7.3 billion is expected to reach 8.5 billion by 2030, 9.7 billion in 2050, and 11.2 billion in 2100.

Most of the projected increase in the world's population can be attributed to a short list of high-fertility countries, mainly in Africa, or countries with already large populations. During 2015–2050, half of the world's population growth is expected to be concentrated in nine countries: India, Nigeria, Pakistan, Democratic Republic of the Congo, Ethiopia, United Republic of Tanzania, United States of America (USA), Indonesia, and Uganda.

Much of the world is ageing too.

The same UN study notes that, even though there are some countries and regions currently experiencing a demographic 'dividend' of younger populations, a significant ageing of the population in the next several decades is projected for most regions of the world, starting with Europe where 34% of the population is projected to be over 60 years old by 2050.

In Latin America and the Caribbean and in Asia, the population will be transformed from having 11% to 12% of people over 60 years old today to more than 25% by 2050. Africa has the youngest age distribution of any major area, but it is also projected to age rapidly, with the population aged 60 years or over rising from 5% today to 9% by 2050.[119]

The story is certainly true for Australia.

In 2016, there were 3.7 million (15%) Australians aged 65 and over, increasing from 319,000 (5%) in 1926 and 1.3 million (9%) in 1976. The number and proportion of older Australians is expected to continue to grow. By 2056, it is projected there will be 8.7 million older Australians (22% of the population); by 2096, 12.8 million people (25%) will be aged 65 years and over.

As Australia's population ages, its age profile is also projected to change.

In 2016, half of Australia's older people (57%, or 2.1 million) were aged 65–74, one third were aged 75–84 (30%, or 1.1 million), and 13% (487,000) were aged 85 and over. By 2046 it is projected there will be more than 3.3 million people aged 65–74, though this represents a smaller proportion of all older people (45%). People aged 75–84 will account for 35% (2.6 million) of the population and almost one in five older people will be aged 85 or over (19%, or 1.4 million).[120]

Where will these older, possibly healthier and fitter people live? How will they live, bearing in mind their need not just for health and social care but, just as importantly, their need in many cases for work and in all cases for connection and community? It's now well established that loneliness can kill and, less dramatically, incubate the kind of physical, social, and psychological harm that is already testing the limits of our health, pension, and care systems.

The ageing of Australia's population is hardly a surprise, or heading in unpredictable directions. While we should avoid catastrophising the situation and assuming, wrongly, that ageing is always and everywhere a difficult and negative trend, it's also fair to put demography close to the centre of the policy and public work agenda for the period ahead.

A digital-transformed government will manifest some clear evidence that it can respond with a mixture of practical creativity, affordable design, new infrastructure for greater connectedness, and rising care and empathy. As the world's population grows, so, too, does its urban population.

A World Health Organization report notes that the urban population in 2014 accounted for 54% of the total global population, up from 34% in 1960, and continues to grow.[121] The urban population growth, in absolute numbers, is concentrated in the less developed regions of the world. It is estimated that by 2017, even in less developed countries, a majority of people will be living in urban areas.

Governance and democracy

The second cluster of trends speaks to changing methods and models of public governance and larger questions of trust and legitimacy from which they need to draw and which at the same time they need to replenish.

7.   Collective intelligence

It's not original to argue that harnessing the combined expertise, insights, and experience of lots of different people to solve a problem is a good idea.

> 'What does collective intelligence mean? It's important to realize that intelligence is not just something that happens inside individual brains. It also arises with groups of individuals. In fact, I'd define collective intelligence as groups of individuals acting collectively in ways that seem intelligent.'[122]

Professor Thomas W. Malone went on to say:

> 'By that definition, of course, collective intelligence has been around for a very long time. Families, companies, countries, and armies: those are

all examples of groups of people working together in ways that at least sometimes seem intelligent.'[123]

That's from Malone's talk about his engagement with the idea of collective intelligence. Massachusetts Institute of Technology (MIT) has a Center for it, with a simple research question, 'How can people and computers be connected so that – collectively – they act more intelligently than any person, group, or computer has ever done before?'[124] (See chapter 4, where the relevance of collective intelligence as a capability for public servants is covered.)

IBM has its own centre too, 'capitalizing on the crowd'.[125] There are conferences, this one having held its fifth in New York.[126] And there's a Facebook collective intelligence group, perhaps not surprisingly.

Although it's not a new subject (we've been talking about it for decades, according to the MIT website), the focus on collective intelligence has been sharpened by Geoff Mulgan's latest book, *Big Mind*. He has pulled together the intellectual and theoretical foundations of collective intelligence with examples, guides, and hints about how to create 'assemblies' of skills, knowledge, and expertise to solve complex, connected challenges and realise new opportunities for innovation and people-powered reform.

Mulgan argues that the answers to these big public challenges are going to come from our capacity to think, imagine, and act together in more interesting and often unusual combinations of skill, experience, knowledge, decision-making, and delivery.

It turns out we're not short of intelligence. So many of these big dilemmas turn out to be problems of doing, not problems of knowing. The big problem is how hard it is to direct all of the intelligence and insight we do have with purpose and persistence at the problems we want to fix. That is the hard bit. Digital transformation must have something to offer in that endeavour if it is going to be valuable.

Mulgan argues that 'collective intelligence depends on functional capabilities: distinct abilities to observe, analyse, remember, create, empathise, and judge— each of which can be enhanced by technologies, and each of which also has a cost.'[127]

These are then supported by infrastructures that make collective intelligence easier: 'common standards and rules, physical objects that embody intelligence, institutions that can concentrate the resources needed for the hard work of thought, and looser networks and societies of mind.'[128]

That work is always the same – hard thinking and analysis, communication and diffusion, alignment through incentive structures (which are often either unhelpful to the common cause or positively antagonistic to it), and delivery.

The problem is that the way our institutions and systems are currently configured is often antithetical to the interests of a collectively intelligent outcome. This is the phenomenon that often confronts us with individually smart pieces of a 'dumb' system. How is it possible for organisations sometimes to act in ways which are egregiously stupid despite overflowing with individual smartness, even brilliance? Technology – digital transformation, in our language – is right in the frame. 'The spread of the Internet along with ubiquitous tools for analysis, search, and memory', he argues, 'have greatly enhanced the world's capacity to think.' The problem remains that 'many more resources are devoted to collective intelligence in competitive fields than cooperative ones, however, and the world suffers from a huge misallocation of brain-power....'[129]

Using new digital tools and platforms, he suggests that the successful examples of collective intelligence 'are best understood as assemblies of multiple elements. Discovering which assemblies work best requires continuous shuffling of the elements, since capabilities, infrastructures, and organizational models have to coevolve with environments.'[130]

Digital transformation needs to be pressed into the service of government's increasingly important role in assembling collective intelligence to solve complex public problems. That makes intuitive sense. We need to render the pieces – knowledge, expertise, physical and virtual assets, platforms, money, policy, power, and authority – more intelligent as they assemble themselves into something that starts to look like a purposeful and decisive puzzle.

Progressing collective intelligence 'is in many ways humanity's grandest challenge since there's little prospect of solving the other grand challenges of climate, health, prosperity, or war without progress in how we think and act together.'[131]

There is an uncomfortable paradox in this conversation.

'The very properties that help a group cohere can also impede intelligence,' Mulgan offers.

What are they?

He suggests things like shared assumptions that don't hold true, a shared willingness to ignore uncomfortable facts, and the prevalence of 'groupthink, group feel, and mutual affirmation rather than criticism.' Often, shared or collective thinking 'includes not only knowledge but also delusions, illusions, fantasies, the hunger for confirmation of what we already believe, and the distorting pull of power that bends facts and frames to serve itself."[132]

If, increasingly, the purpose of government in the light of these trends is to be an effective assembler and activator of collective intelligence for public work, then that gives us another measure against which to test the value of the digital transformation project.

Is the shift to digital making it easier or harder to assemble, direct, and amplify the work of new assemblies of collective intelligence? If it is making it easier, because of the way digital offers new ways to observe, to know, to remember, to analyse and discern, to act, to measure and learn, and then to do it all over again and each time getting better and stronger in the instincts and practices on which this process relies, then we are transforming.

If not, we're doing something else.

8.   *Lots of pieces, no puzzle*

In any complex system that relies on the actions of lots of different players – and this can be at the level of an organisation, a local community, a city, a nation, or the world itself – a big challenge is to worry about the health and functioning of the whole, rather than the individual pieces.

There is a growing concern that the capacity for local, national, and global cooperation across and between communities and nations is being eroded by the rise of 'nativist' instincts to turn inwards and build walls, real and metaphorical, as a form of protection and security.

In the 2017 WEF Global Risks Report, the risk was called out bluntly as a decline in the systems and habits of global cooperation. It picked out five contributing factors:

1. International cooperation is giving way to unilateral or transactional approaches to foreign policy just as a host of issues – such as global growth, debt, and climate change – demand urgent collective action.

2. The interconnected nature of the global system produces cascading risks at the domestic level. (As an example, failing to contain the Syrian civil war since 2011 forces migration flows to countries already experiencing low growth and rising inequality, fuelling the risk of frustration and further acts of violence.)

3. A declining sense of trust and mutual good faith in international relations makes it harder to contain the resulting pressures through domestic policy.

4. Technological innovation exacerbates the risk of conflict. A new arms race is developing in weaponised robotics and AI. (And this includes the rapidly rising significance of cyberspace as a new 'domain of conflict'.)

5. While risks intersect, and technologies develop quickly, too often our institutions for governing international security remain reactive and slow moving.[133]

For governments, three big challenges emerge.

One is about the nature and quality of conversations with citizens and communities about issues of direction, policy priority, and complex decision making.

A second is about how open and legible the processes of governing needs to become – through initiatives like the Open Government Partnerships[134] perhaps, and new ways of using the instincts and practices of an 'open data' model – as an investment in new assets of trust and engagement.

And third is the need for innovation and reform that lifts the metabolism of national and global institutions (speed, intensity, and responsiveness) to more obviously match the nature of the problems they are trying to solve and the surrounding conditions in which they arise.

9.   Rediscovering the possibilities of 'public'

In a recent interview, Tony Shepherd, a businessman, former chair of the Business Council of Australia, and chair of the Commission of Audit whose report formed one of the cornerstones of the incoming Abbott Government's 2014 budget and public sector reform strategies, suggested that downsizing the public sector had gone too far.

In the interview, he said of the public sector, 'I really think we need to reinvigorate it at the federal and state level in terms of its capacity and its quality.' He went on to suggest that 'with outsourcing and privatisation ... we have probably run it down a bit too far. I think it needs to be adjusted. Backwards, upwards.' And to confirm the underlying point, he observed that 'we tend to talk down the public service in Australia. I think that's a really big structural issue for us, because our form of democracy really does require a strong and very competent — and independent, I might add — public service.'[135]

Perhaps we're witnessing a shift in sentiment and practice at the heart of our notions of good government and the work of the public sector

After 30 years or more of public sector reform under the rubric of 'new public management' and similar models – which we review in more detail in chapter 4 – advocating a range of private sector and commercial tools and cultural habits to reform, and, inevitably, downsizing the public sector, the tide seems to be turning.

Notably as the pace and intensity of global, regional, and national change piles up new risks and opportunities, the role of government and the public sector as an important and, in some situations, inescapable player in determining how to respond is beginning to change.

We mentioned earlier the work of Mariana Mazzucato charting a new conversation about the role of the public sector and the state in pursuing mission-led innovation, a more creative and realistic industrial strategy in the service of outcomes that include competitiveness and inclusive growth.

The rediscovery of the value and importance of the public dimension in our lives engages a mix of ideas and instincts.

One is the renewed interest in how, in the face of economic, cultural, and technology forces for divergence, difference, and dispersion, we can continue to forge a sense of common good. Where do we get a sense of our common identity and interests? How do we define and privilege, in a world of fracturing institutions and radical individualism, a sense of public purpose?[136] (The organisation that Mariana Mazzucato now heads up at University College London is called the Institute for Innovation and Public Purpose.)

Another element is the need to match a rising interest in the role of 'public' in many of the big issues we need to tackle as a community with substantial reform in many of the operating models and aspects of the culture of the public sector.

Accepting, in line with Tony Shepherd's admission, that we may have overshot the mark in the more or less ideological drive for a leaner and more efficient public sector doesn't deny there remain important changes to secure the right mix of talent, productivity, effectiveness, and culture in the public sector.

And there's a larger issue at stake here too, which is the concept of 'publicness' itself.

Part of the challenge for digital transformation is to demonstrate how it will engage with, and perhaps change profoundly, the architecture of values and assumptions that shape a sense of 'public' in the first place – common interests, equity of access, engagement and service, and the ability to articulate the distinctive role of public institutions and governance, partly as platform but also as direct and significant players.

10. Shifting patterns of global power and influence

The largest canvas on which we can write the story of digital transformation is the decay of the liberal world order whose values of openness, innovation, and fairly distributed progress appear to be eroding.

According to one analysis:

'After a run of nearly one thousand years, quipped the French ... writer Voltaire, the fading Holy Roman Empire was neither holy nor Roman nor an empire. Today, some two and a half centuries later, the problem ... is that the fading liberal world order is neither liberal nor worldwide nor orderly.'[137]

Citing a combination of economic forces (declining real wages for many in the midst of apparently booming economic conditions), cultural introspection, and institutional fracturing, the analysis is blunt:

'Liberalism is in retreat. Democracies are feeling the effects of growing populism. Parties of the political extremes have gained ground in Europe. The vote in the UK in favour of leaving the EU attested to the loss of elite influence.[138]

Haass went on to say:

'Even the US is experiencing unprecedented attacks from its own president on the country's media, courts, and law-enforcement institutions. Authoritarian systems, including China, Russia, and Turkey, have become even more top-heavy. Countries such as Hungary and Poland seem uninterested in the fate of their young democracies.'[139]

Another analysis, by Joseph Nye, just before Trump became US President, noted that 'recently, the desirability and sustainability of the order have been called into question as never before.'[140]

The bigger claims, beyond the peculiar conditions of the US presidential election are that 'the foundations of the order are eroding because of a long-term global power transition involving the dramatic rise of Asian economies such as China and India.'[141]

And others still, the analysis suggests, see the foundations of an open, liberal order 'threatened by a broader diffusion of power from governments to non-state actors thanks to ongoing changes in politics, society, and technology.'[142]

The conclusion? 'The order, in short, is facing its greatest challenges in generations. Can it survive, and will it?'[143]

Partly as a consequence of these big shifts, broadly speaking, global power and influence is shifting east and south (Asia, China, South America and Africa) from the north and west (US, Europe) whose long dominance, driven largely by economic and scientific prowess, is diminishing.

Of course, nothing in life, and especially in the world of geopolitics and the contending architectures of global power and influence, is ever that simple.

But the facts are undeniable and the trends at least provocative:

- China's State Council has determined that, by 2030, China will become the world's leading AI innovation centre, supporting an industry that will be worth $150 billion, blending with investments in quantum computing and chip design. The 'brute numbers' are tilting in China's favour – in 2016, the total US unclassified AI research totalled $1.6 billion. China is planning a $2 billion AI park in the suburbs of Shanghai.[144]
- The US remains the dominant global power, but since 1950, its share of the world economy has dropped by almost 50%, from 27% to 15%. By contrast, China's share has grown from 2% in 1980 to almost 18% today.
- China, with other rising economies, like Indonesia, India, Nigeria, and Brazil, are claiming more weight and influence in world affairs.[145]

There are shifts, too, in patterns of economic influence and intensity, offering up unexpected dynamics of politics, culture, finance, and opportunity.

And it turns out that it's not the US which, despite leading the world in the availability of venture capital, leads the world for the role of start-up and young business as economic generators ... for that you might have to look to Sweden, Brazil, Italy, Austria, or the Netherlands.[146]

Chile, Botswana, Jamaica, Angola, Vietnam, Cameroon, Brazil, Thailand, and Uganda are all leading in the proportion of employment from start-up or self employment.

Again, the list is open to contest and debate and other lenses shift the answers. The point is that innovation and economic intensity and energy are spreading and shaping policy in new patterns.

There is considerable commentary about the rising influence of China and India particularly, but of other rapidly developing economies and countries too, laced with some contest from those who argue strenuously that news of the demise of the west, and especially of the dominance of America in terms of economic strength, military dominance, and innovation capability, is greatly exaggerated.

China has already 'voted' for a lifetime President, whose promise to his citizens is to recapture China's rightful place in the world after centuries of being dominated by the rising west.[147]

The 'One Belt, One Road' initiative seeks to circle the globe with a $1 trillion chain of infrastructure assets that tie China to the world and, presumably, the world to China.[148]

The initiative will connect ports, railways, and road, and much besides, from China to Europe, running through more than 60 countries which account for over 60% of the world's (2015) population and which are responsible for producing over a third of global GDP population. It will facilitate over a third of the world's merchandise trade.[149]

Debate about how that plays out in a kind of 'Australia in the middle' strategy is growing as successive governments seek to play our geopolitical cards in a changing game of power, both soft and hard.

In the Australian Government's most recent foreign affairs white paper, for example, the shifting nature of the world's influence and power structure was mapped back to some big challenges for Australia. Shifts in sentiment about the impact and fairness of globalisation is leading to renewed interest in various forms of economic nationalism and protection, moves that harm an open trading economy like ours. And this at a time when the balance of economic and trading activity is shifting east.

Global governance and the formulation of, and adherence to, commonly accepted rules and norms of international behaviour are both becoming harder.

A 'more inward-looking and contested world' will inevitably render the task of governments to 'deliver access for their citizens to the benefits of national prosperity' more difficult. Sustaining the living standards we have become used to, never mind expectations that they might improve steadily over time, looks set to be especially tough.[150]

11. *Who can you trust: the future of democracy*

Measures of trust are moving in some alarming directions, mostly down, although according to one recent analysis, not so much out as across.

A 2017 Gallup poll found only 35% of Americans express 'a great deal' or 'quite a lot' of confidence in 14 major institutions. In other words, almost two thirds of Americans don't have much confidence in institutions that play a critical role in the life of America.

Eighty-eight per cent of Americans don't trust the US Congress; 79% don't trust big business, 73% don't trust the media, 72% don't trust organised labour, 68% don't trust the presidency, 60% don't trust the US Supreme Court, and 59% of Americans don't trust churches or organised religion.

In the Lowy Institute's analysis of Australian attitudes to democracy, the analysis notes that 'the numbers have not shifted much this year, but the ambivalence about democracy shown again in 2017 was enough to provoke comment from *The New York Times* in an infographic headed "Australia's Dark Vision of the World". Particularly alarming was the fact that support for democracy was appreciably lower among younger people. Only 52% of younger Australians aged 18–29 years agree that democracy is the preferable form of government, against 60% overall....'[151]

As this book was finalised in early 2019, we found the world in a new phase in the loss of trust: the unwillingness to believe information, even from those closest to us. The loss of confidence in information channels and sources is the fourth wave of the trust tsunami. The moorings of institutions have already been undermined by the three previous waves: fear of job loss due to globalisation and automation; the Great Recession, which created a crisis of confidence in traditional authority figures and institutions while undermining the middle class; and the effects of massive global migration. Now, in this fourth wave, the world is losing faith in the search for common facts and objective truth, weakening trust even as the global economy recovers.[152]

The same analysis points out that shifts in the raw numbers are matched by changing definitions of democracy itself. Specifically, 'the moral values on which people base their democratic support have turned dramatically more liberal over the generations'.[153]

As a consequence, 'support for democracy has changed its meaning: while older generations continue to endorse illiberal notions of democracy, younger generations support an unequivocally liberal notion.' At the same time, it seems, younger people especially have less faith in democracy but expect more from it.[154]

In 2017, for example, the Edelman report was uncompromising in its analysis of the eroding foundations of trust for government, business, and civil society. It was a bleak picture.

It revealed the largest-ever drop in trust across the institutions of government, business, media, and non-governmental organisations (NGOs). Trust in media (43%) fell precipitously and is at all-time lows in 17 countries, while trust levels in government (41%) dropped in 14 markets and is the least trusted institution in half of the 28 countries surveyed. The credibility of leaders also is in peril: CEO credibility dropped 12 points globally to an all-time low of 37%, plummeting in every country studied, while government leaders (29%) remain least credible.

The Trust Barometer found that 53% of respondents believe the current overall system has failed them — it is unfair and offers little hope for the future — while only 15% believe it is working, and approximately one third are uncertain. Even the elites have a lack of faith in the system, with 48% of the top quartile in income, 49% of the college-educated, and a majority of the well-informed (51%) saying the system has failed.

The gap between the trust held by the informed public and that of the mass population has widened to 15 points, with the biggest disparities in the US (21 points), UK (19 points) and France (18 points). The mass population in 20 countries distrusts their institutions, compared to only six countries for the informed public.[155]

The 2018 report provided little relief from an overall sense that trust continues to leak alarmingly from many of the systems and institutions in which we've traditionally invested a high level of confidence in their ability to privilege a common or public shared interest.

The 2018 report noted that:

- Volatility brews beneath a stagnant surface. If a single theme captures the state of the world's trust in 2018, it is this. Even as people's trust in business, government, NGOs, and media across 28 markets remained largely unchanged, experiencing virtually no recovery from 2017, dramatic shifts are taking place at the market level and within the institution of media.
- Globally, 20 of 28 markets lie in distruster territory, one more than in 2017. Trust among the informed public – those with higher levels of income and education – declined slightly on a global level, from 60% to 59%, thrusting this group into neutral territory from its once trusting status.[156]

The 2018 survey reported the emergence of what Edelman describes as two poles which are drifting further apart. Whereas in previous years market-level trust has moved largely in lockstep, it notes, for the first time ever, '[T]here is now a distinct split between extreme trust gainers and losers.'

No market declined more steeply than the US, with a 37-point aggregate drop in trust across all institutions. And the loss of trust was most severe among the informed public – a 23-point fall on the Trust Index – 'nearly erasing the 'mass-class' divide that once stood between this segment of the U.S. population and the country's far-less-trusting mass population.'[157]

In her analysis, Rachel Botsman argues that trust (which she defines as 'a confident relationship with the unknown') is shifting from intensely local (who do you know in the village) to deeply institutional as the world became bigger and more complex to a third phase in which trust is highly distributed through new networks of peer and other connections often mediated by new digital tools and platforms.

Rachel's point is that trust may not be disappearing so much as decentring, shifting sideways through new connections to those we know and whose opinions, which themselves are subject to the bracing scrutiny of the crowd, we have learned to rely on.

'So should we be mourning the loss of trust?' she asks. Yes and no. She suggests that '[W]hatever the headlines say, this isn't the age of distrust – far from it. Trust, the glue that holds society together, hasn't disappeared. It has shifted....'[158]

And it has shifted in distinct ways. Trust that used to 'flow upwards to referees and regulators, to authorities and experts, to watchdogs and gatekeepers', she explains, is now 'flowing horizontally, in some instances to our fellow human beings and, in other cases, to programs and bots'.[159] Trust is being turned on its head.

And from our perspective, the important implication is that 'the old sources of power, expertise and authority no longer hold all the aces, or even the deck of cards'.[160] Digital transformation's impact can't be separated from its ability to respond to, and noticeably improve, these new dynamics of trust as they impact governing and the work of the public sector.

None of this is without risk, of course. Self-serving bubbles of narrow opinion and amplified prejudice, all of the potential dangers of fake news and confected opinion that have become something of a staple in recent times, are all real and present dangers.

And they play directly into the role of government and the public sector as they seek to balance competing interests, uphold a sense of public or shared interest, and mediate equal and sometimes opposite instincts for competitive advantage rest on the one hand, while ensuring safety and security.

These trust shifts lead to some difficult assessments about the way we do democracy, and the underlying business of government and the public sector. They remain hostage to the search for an increasingly elusive combination of high trust, deep empathy for, and engagement with the experience of ordinary citizens across all aspects of their lives and better performance in terms of competence and productivity.

There's a strange paradox, which is often the currency of transition, at the heart of any attempt to make sense of the degree to which contemporary government works effectively.

It's not hard sometimes to get the feeling that government, at least in its broadly liberal democratic form of the sort we're familiar with in Australia, doesn't work anymore.

These are some common perceptions – policy stagnation and gridlock, and a crowded and increasingly tangled agenda of 'wicked' problems. Their mounting complexity keeps spiralling out of control, apparently beyond the reach of the institutions and practices of our public governance processes. The result is deep disaffection and disengagement that pervades the relationship between government and citizens.

But there's other evidence too that we can't ignore – for example, that programs and services are still being designed and delivered, often in very difficult circumstances and under great pressure, and that sincere and energetic efforts are being made to tackle problems and come up with improvements with a mixture of invention, pragmatic innovation, and determination. Especially under circumstances of volatility, unpredictability, and intensity (think floods, fires, terrorism), it's also true the public sector can not only pull out impressive levels of concerted, coordinated, and highly effective action, but is often where we still turn reflexively for help and reassurance when things get tough or we find ourselves in trouble.

So, government is working well and falling apart at the same time; bringing patient and occasionally inspired persistence to wicked problems that are drifting further away from existing practice and reflexes; showing a degree of brilliance and resilience under the pressure of volatile unpredictability; and inert with doubt and even despair sometimes, in the face of incontrovertible evidence that big licks of money, effort, and passion seem too often to achieve little.

Work and technology

The third and final cluster of big trends focuses on the intersecting worlds of work and technology.

12. *Deep digital disruption*

It would be odd if a book charting the course of digital transformation of government in Australia didn't pick up the digital transformation of pretty much everything else as a potent trend in its own right.

There are plenty of arguments about how far and how fast the disruptive potential of digital is moving in and through government and the public sector.

One assertion from the Australian Productivity Commission is that we're not seeing anywhere near as much actual disruption as some claim and that, by and large, we're still in the foothills of a venture that has failed to do much more than digitally embroider stubbornly analogue systems and processes.[161]

This critique suggests that we're still, largely, 'doing' digital rather than 'being' digital. Some measures of convenience, speed, and integration are served by some of the better examples, but there are few examples of the wholesale and creative embrace of digital driving, as it has in other sectors, totally new ways of doing things and, in some cases, doing totally new things.

The rapid emergence of technologies and capabilities has ramped up both the speed and intensity of digital's disruptive potential.

A roll call of the developments of the past few years reinforces the point – AI, machine learning, the Internet of Things, and the spread of embedded sensor networks in pretty much every piece of physical infrastructure from fridges to cars to bridges and planes, self-driving cars, medical science breakthroughs including the invention of nano-bots that can be injected into the human body to do their forensic search and repair work, blockchain, and the promise of quantum computing. Chapter 3 explains what some of these are as well as explaining that some other elements in the current and emerging digital toolkit are for government.

Partly as a function of that rapid increase in the metabolism of digital and technology invention and spread, the prospect of disruption is being tested against measures of human flourishing, ethics, and the responsible use of power and influence.

The name Cambridge Analytica has already established itself as a symbol of all that is troubling about a world in which a few very large players have become dominant and dangerous.[162]

The use and misuse of personal data for a mixture of unethical, immoral and criminal attempts to influence politics, for example, is drawing a new discussion about appropriate ways to regulate these new players.

At the Davos WEF meeting in 2018, the then British Prime Minister Theresa May and billionaire hedge fund investor George Soros were among those voicing concerns about the risks of unaccountable digital domination. The risks range from economic (narrowing choice and competition in key areas like retail, entertainment, search) to the intensely personal, almost moral (platforms, devices and software developed to deliberately addict as many as possible to use them and use them too often and unwisely).

A recent analysis suggested, rather bluntly,

'From Washington to Europe to Australia, so-called Big Tech has never been bigger, richer or more powerful. It has also never been more on the nose'.[163]

The litany of accusations makes for some depressing reading. 'These giants are accused of ruthlessly invading our privacy, killing off brick-and-mortar retailers, monopolistic practices, stealing news and advertising from traditional media, allowing nefarious players – from Russian intelligence to neo-Nazis – to exploit their sites, and refusing to help intelligence agencies access encrypted sites to hunt down terrorists.'[164]

Talk about the 'enabling' role of digital technology masks the much more profound changes across society and the economy wrought by these new tools and platforms, and their associated culture and mindset, to which we remain too slow to respond, especially in government.[165]

There's something reassuring about the notion that digital technology is an enabler. It's a frame that implies the absence of any serious disruption to the underlying methods, structures, and, particularly, power distribution implicit in the way things are being done now. According to the 'enabling' frame, its real value is to help us do what we're doing now, perhaps faster and more conveniently, and sometimes more safely.

Digital technology can be an enabler, for sure. And there is nothing wrong with the ambition to do what we do now better or faster or more productively. Improving how we do what we do in government is fine.

But enabling doesn't intrude awkward questions about what we are doing in the first place, why we are doing it, and whether there is something in the promise of digital transformation that invites a more fundamental review of role, purpose, and intended impact. Putting aside for the moment the arguments you could have about each of these examples, Uber has enabled a quicker, cheaper (mostly), and safer (arguably) experience of getting from A to B, but it hasn't fundamentally changed the business of getting from A to B.

Airbnb might argue that they haven't, as some others have, just made the business of booking a hotel room quicker, cheaper, and more convenient. They have used digital technologies to transform the basic 'production' of a quite different experience of finding somewhere to stay when you travel. Checking into a room in someone's house, possibly interacting with them as you get to know the local area, and perhaps even forming longer-term relationships is not another way to find a hotel room. It's not a hotel room at all. It's an experience that wasn't possible before, at least at the scale and convenience that is now commonplace.

MOOCs, or Massive Open Online Courses, at least in one version, are not a different way of attending an existing university, although they are that too. They are, at least conceptually, a totally different way of thinking about the business of higher education, from the digital ground up.

13. *The new work order*

Books, articles, and research about the new world of work, or the 'new work order',[166] are bursting out at an alarming rate. Everyone, it seems, has worked out that something big and important is happening to the structure and culture of work. The very concept of work in the post-industrial world is being tested by an unprecedented confluence of economic, social, and technology conditions.

Broadly, the new work order is characterised by these attributes:

- The rise of contract or 'gig' work in which more people operate as independent workers with no formal or structural organisational affiliations and trade elements of security and protection for flexibility and choice.
- New modes of working that allow, and even encourage, more flexibility in the physical location of work – home, office, 'third spaces' like work hubs and shared spaces.
- New methods of working that harness the flexibility and efficiency dividend of ubiquitous digital connectivity and shared virtual platforms of collaboration.

Deeper cultural shifts are redrawing lines of power and authority for leadership and management in new forms of organising.

So far as government and the public service are concerned, these are some of the dilemmas that are starting to emerge:

- How does the public sector reconcile the growing demand for work, and workers, that are more fluid and agile, with a system of recruitment, training, and accountability that often traps public servants in work systems whose incentives and sanctions remain grounded in the demand for predictability, hierarchy, and relatively rigid work classifications?
- How does public work cope with the need to retain longevity, persistence, and proper records of work over the long haul with an increasingly transactional approach to projects in which people and teams form, perform, and then un-form rapidly and with a much more varied mix of workers and resources in the mix?
- How does public work engage a more open and experimental approach which involves more 'mistakes' and an ability to try new ideas that

often engage controversial or politically sensitive issues while leaving unchanged many of the constraints on public servants' ability to work that way?

We're going to deal with some of these challenges in more detail in chapter 4. But for now, it's important to note that shifts in defining and doing work are already testing some of the traditional rhythms and structures of public work.

What we're noticing, for example, is that enduring values and capabilities of public work – rigour, impartiality, ethics, fairness, a care for and pursuit of the public or common interest, a concern for the long term – are now being mixed with aspirations for a new set of 'traditional' skills that are becoming just as valuable for effective public servants.

These include the ability to think beyond the usual, a capacity for speed and agility, the capacity to lead whole systems and curate complex communities of skills and expertise to achieve big public results – better health, skills for work, safer and 'smarter' cities, and climate adaptation – that can no longer be 'delivered' in a simple production model.

Digital transformation needs to have something useful to offer those who are grappling with these shifts. In particular, the tools and culture of digital need to play into the institutional domains – talent, structure, culture, leadership – from which the modern public service is emerging.

There are two cases to make for the significance of the digital transformation of government and the public sector, and for continuing to invest money, time, and institutional capital in its accelerated trajectory.

One is the 'thin' case.

In a world turning deeply and inexorably digital, at a speed and with a mixture of social, economic, and ethical consequences that seem often to outstrip our collective ability to absorb and respond, there is little choice for government but to follow suit.

As fast as it can, government has to engage the new digital world, both in its role as framer and policymaker for the work of the rest of the digital revolution and in its capacity as one of those institutions that has to get on board the digital train in its own right.

But there is a 'thick' case to be made too.

This case relies on a more ambitious definition of the transformation task. It argues that governments can't be content to be swept along in the digital tide and, more or less, keep up with the rest of the world.

Our argument in this chapter, and in this book, is that the digital transformation project needs to see itself and be judged according to a more purposeful intent to actively shape and respond to the big forces for change in the wider world.

Paradoxically, we think prosecuting the case for digital transformation becomes easier, and certainly more satisfying, when its terms and scope become more expansive. Digitally transforming the way we govern and confront the contests and opportunities of public work that shape our lives in common should bring something distinct to the task of rising to the demands of a changing world.

That, in the end, is the point.

Why do these trends matter?

These big trends suggest three tests for digital transformation in and of government, which needs to demonstrate how it can:

- Materially lift levels of trust in government and the public sector which need to be rescued and repaired as the foundation for tough decisions, and complex reforms
- Manifest much higher levels of empathy for the citizens, businesses, institutions, and communities with which they interact so that policy and decision-making respond to the contours of people's lives and the experiences and expectations from which they derive meaning and purpose
- Noticeably improve the quality and impact of the work governments do in policy, regulation, the provision of infrastructure and services so that good performance (in other words, competence and customer service) becomes more consistent, which feeds relevance and respect in the relationship between government and citizens.

Rather more importantly, we might expect to witness new ways in which emerging digital tools, practices, and culture connects those three elements – trust, empathy, and competence – into a new experience of good government done well.

The world is changing at the speed of innovation and necessity, while government (sometimes for very good reasons) moves at the speed of stability and predictability.

This is a problem, but it doesn't have to be.

The trick, first of all, is to hang on to the enduring values of public work. Whatever else we do in our efforts to digitally transform, we can't compromise these. Probity, fairness, transparency (or, as we might argue, legibility), rigour, accountability, and a lively sense of the public interest or common good – these are not up for negotiation.

With that anchor, we must confront a conversation about the institutional practices and instincts of government, some of which have become inexcusably slow, backwards-looking, and stubbornly change-resistant, and call them out for reform. How can we separate out the form from the substance of these practices, so we work out apt ways to give these important attributes suitably modern digital form and practice?[167]

The point of presenting these trends is not the trends themselves, fascinating though they are alone and in various combinations.

If the impact of digital tools, platforms, and culture on the work of government and the public sector in Australia doesn't dramatically improve the rate and intensity with which they can respond, with creativity and impact, to a world of opportunity and risk which these intersecting trends represent, then we are not 'there'.

The digital transformation of government can only be judged by engaging with government's changing role and purpose in a world of conditions and demands which themselves are changing dramatically. There is nothing wrong with the contribution of digital to incremental and operational changes that help governments do some of the things they need to do a little faster, more conveniently, or more safely.

That is all good. As Paul Shetler, the former CEO of the Digital Transformation Office (DTO) in the Australian government, might argue, be careful that the pursuit of 'high tech fantasies' doesn't distract from more mundane but important tasks like cleaning up your website and answering the phone quicker with better answers to the things people want to fix.[168]

But 'there', in our view, is a function of something more ambitious if it is to qualify as transformation. We bring these questions together – what, in the end, is the digital transformation project and how will we know if it is 'there'? – in the manifesto with which this book opens and also provides as its final chapter.

As an indication of the tests against which we might measure the significance and trajectory of the digital transformation project, these are four implications from these trends for the digital transformation project.

Policymaking, legislation, and regulation

In the face of the rising speed and intensity of the changes being made in the world, not only but especially by technology, the way governments make policy, write, and enforce legislation and create fit-for-purpose regulatory frameworks has to reflect the same speed and intensity in order to maintain relevance and improve impact.

There is a strong case to be made (and we are broadly supportive) for the use of many of the tools and mindsets of digital transformation – for example, agile methods and processes, human-centred design, greater reliance on experimentation and prototyping, judicious use of the 'crowd' for insights and expertise – in the mainstream policy process that remains a large part of the distinctive role of government.

The opportunity is to engage the capacity of these tools and methods to accelerate the speed and intensity with which problems can be solved and new ideas surfaced, tested, and adapted. The risk is that some of the fundamental assumptions of good policy making, including time to undertake deep and often complex research and analysis, and the requirement for outcomes that are reliable and authoritative might be either compromised or discounted.

Our view is that the risks can be mitigated, and the opportunities realised in a pragmatic and gradual process of opening more of the core policymaking tasks and functions of government to a set of capabilities and culture that a digital mindset can bring. In particular, we think the quality and impact of policy making could be considerably improved if the implications for, and the experience of, those people and communities whose lives would be most directly impacted are more explicitly and persistently held at the centre of the policymaking process.

Decision-making

Partly under the influence of a pervasive instinct for co-creation, how public decisions are made must become more legible so that people and communities cannot just see but understand – almost literally 'read' – how the process emerges with the answers and proposals that it offers.

That doesn't mean transgressing the need for requisite security and confidentiality of some dimensions of that process. But its underlying instincts must shift from what has essentially been an exclusive and minimally open process to one whose instincts are more reflexively open and inviting.

Designing and delivering services

Increasingly, public services must combine clever and beautiful technology with smart and inclusive design to improve the way evidence of all sorts (formal, experiential, hard, and soft) connects and add the simple 'nothing about us without us' rule that puts the experience and circumstances of those whose lives are most directly affected at the core of the service endeavour.

We should start to see more and more evidence that new platforms and tools, including the use of data and better analytics, create services and service experiences for people that go beyond incremental improvements.

New relationships of communication, influence, and accountability with citizens and communities

The way in which information and knowledge flow between people, communities, and governments, and then within governments themselves, should manifest a more open, equal, and mutually respectful attitude. Well beyond the confines of traditional 'consultation' and 'engagement', the rhythms of governing and public sector work should take on a more open and conversational style.

There are reforms already happening in government, aided and accelerated by the use of good digital practices, which suggest this new conversational and engaging form of communication can become the norm. Transforming means we need to see not just more examples but more evidence that these examples reflect a determined effort to entrench these instincts into the culture and practice of good government.

How this analysis frames the rest of the book

Three big conclusions frame the rest of this book.

First, it is a big mistake to assume an unchanging model of government to which digital transformation of government simply applies the same tools and methods.

Both pieces of the puzzle – the 'digital' piece and the 'government' piece – are transforming. As a consequence, they are transforming each other in significant and sometimes unexpected ways.

Second, the story of digital transformation of government should be the story of trust and relevance which fuel and sustain legitimacy – government's only defensible currency. Underneath the discussion about government's changing role and purpose, its persistent values and functions, and its variable performance and impact is the inescapable story of the implosion of trust in and about the work of government and much of the work of the public sector.

What that means is that a very big part of the answer to the question 'Are we there yet?' in the journey to digital transformation of government must be framed with evidence that transformation is rescuing stocks and flows of trust on which the legitimacy and efficacy of government depends.

And third, the practical effects of digital transformation must extend well beyond, but obviously need to embrace, questions of efficiency, productivity, and effectiveness.

Digital transformation is hard work, and there is a lot of detailed design and implementation to be done for the platforms and tools of digital transformation to work well. A lot of often dull but critical work is required to build these tools and make these new ways of working reliable and safe.

But the real impact of the digital transformation is not ultimately measured in the currency of operational efficiency or technology sophistication. Its only real test will be the extent to which it actively enables and accelerates some fundamental changes in the relationship between citizens and government, and between citizens themselves.

In that sense, digital transformation of government is situated at the heart of a new architecture of power and accountability in the business of governing, itself determined increasingly by the ability to respond to the trends which we outline in this chapter.

Noticeable and sustainable shifts in trust, power, and accountability are likely to be the markers to judge how we are tracking in the pursuit of transformation, or at least the source of questions we need to ask about its progress and ultimate impact.

Finally, an implication for the approach to digital transformation that we advocate is the need for 'futures' and future-thinking capability that runs deeper than the occasional consulting report or conference.

Not unlike the Singapore Government's Centre for Strategic Futures, we would expect that, especially as part of the ambition to mount a serious 'national mission' for deep digital transformation, the public sector will invest in a more embedded and persistent 'futures' function.[169]

In particular, the digital transformation agenda should be driven by a sophisticated and contemporary understating of the changing nature of public work and the way in which many different players and interests, and not just the public sector itself, experience considerable change and are now deeply implicated in the quality and impact of that work.

Three important messages

There are three important messages for readers in this chapter.

First, that the digital transformation of government can't only be about transactions and efficiency. It must also have something to offer governments and the public sector in their attempts to respond to a rapidly changing world, which the trends outlined in this chapter, individually and by their interaction, illustrate.

Second, those designing digital transformation strategies and programs need to cast the significance of their work in this larger context. They need to accept that the job is only half done if it fails to engage digital transformation's role in helping government and the public sector to engage these strategic challenges.

Third, the bedrock challenge for governments in a changing world is a combination of trust, empathy, and competence. That is digital transformation's challenge too. What does it bring to the table by way of tools, methods, mindsets, and capability that actively invest in those attributes of success?

Appendix: Further reading on trends

These are the foresight reports we reviewed as part of the research for this chapter:

CSIRO, 2018, 'Our Future World: global megatrends report', https://www.csiro.au/en/Do-business/Futures/Reports/Our-Future-World

PwC, 2016, 'Five Megatrends and Their Implications for Global Defense & Security', https://www.pwc.com/gx/en/government-public-services/assets/five-megatrends-implications.pdf

Transport NSW, 2017, Future Transport, 'Global Megatrends: The seven global megatrends that will transform transport', https://future.transport.nsw.gov.au/designing-future/global-megatrends

World Economic Forum, 2017, 'Global Risks Report', http://reports.weforum.org/global-risks-2017

Chapter 3

Digital Technology: Current & Future Tools, Methods & Digital Central Units

'The approach of governments to date has been to tell citizens "there's a form for that". Well, it's time they start saying "there's an app for that".'

Former Australian Government Communications Minister,
the Hon. Malcolm Turnbull MP

It might seem a bit odd that a book that is supposed to be about the digital transformation of government is only getting to the digital part in chapter 3. To set the scene for this, we're arguing that we can't expect to get 'there' in the digital transformation project until we understand how digital technology is causing, and responding to, the big social, economic, political, and cultural shifts which we sketched in the last chapter. Nor can we claim we're 'there' until we get a clearer sense of the interaction between the digital 'lifeworld' and some pretty big questions about the role and purpose of government itself, which we talked about in chapter 1, where we argued the need for a new 'theory of the business' for governing and government in the digital era.

To restate the case, the success and significance of the digital transformation project in government and the public sector should be judged not only by the standards of incremental reform and transactional change but also by the extent to which it permeates deeply into a new way of governing and public work. The reason we are searching for new ways to do governing and public work is because the larger trends, most of which are themselves being driven and transformed by developments in digital capability and culture, test the limits of many of our current institutions of public governance. But, obviously, in a book about digital transformation, we need to talk about digital.

This is the third point of our 'digital diamond'. There is a considerable risk in attempting to set out the tools and methods of digital technology for public servants in a single chapter of a book when there are literally hundreds of books and articles available that treat the same topic at great length and in much greater detail than is done here. It might seem a little superficial and too sketchy, especially for those who have some familiarity with the technologies we discuss. So, it's important to be clear about our intent, which can be defined by three propositions.

First, this is a sketch of a large, rapidly changing, and very diverse field. Our purpose is not to be definitive or detailed but to offer a review of some of the main contours and content of this domain, about which all public servants and others working in and with government need to be familiar, and about whose use and value they should be increasingly confident. This chapter is more of a 'ready reckoner' for those who want a quick guide to the tools and methods being used now (e.g., cloud computing); how these have been developed in government, including through newer Digital Central Units (like the Digital Transformation Agency, or DTA); and those technologies that will fuel the fourth industrial revolution (AI, etc.).

We use plain English and have done our best to be hype free. In each case we offer examples and stories from our experience and from around the world. We indicate the source of the definitions, which have either come from quotable sources or are ones we've fashioned – it was surprisingly difficult to find some of these.

We include some suggestions for further reading as well, grouped as follows:

Australian-produced essential reading
Global example(s)
Other (random) material that we found helpful

Peter Drucker once remarked that, sooner or later, all good ideas degenerate into the need for hard work. If you are working in or with government and contributing to the digital transformation project, these are some of the tools and digital capabilities you will be working with now and in the years to come. Think of it as an overview of the 'small picture' toolkit of practical methods and technology tools necessary to engage the 'big picture' changes and trends set out in the preceding chapters.

Finally, the chapter goes at least a few layers down in the 'changing technology' node of our initial explanatory 'diamond' to show you what we think that means in practice.

What digital technology is mainstream now, and how is it being used

Digital technology – types
a. Websites, online services, apps, and content
b. Software, hardware, and enterprise architecture
c. Cloud computing and platform as a service
d. Data, open data, registers, application programming interfaces (APIs), analytics, and dashboards
e. Security: cyber and identity management
f. Social media and blogs

The next instalment: What's coming in the fourth industrial revolution, and why is it important?
a. Artificial intelligence (AI)
b. Automating trust: blockchain
c. Virtual and augmented realities
d. Internet of Things

Digital technology transformation methods
a. Waterfall project management
b. Agile
c. Design methodologies: design thinking, service design, and user experience

Centrally driven transformation: The revolution to date
a. Overview of Digital Central Units* around the world
b. The Government Digital Service (GDS), UK
c. The Digital Transformation Agency (DTA), Australia

*Where we use the term 'Digital Central Units', we refer to groups of public servants within government departments or agencies who have (varied) responsibilities and remit to drive forward digital transformation in these organisations and across governments.

The future is already here: a quick tour of the current digital landscape

Many Australian public servants can't explain what apps are or how to use cloud platforms.

Anonymous senior public servant

It's ok. The high-ranking official sitting next to you at the Steering Group meeting doesn't understand the details of what the guy wearing trainers, with his MacBook covered in stickers, is saying either. You both just about know how to use Microsoft Office.

Only recently have the terms *apps, cloud platform, APIs, cyber,* and *social media* entered the public sector lexicon. Didn't digital technology used to be called 'IT' and, before that, 'e-government'?

Previous generations experienced similar shifts as word processors came in during the 1980s, networks, PCs, and email hit in the late 1990s, and people started to use laptops at the turn of the century, fuelled by the power of the Internet during the dotcom boom. The digital era really began from around 2004–2005, with the advent of social media (Facebook in 2004, and Twitter in 2006), smartphones (iPhone in 2007), and cloud computing (Amazon's Elastic Compute Cloud in 2006) providing the rocket fuel.

Much like any new trend or terms, these labels and descriptions can be used and abused either deliberately or out of ignorance. Gone are the days when understanding digital technology was the domain of the IT department or outsourced. It's hard to find a service or a policy that doesn't need some form of digital technology or a digital mindset (complete with terms like *agile, design, prototype,* and *pivot*) either to help design it, consult on it, deliver it, or run it.

Our overview of the digital technology that is now becoming mainstream in the Australian government is based on our experience and research. The application, use, and understanding varies from state to state and organisation to organisation.

Digital technology – types

a. Websites, online services, apps, and content

Government websites in Australia have been around since 1997, with information on how to pay your taxes – predictably – being one of the first[170] These have slowly evolved from providing static basic information – you know, the kind which just had opening hours and often looked and felt much like a leaflet posted on the web by the work experience student.

> **Websites:** A connected group of pages on the World Wide Web regarded as a single entity, usually maintained by one person or organization and devoted to a single topic or several closely related topics. Usually focused on providing information. (Techopedia)

Every government entity has developed websites over the last 20 years, forming part of their brand and identity. Progressively, information previously provided in paper form has been digitised and put online.

The problem now is that there are still too many of them, all looking and feeling different. Content is often long and dull, written from a government perspective (think each individual agency and a legal and policy voice with a reading age of 16+). It is often out of date, has a cumbersome process for updating, and, in some cases, has never changed.

The Federal Government, at last count, has over 1,500 individual websites and apps and there are 4,000 at the State and local government level.[171] That's five and a half thousand websites!

> **Government Portals:** A single interface that allows users to access in one place information or complete service transactions. (Stewart-Weeks & Cooper)

Better practice is the UK's award-winning GOV.UK which, since 2011, has had all digital interactions (information and services) for national government in one place, is presented in a clear and consistent format, and meets citizens' expectations of regularly being updated and usable.[172]

Governments in Australia are well on the journey to be digitally transformed when it comes to online services. Whilst the term 'government portal' is considered by some to be outdated and government-centric, it is widely used. These are web-based platforms that collect information from different sources into a single presentation to users and provides them with the most relevant information for their context. Examples include the Federal Government's MyGov, Service NSW, and the ImmiAccount (developed by the Department for Immigration and Border Protection, which is now part of the Department of Home Affairs). Paying taxes, effective regulation, service provision, security, enabling tourism, and businesses have all been prioritised and benefited from this digital focus and streamlining.

People in Australia have benefited since 2004 from the ability to submit tax returns using digital forms. ('Making tax less taxing' was no doubt in some communications brief at the Australian Tax Office, the ATO). These were then upgraded to provide automated calculations and refunds in days, not months, through the ATO's system as part of MyGov since 2013.

Whilst probably the least popular government interaction, the taxpayers of Australia have a world-leading service to use, something the UK – noting the 50 million population difference – have only just got around to doing and which was inspired by the Australian pioneers. What's more, the ability to use one password or way to identify yourself (the so-called single-sign-on authentication) affords users simpler and faster access to services – provided that you manually link to each service and identify yourself to each one – such as welfare payments, medical rebates and e-health records, disability support, child support, and veterans affairs.

Similarly, the 'one-stop shop' of Service NSW is where you can apply for licences, check information, and update the Government. It consolidated 100 websites, 400 different shop fronts, more than 100 call centres, and 8,000 phone numbers into one place.[173] That's before you consider the titanic struggle to get government agencies to cede control of services since the new agency was created in 2013.

Queensland's Smart Service Queensland (previously called 'One-Stop Shop') has been going since 2014 in various formats, offers 400 services, and includes a 'tell us once' feature for address changes. Service Victoria launched in 2018, and whilst seeking to increase digital transactions from a baseline of 2% of interactions, has a focus on 'making interactions with government less bad'.[174] However, State service portals are not linked. Despite Australians being able to freely move across state boundaries, unfortunately their data doesn't. These service platforms trap data between different technology platforms with different standards and limited connectivity between the three tiers of government.

Australia is world-leading in the experience of applying for visas, including e-visas, automated intelligence and risk checks, uploading of documents, and digital communications. The single digital interactive platform ImmiAccount is designed to allow the user – for common visa types – to manage all of their interactions in one place. Whilst paying $5,000 for a visa was painful, the experience was paperless, one of the authors (Simon) didn't have to repeat information, and the content, for the most part, was clear enough that he didn't have to pay an immigration agent to do it for him.

Over the last 10 years, a proliferation of software applications, known as apps, for smartphones has been developed. These started out as games on iPhones, began to become more useful (Google Maps, WhatsApp, etc.), and gradually every government department now features apps ranging from simple information to encourage you to wear sunscreen through to MyGov and Service NSW. Unlike websites, apps require users to know how to find and download them, register, and then interact with them to be of any use.

> App: An app (application) is a type of software that allows you to perform specific tasks. Applications for desktop or laptop computers are called desktop applications. Those for mobile devices are called mobile apps. When you open an application, it runs inside the operating system until you close it. (Goodwill Community Foundation, Learn Free)

Thankfully the phase of 'let's build an app' for any problem or topic, which Ministers announced, and then more often than not, the uptake didn't match the ambition, has gone out of fashion. For example, the Victorian government says it has 70 mobile applications available ranging from 'Choose Tap' to 'Show Dates'. In the case of these examples, whilst they may have niche uses, both have low download rates and provide information that can be found on websites (at a lower cost) or is already provided by commercial entities. The UK's GDS had a 'by default, no apps' approach because they felt that user needs (and government resources) would be better served through developing a core web service that works well on mobile devices.[175]

Where apps do make sense, it's better for governments to open up the problem, provide some data (more on open data below) and maybe even some funding. A good example is the 'SnapSendSolve' app that was born out of a competition run by the Victorian government in 2010. It now has 200,000 users across Australia, who digitally report issues like graffiti to the relevant local authority to resolve – removing the need for grumpy phone calls and letters.

This has been transformative because local authorities have changed their systems to be responsive to data received from the app and have reaped the benefits of less correspondence and higher satisfaction rates.

Experience WA, Western Australia's app for tourism, the Fishing Mate app for fishing regulations in the Northern Territory, and ABC's Iview are good examples of apps that offer reliable platforms for users to transact or engage quickly and easily.[176]

The capabilities of web browsers are catching up quickly to mobile apps with progressive web apps. These are web applications that are regular web pages or websites but can appear to the user like traditional applications or native mobile applications, such as including camera access or offline support.[177] Such capabilities may mean the end of government apps.

Content: Digital content is the textual, visual, or aural content that is encountered as part of the user experience on websites. It may include – among other things – text, images, sounds, videos, and animations. (Steve Krug)

Good websites, online services, and apps don't expect citizens or businesses to have a mental map about how to navigate government. They provide easy to digest information and transactions in formats and languages that suits them. Government is the government as far as they are concerned, and they rightly expect all three levels to be joined up and consistent. Government websites, services, and apps really do need to take heed of the 'more is less' mantra. The content certainly shouldn't be the last thing produced before a website goes live, and it should be tested on real people. Plain English, not policy-wonk terms, are a must.

Content should be organised around citizens' needs, and in doing so, become services that enable interaction. For example, there are at least three different, seemingly competing 'how to start a business' websites provided by the Northern Territory. They provide information rather than actually helping a user to progress, e.g., to apply for a grant. Designing for mobile (smaller screens) has helped. A lot of website content could be reduced and any information can be provided as the pre-cursor to starting an interaction.

Content also includes the emails and electronic notifications. Figure 04 shows an example of an email sent by the Australian Tax Office through the MyGov system. It is pretty basic and certainly not attractive, with no styling, colour, or branding. Tom Burton goes a step further to suggest that MyGov 'still feels clunky, a '90s style top-level portal ... with poor navigation, a cacophony of stylesheets and design palettes, and zero brand personality.'[178] It does not meet the standards that citizens get from commercial organisations, such as banks. For example, every time the Federal government wants to communicate with users using MyGov, it sends an email like the one below, in figure 04, with the 'You have a new message in your myGov inbox', creating fear in users as it could be anything from a tax bill to a privacy policy notification update, and this is one of the reasons the government, through the DTA, are looking to change it.

Figure 04: Example of government-generated content

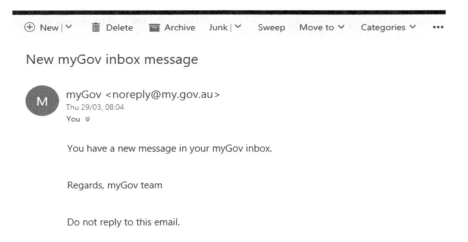

Further reading:
- *Australian:* Federal and State Government websites – search online (you'd be surprised by how few public servants actually look at their own department/agency websites)
- *Global:* www.gov.uk – international best practice, so much so that New Zealand and other countries have copied the format
- *Random:* Steve Krug's book *Don't Make Me Think: A Common Sense Approach to Web and Mobile Usability* does exactly what it says in the title. You'll never consume content in the same way again.

b. Software, hardware, and enterprise architecture

These terms are bandied about, but what do they mean?

Software: A part of a computer system that consists of data or computer instructions. Examples of providers include Java, Oracle, Microsoft, Drupal and Common Language Infrastructure. (Techopedia)

Software as a Service (SaaS): Allows users to connect to and use cloud-based apps over the Internet. (Microsoft).

Hardware from which the system is built, includes the operating system (like Microsoft's Windows, or iOS for Apple) data display (what you see), and microchips (how the data is computed). An iPhone is a piece of hardware, as is your desktop computer. (Adapted from Techopedia)

Technical architecture: Computer system architecture 'layer' which defines and specifies the interfaces, parameters, and protocols used by product architecture and system architecture layers. (BusinessDictionary.com)

Software is what you, as a citizen or public servant, are likely to see and use at the so-called 'front end', such as through websites, apps, or packages like Microsoft Office (PowerPoint, Word, Outlook, etc.), making it the biggest differentiator in government service delivery quality.

Previously, software had to be installed on individual computers or configured for each instance of use. These days, software as a service (SaaS) is purchased as licences, with the service provider managing the software hosted in their data centres in the cloud – see definition below – rather than it being installed on computers.

Hardware are the physical pieces of equipment or kit that are used to operate the software – desktop computers, laptops and notebooks, mobile phone handsets, servers, etc.

How the software and hardware work together is determined through the technical architecture. In this sense, architecture means an overall design with associated rules that make sure different elements of an overall system make sense and work together.

Decisions around whether to buy, adapt, or build are made on a project/program/ service and department (or occasionally on a whole-of-government) basis. Those tasked with delivery of such changes largely argue for what they believe will work or where they can spread the risk. Cost, time, risks of duplication, existing (or legacy) system issues, and quality factors are all considered.

One technique is to create a Wardley Map.[179] This starts with articulating what users need (or the problem being solved for), determining what components will meet those needs, and then mapping them to where unique value can be created. This starts with (industrialised) commodities, such as data storage, products that can be rented, like servers, and custom-built software or genesis, where you build your own from completely new. Using such mapping helps to determine where it makes sense to develop your own – such as where there is no existing software, or you have unique needs – and where it does not make sense; e.g., there's no point in government departments developing their own email or web-hosting capabilities, because that problem has already been solved for.

Three types of projects that you might have heard about relate to back-end systems, off-the-shelf solutions, and build your own.

At the back end (the bit that citizens or public servants don't see) are enterprise resource planning (ERP) systems which use software to streamline processes and information across an entire organisation by integrating functions like payroll and customer contacts. Such systems have a single database that is shared across business units which can be relied upon to meet their needs. These tend to be multi-year projects that improve efficiency, quality, and accessibility of their data, e.g., from reporting and automation because they pull from one system rather than multiple systems. SAP and Oracle are examples of ERP suppliers.

These off-the-shelf solutions are customised to varying degrees and used for applications that have multiple users across an organisation or enterprise. Examples include Salesforce for customer relationship management (CRM), Concur (for expenses), Microsoft 365 (e.g., for email and calendar), and Google Apps (e.g., Google Drive) and earn revenues from subscriptions to them for updates and use.

Alternatively, government departments are increasingly building their own software using different components developed themselves (in-house), from open sources or from commercial vendors.

Further reading:
- *Australian:* LinkedIn learning, Software, https://www.linkedin.com/learning/topics/software-development?u=1504

- *Global:* BMC Enterprise Architecture Frameworks (EAF), The Complete Beginner's Guide, https://www.bmc.com/blogs/enterprise-architecture-frameworks
- *Random:* TechTarget's WhatIs.com?, http://whatis.techtarget.com/, Technology terms in non-technical language

c. *Cloud computing and platform as a service (PaaS)*

Cloud computing is a type of computing that relies on shared computing resources rather than having local servers or personal devices to handle applications ... The services are delivered and used over the Internet and are paid for by the cloud customer on an as-needed or pay-per-use business model. (Webopedia)

Platforms as a Service (PaaS) is a cloud computing model in which a third-party provider delivers hardware and software tools – usually those needed for application development – to users over the Internet. A PaaS provider hosts the hardware and software on its own infrastructure. (TechTarget.com)

'Cloud providers' like Amazon Web Services, IBM, and Microsoft have offered these computing services from around 2010/11. Using the cloud removes the need for physical hardware, much like removing the need to have individual water storage or your own generator. Companies typically charge for cloud computing services based on usage, similar to how you're billed for water or electricity at home. There are different cloud computing models, each shifting increasingly more work onto the cloud provider, and less responsibility for the user.

Infrastructure as a Service (IaaS) is where you can rent usage of individual servers from a cloud provider, instead of running your own physical servers in a data centre.

This provides the benefit of huge on-demand capacity and the flexibility of per-minute billing, so government agencies can quickly scale up and down to respond to changes in traffic.

IaaS removes the responsibility from the user to keep the physical infrastructure online (e.g., making sure power, networking is available) but the user still needs to manage the operating system, databases, and other services required to host an application.

Platform as a Service (PaaS) is a model that goes further: a cloud provider will not just provide the server but also take care of running your code, including the processes to release new code, the security and availability of the underlying infrastructure, and maintaining databases, storage, and other backend services. This frees up teams to focus on building services and reduces the need for dedicated web operations employees.[180]

In government, when building on a security-accredited PaaS provider, the processes to secure and accredit your infrastructure are much simpler, as typically only the application layer (the code you wrote) requires assessment.

The terms 'private cloud' and 'hybrid cloud' refer to an emerging model where cloud-like technologies can be offered in an organisation's existing data centre. Where there are specific security or privacy requirements that impede an organisation from using the "public" cloud, this model can provide some of the benefits of cloud computing.

However, private clouds do not provide the on-demand capacity and global reach of a public provider, they need significant capital investment upfront, and require that you estimate how much capacity you'll need in the future. For almost all common use cases, public cloud is a better option.[181]

As such, the ease of adding capacity, scaling, sharing – and the falling cost – has provided a supercharger to speed up digital transformation in government (and the rise of technology start-ups) since circa 2011. No longer must IT teams do lots of legwork to buy equipment and set it up, such as buying, running, maintaining, and protecting servers.

All of the AI, blockchain, social media, etc. trends discussed below are made possible because of the cloud. So, has Australia made the most of this opportunity of connectedness and speed that comes with cloud computing? Yes and no.

Numerous government agencies have transitioned to the cloud. They've realised the fallacy from a security and business continuity perspective of having to own, store, maintain, and manage data servers in their buildings. Indeed, everything you write is easily accessible (and disclosable under the Freedom of Information Act) in the cloud. The Australian Government has been a global leader in adopting a 'cloud first' policy since 2013/14 to encourage using cloud services. Driven by the Department of Finance, this has focused on reducing costs as well as lifting productivity and enabling the development of better services.[182]

Cloud computing[183] powers platforms – shared infrastructure – on which services and products can be flexibly built, tested, and adapted. They provide a service or interaction. For example, Uber is a platform for connecting passengers with drivers, Apple's iTunes is for apps, Amazon as a marketplace is for commerce, and Airbnb is for travellers and places to stay. They all allow third parties access that increases the value of their platforms. These are powerful services that have quickly joined together and expanded multiple data sets and components. Such platforms use data to engage (or entice) the consumer, to push content, save time, and generally make the transaction as painless as possible.

As Damon Rees, NSW's first Chief Government Information and Digital Officer advocated, if you don't know what these apps and services hosted in the cloud are, have a fiddle around with them or ask your children to show you.[84] Now.

Further reading:
- *Australian:* Digital Transformation Agency, Secure Cloud Strategy, https://www.dta.gov.au/our-projects/secure-cloud-strategy
- *Global:* Quentin Hardy, *Harvard Business Review,* 'How Cloud Computing Is Changing Management', https://hbr.org/2018/02/how-cloud-computing-is-changing-management
- *Random:* Microsoft Azure, 'What is cloud computing? A beginner's guide', https://azure.microsoft.com/en-au/overview/what-is-cloud-computing

d. Data, open data, registers, APIs, analytics, and dashboards

Open data: If data is described as 'open', it means anyone can access, use, or share it. (data.gov.au)

Public administration has been in the data business since it was invented in China and ancient Egypt. The story of Christmas might have been very different had the census not been going on in Bethlehem. The difference between those paper-based scroll records and the floppy disks, mountains of paper, and the database stuck on your hard drive is that there now exists a phenomenal amount of data. It includes text, images, videos, transactions, and web searches that government, citizens, and businesses generate, collect, and store.

Uses comprise everything from informing policy development and reporting, intervention, protection, and enforcement to service design and the operational delivery of services.

Data generated, collected, and stored by the Australian government tended to be siloed, used intermittently, and not open for use. This has changed since 2015, with https://data.gov.au providing a way to find, access, and reuse public data with nearly 30,000 discoverable assets. However, as the limited number of case studies relating to the value created from opening up these assets attests to, a lot of this data is in portable document format (PDF), which makes it hard to access and costly to extract often static data from it, i.e., it's not really open.

In response, APIs are increasingly being provided by government agencies to enable data to flow from interface to interface; 6,200 are available at Federal level, ranging from land titles to rubbish collection and regulations, as part of 58,000 data sets.

Open data is a big part of the digital transformation project. All governments in Australia, and many around the world, have open-data policies and strategies. There are challenges still, with a mixture of technical, organisational, and cultural dimensions of the shift to a more reflexively open approach to using and sharing public data. And there are new challenges too, from the need to broaden the reach of the open-data approach

> 'Application programming interfaces' (APIs): An application programming interface (API) provides a software-to-software connection so that two applications can communicate directly without any user intervention. APIs enable agencies to efficiently share and release data in the most usable forms and to reuse existing technology for a variety of purposes. (digital.nsw.gov.au)

to include important stores of data held by private companies, especially in areas like transport and energy, which are important input to public problem solving.

Issues of relevance, security, privacy, ease of access, and citizen engagement remain significant elements of the open-data policy and delivery space. It's important to be realistic about the speed and intensity of progress which, for some proponents, can often feel much slower and more ponderous than it need be. But the general direction towards a more open-data environment for government and the public sector seems inevitable.

The idea behind open-data government data registries and APIs is that the private or third sectors, as well as governments, can try and create value from the data. This includes surfacing information within a current user experience rather than having to navigate or check a different website, for example. (See the section on platforms.)

The MySchool website run by the Australian Curriculum, Assessment and Reporting Authority is one example.[185] Schools' data, such as the geographic list of schools, inspection outcomes, and exam results, are put together. That helps to meet the needs of parents deciding what schools to send their kids to and

Data registers: Lists of information that are a single source held once across government. Example data range from lists of companies and charities to registered social workers and schools. (UK Government Digital Service)

enabling activist parent–teacher associations to raise standards. But the use of schools' data in this way is not without contest, especially by those anxious that data-driven comparisons can feed the political imperative for variations on the 'league table' models of school performance, which some argue drive an unhelpful 'teach of the test' culture that undermines wider educational and learning values.

NSW's FuelCheck app allows users to compare the real-time price of fuel across the state.[186] Whilst it is a good political story, the purpose, explained Minister Dominello, is to stimulate competition through making price information easier to find.[187] In this case, government changed legislation so that fuel companies have to update an API every time they change their prices. Whilst this feels like government intelligently using data to save consumers money, it remains to be seen if people will change their habits and drive further for cheaper fuel or not. The app is emblematic of what is possible and encourages people, including public servants, to go further with innovation.

Data.gov.au is a good start, but it could improve to be more like the UK's approach, with a focus on building national data infrastructure that they call registers. These lists, or registers, ensure that data is easy to create, maintain, discover, and use; i.e., single source. Different departments take responsibility for creating a register and making it available, and that helps get out of the tangle of data only being used within the organisation that collected it. For example, the Foreign and Commonwealth Office manage the global lists of countries and territories.

Data analytics refers to qualitative and quantitative techniques and processes used to enhance productivity and business gain. (Techopedia)

Data analytics uses computers to make sense of different types of data on a scale that humans can't. Very rarely does data fit in a (structured) database. Unstructured data means it's in a variety of formats, like emails, images or documents, without any logical arrangement. Data is extracted and categorised to identify and analyse behavioural data and patterns, and techniques vary according to organisational requirements. This can include using machine learning, which we discuss later.

In NSW, the analytics dimension of digital transformation has been carried especially by the Data Analytics Centre, or DAC, as it's known as. The first of its type in Australia, and with its own enabling legislation, the DAC is pursuing the promise implied in its belief that 'data analytics has the potential to deliver innovation in service provisions and improve outcomes by generating new perspectives on complex problems.'[188]

One of the important dimensions of its work has been to develop better ways to tackle the challenges of data collaboration within and between government agencies, and often between government, individuals, and organisations, private and non-profit, outside of government.

Thanks to cloud computing, it is no longer the preserve of organisations with the scale and resources like the Australian Security Intelligence Organisation (ASIO), or Coles supermarkets with Flybuys, to do something useful with this data.

For example, police departments use data to predict times and locations of crimes likely to happen and then deploy officers to prevent them. In New York City, the illegal disposal of grease has been reduced by 30% through public servants using analytics tools and data from three different agencies to help choose targets and enforcement action rather than manually determined inspections.[189]

The ATO accrued $500 million in savings in just one year through prevention of fraud and error by using advanced analytics.[190] For fleet management, such as emergency vehicles, data analytics can take all of the information about a vehicle, maintenance requirements, warranty dates, known issues from that or similar vehicles, and times of least use so that vehicle downtime has minimal impact. Various health districts, such as in Melbourne, have trialled and use analytics to predict intake, including in emergency departments, and roster their employees accordingly.[191]

My Health Record is a database that contends it will save lives.[192] It is helpful for a doctor in an emergency department in Perth, for example, to access your medical history if you have accident whilst on holiday from Townsville. The controversial part relates to privacy issues about how data is accessed and stored and how these concerns are considered in relation to the potential wider public benefit.[193]

The more unknown, still to be discovered part is how researchers can apply data analytics and AI to a large unstructured data set relating to anonymised health data that could be analysed over time to identify correlations and patterns that can lead to macro-level prevention and cure. This could range from identifying correlations between different types of illnesses or seemingly unrelated symptoms and geographic data being used to focus on healthy-eating campaigns in overweight suburbs to determining which cancer charities receive more research funding.

Within data, metadata is the term used to provide information about a certain data item's content. For example, within photographs, the metadata describes how large the picture is, the colour depth, the image resolution, when the image was created, and other data. A 'data lake' is a repository that holds data in its original format and a 'data repository' is the destination for designated data storage. The 'data warehouse' is the system used for reporting and data analysis. The bit that you'll often get to see is the depiction of the data as a 'visualisation' which provides some accessible and usable insights from one or more data sets with correlations of particular value.

Digital Dashboards are places for government to publicly report how its services are performing. The dashboard makes this data accessible to increase transparency and drive the continuous improvement of government services. (Australia's Digital Transformation Agency).

Up to date Government performance data is slowly making its way online. The digital dashboards pioneered by the UK's GDS [https://www.gov.uk/performance] showing real-time performance data of completion rates, user satisfactions, digital take-up, and cost per transaction is available for nearly 800 services. The Australian version has 11 [https://dashboard.gov.au], not because of technical restrictions but organisational and cultural ones where the data hasn't been released.

Further reading:
- *Australian:* Australian government open data, www.data.gov.au
- *Global:* UK Government's Performance Dashboards, https://www.gov.uk/performance
- *Random:* Govtech.com, How to Do Data Analytics in Government. http://www.govtech.com/data/How-to-Do-Data-Analytics-in-Government.html

e. Security: cyber and identity management

Government needs to protect its own systems and data, provide resilient responses during security incidents, and support and advise Australian businesses and citizens in order to be protected from these threats. Increasingly connected and networked systems combined with more data means increased assets to protect. According to the Australian Cyber Security Centre (ACSC), threats might include cyber espionage that gathers intelligence in support of state-sponsored activities, cyber-attacks that aim to destroy critical infrastructure, or criminals using the Internet as a means to defraud or steal individual identities.[194]

> Cyber security is the practice of defending computers, servers, mobile devices, electronic systems, networks, and data from malicious attacks. (Kaspersky)

ACSC warn that there were 47,000 identified cyber security incidents in 2016–17, including online fraud such as phishing emails (fake bank emails getting you to send your account details), malware (software which steals data, like your passwords, for example) and more sophisticated hacks (stealing employee data, for example).[195] The cost is estimated to be $1 billion annually to the Australian economy.[196]

Knowing an individual or organisation is who they say they are is critical to maintain the fidelity and security of online interactions. This stops fraud and unauthorised or accidental disclosure of information. Being able to do this digitally and securely, without the need to verify people or their documents in person, is vital to reducing duplication, generating efficiencies, and enabling straight-through processing (where the transaction process is speeded up and can be processed without manual intervention).

> Identity management is about proving you are who you say you are in order to control information about users on computers, such as information that authenticates the identity of a user, or that describes information and actions they are authorised to access and/or perform. (Stewart-Weeks & Cooper)

Passwords, biometrics, and smart cards are examples of identity management. Many will be familiar with the MyGov two-step verification where, during the log-in process, they send you a text message with a code which you must enter to gain access to your MyGov account. Many banks have the same. However, different passwords and logins for many services see people irritated and constantly having to reset passwords, or use the same passwords across different platforms and services, creating additional vulnerabilities.

Achieving consensus on the development and use of one single digital identifier which is both practical and technically feasible is one of the reasons why, over the previous 30 years, it has proved to be a challenge that has defied the Australian government, including the 1980s' proposal for an Australia Card.[197]

The Australian Government's GovPass program is building a trusted digital identity ecosystem to support online access to high-volume Federal Government services. This is a new federated identity system with the DTA developing the underlying Trusted Digital Identity Framework, which is a set of rules and standards that aims to make sure the system is secure and accessible.

The vision is to give Australian citizens and permanent residents a single and secure way to create a digital identity which can be used to access online government services – i.e., a single digital identifier to enable them to interact with government once, without having to re-enter information, and to pre-populate information based on what has already been provided.[198] An example digital identity provider is the myGovID, currently in development, which is intended to be the Australian Government's safe, secure, and reusable identity provider for government departments to use.

This approach has learned from the UK Government's GOV.UK Verify. This identity assurance system was developed by the GDS in 2015. The system is intended to provide one single trusted login across all UK government digital services after verifying the user's identity in 15 minutes during the registration process. It allows users to choose one of several companies (like credit checking agencies) to verify their identity to a standard level of assurance before accessing 12 central government online services, like the tax department, or checking your driver's licence. However, it can struggle to identify people who haven't been in the UK for that long or who live 'off the grid', without interacting with government or using infrastructure such as banks. It is unclear if the system will continue.[199]

Further reading:
- *Australian:* NSW Government: Cyber security matters in a digital world, https://www.digital.nsw.gov.au/article/cyber-security
- *Global:* GOV.UK Verify, https://www.gov.uk/government/publications/introducing-govuk-verify/introducing-govuk-verify

- *Random*: 'The Dark Side of Hacking: Confronting the Cybersecurity Challenge' in *Delivering on Digital: The Innovators and Technologies That Are Transforming Government*, by William D. Eggers

f.   Social media and blogs

Australians are some of the most prolific consumers of social media in the world.[200] Facebook, Twitter, Instagram, and LinkedIn are not only used by pre-teenagers to octogenarians across the country but by government departments for communications, sharing views, documents, articles, and videos.

> Social media are websites and applications that enable users to create and share content or to participate in social networking, such as Instagram, Facebook, and Twitter. (Stewart-Weeks & Cooper)

Many politicians, including those more digitally savvy like former NSW Premier Mike Baird, and the new Minister for Customer Service, the Hon. Victor Dominello, in NSW, and former Prime Minister Turnbull, have extensively embraced social media as a form of engagement and promotion, and not just to disseminate information. They use it

> Blogs, short for 'weblogs', are typically informal, diary-style text posts often covering discussions or discrete topics. (Wikipedia)

as a means of dialogue and to demonstrate their passion for public service. Mark Scott, the Secretary of the NSW Department for Education (and former Managing Director of the ABC, Australia's national public broadcaster) has 122,000 followers, which provides him with a direct link to the schools and teachers he engages with.

Tom Fletcher CMG, a UK diplomat, famously did this as the British Ambassador to Lebanon. He was nicknamed the 'digital diplomat' because he used Twitter and blogs to not only promote the UK but draw attention to issues in the region during the Syrian war. He almost single-handedly opened up what some might say is a famously closed and stuffy institution, the UK's Foreign and Commonwealth Office, bringing diplomacy into the digital age. This may have inspired others, including Sir Mark Sedwill, and Clare Moriarty CB, Permanent Secretary for the Department for Exiting the European Union, as well as an array of diplomats including Menna Rawlings CMG, the UK High Commissioner to Australia 2015–19.

The UK's GDS openly published blogs at all levels of public servants about what they were working on, lessons learned, and to promote achievements from 2012.[201] This helped inspire public servants (including Simon) to find out more, build capabilities, and to encourage people from outside the public service by showing them what kind of problems and work they would be doing. Most of the Digital Central Units, including in NSW and the DTA (which we discuss later on this chapter) use blogs as a way of working in the open.

The exception to this is where you get the occasional public servant who decides the risks of saying something controversial are outweighed by using social media or blogs as a platform to advocate for and drive transformational change.

Public servants have to navigate mixed messages in that, on one hand, engagement is important, but on the other, social media guidelines often make it difficult to say anything of interest or personal.[202]

Further reading:
- *Australian:* Stephen Easton, 'New advice for public servants posting on social media, same old rules', The Mandarin, https://www.themandarin. com.au/82248-new-advice-public-servants-posting-social-media-no-new-rules
- *Global:* Tom Fletcher, Twitter, http://tomfletcher.global; Menna Rawlings, Twitter, https://twitter.com/MennaRawlings
- *Random:* Tom Fletcher's book *The Naked Diplomat: Understanding Power and Politics in the Digital Age*, Harper Collins, 2016

The next instalment: What's coming in the fourth industrial revolution (4IR) and why is it important?

Just as public servants are getting their heads around current digital technology and the impact they're having on the provision of government services, a new wave of technologies is emerging associated with the 4IR. These are accelerating where digital technology is an enabler to replace (automate) or do something humans can't do themselves, either at all or fast enough to be valuable.

We consider three types of AI – reactive, proactive, and personal.[203] We also consider other emerging technologies – blockchain, AR, VR, and the Internet of Things (IoT).

Artificial intelligence (AI)

Perhaps the most hyped – or feared – trend is AI. Government agencies across Australia have been busy considering AI, including the required capabilities, potential uses, and the economic potential, as to how AI can generate value through mimicking human intelligence.[204]

AI works in four ways:[205]

> Artificial intelligence (AI):
> A collection of interrelated technologies used to solve problems autonomously and perform tasks to achieve defined objectives without explicit guidance from a human being (Data61).

- Automated intelligence: Automation of manual/cognitive and routine/ non-routine tasks undertaken by people
- Assisted intelligence: Helping people to perform tasks faster and better
- Augmented intelligence: Helping people to make better decisions
- Autonomous intelligence: Automating decision-making processes without human intervention, e.g., autonomous vehicles

The use of AI will become as omnipresent in our personal lives as apps and smartphones have. The 'narrow' application AI is already upon us. This is where machines can perform tasks previously performed by humans, especially those which are high-volume and mechanical.

For example, Google's Gmail scans the content of your emails to suggest responses based on the tone and content and identifies spam email (e.g., it learns that penis enhancement invites are likely to be spam). The speech recognition in Apple's Siri or Amazon's Alexa is powered by AI. This AI arms race, with Google, Facebook, Alibaba, and others ploughing billions into this technology to develop its much wider use, is just beginning. Expect to see AI emerge like the app revolution in 2007–08. Kevin Kelly suggests that 'AI will become ubiquitous, embedding cheap smartness into everything we make ... you'll take x and add AI to it'.[206]

Like others in Australia, government is just starting to figure out how to benefit (and regulate) from where AI is now and where it's going to be. Public servants are clear that they can't just look to insert AI into services for the sake of it, that there has to be a net benefit. One analysis suggests that if AI can understand, monitor, reason, predict, interact, learn, and improve, then through these applications 'AI can reduce administrative burdens, help resolve resource allocation problems, and take on significantly complex tasks'.[207] On the security side, the use of AI to predict terrorism, model the impact of weather events, detect fraudulent applications, and prevent crime will be hugely beneficial. Instant translation and digestion of foreign language texts could change diplomatic relations.

The major consultancies and technology firms are pushing the benefits of AI, with most side-stepping the loss of jobs concern with narrative focused on freeing up employees to work on more creative and complex jobs.[208]

a. Reactive AI: automating human tasks

This type of AI is about automating reactive actions, such as completing simple rules-based processes or engagement, that humans would otherwise have to do.

Robotic process automation (RPA): Software tool used to capture and interpret existing IT applications to enable interaction across multiple IT systems. It mimics existing actions undertaken by humans. RPA-suitable processes include pre-populating forms, collecting and reformatting data, and billing. (Deloitte Australia)

Many public service agencies have explored using, and are rolling out, robotic process automation (RPA). RPA doesn't use the kind of robots that you see in movies. RPA can use a combination of clever macros (like the formulas you use in a spreadsheet in Microsoft's Excel) and programming to automate repeatable manual processes. These are actions that humans do but require little judgement, often in back offices, such as invoice processing and appointment booking.[209]

The big banks in Australia have been RPA-ing their repetitive processes as much as possible since 2017 or so, including form completion, data transfer across systems, data validation and collection, document scanning, scrapping data from the web, following if/then decisions rules, and transcripts.[210] Unlike humans, RPA can run 24 hours a day, seven days a week, and, assuming that it's been set up correctly, will have a higher degree of accuracy and productivity; typically, say, a team of 10 who have been doing this work can become a team of one or two who are responsible for supervising and quality assuring the RPA as it runs on computers in an office.

Government is at the stage of exploring the potential benefits of RPA, including how it can help reduce paperwork, backlogs, help with resource constraints, and put employees onto high-value work that requires uniquely human abilities. Some believe it's the cure for the perennial 'more for less' ask of government. However, that narrative gets lost with the word 'robot', which is unhelpful. However, this technology is here and some trials are already showing that RPA could allow many tasks and related jobs to be reassigned or eliminated altogether.

The other, more practical drawback of RPA in government is that the real complexity of automation is defining the processes to a sufficiently granular level, ideally with limited exceptions. Government, operating as it does in many areas as rule-based organisations, should be perfect. However, whilst there are efficiencies to be had from moving workers onto higher-value work or making redundancies, departments are baulking at the time and cost associated with process re-engineering. Some examples of RPA that we've seen actually uncover the inconvenient truth that the process isn't required at all, or that the action, e.g., matching invoices, could actually be better done using a specific app.

Whilst on the topic of robotics, robots – the kind that people seem to have in their mind, like something from the Star Wars or The Terminator films – are instead machines used to perform automated physical functions. These have been around for decades and are getting more sophisticated and cheaper as all manner of sensors are added to allow physical robots to safely work alongside people.

These types of robots are less relevant to 'digital', which is more about transforming interactions rather than using technology to do the same thing repeatedly, but faster. Where robots augment or replace these are in unpredictable environments, with particular relevance to the military, disaster response, surgeons, and drones for shark detection, for example. For everyday interactions, we can't quite see the day – or at least in the next five to 10 years – where Service NSW, for example, replaces human customer service with a robot who replicates what a person currently does.

The rise of the robots will generate work for government, including regulation, safety, and similar concerns, especially as they enter our homes and become real enough to form relationships with.

Why wait on the phone to a call centre, and remember to ring during opening hours, when you can chat to a bot to sort something out? Visit a major bank or airline's website and up pops a chatbot, or 'virtual assistant', inviting you to have a chat by offering to help you with something.[211] They conduct a typed conversation and convincingly simulate human interactions. The idea is

Chatbots: A computer program designed to simulate text-based conversation with human users, especially over the Internet. It mimics or augments qualitative human judgements. (Cooper & Stewart-Weeks)

to emulate citizen–government interaction during the delivery of a public service to a business or a citizen.[212] This is to save, for example, the time and cost of enquiries being handled in call centres, enable first-time resolution, and/or the associated rework costs of incorrect submissions. Examples include the ATO's 'Alex',[213] Service Victoria's 'Vicky',[214] and Germany's 'GovBot'.[215] The Australian Department of Human Services has been deploying chatbots to help with queries and as a way of servicing demand, with 33 million unanswered calls in 2017.[216] The government of Jersey has developed a chatbot to replace the surveys that previously made up public consultations with something quicker, easier, and more effective.[217]

Government chatbots have been based mostly on rule-based expert systems, where there are stock responses to frequently asked questions.[218] As such, there is limited flexibility and responsiveness to unexpected questions. Some can come across as glorified Internet searches. Much more useful are the chatbots that can be trained to translate the input data into a desired output value, i.e., a considered versus stock response. When given this data, the bot analyses and forms context to point to the relevant data to react to spoken or written prompts to serve individuals, based on specific interpretation of their needs.[219]

Cognitive assistant: A computer that helps you understand what is going on around you, and supports decision-making, using technology such as speech recognition and tonal analysis. (IBM)

Natural language processing (NLP): A branch of artificial intelligence that helps computers understand, interpret, and manipulate human language. (SAS)

Cognitive assistants recognise speech, and when you talk to them, it's just like talking to a person. It involves converting the spoken word to text, which goes through natural language processing in order to be understood by a computer. Apple's Siri on the iPhone is an example.

The Amazon Echo (Alexa) and Google Home are household voice assistant devices currently using these technologies, sometimes called 'AI bots'. We use our Echos to tell us the time, set alarms, read personalised news, and play our favourite songs. In time, Alexa will become just like having a personal assistant, assuming we are happy to give up massive amounts of data to Amazon.[220] She'll remind you that someone's birthday is coming up (and prompt you to buy a present – from Amazon). She'll tell you to leave now because the traffic's bad in order to get to work on time. Why bother typing an Internet query when you can just ask out loud? Not bad for $50. This technology will continue to improve with the introduction of screens into these devices, meaning that you could, for example, ask for recommendations for flights, see the options, and then tell the device to book them using voice authentication to charge your credit card.

These devices are becoming more popular in Australia, with as many as 57% of searches now executed through voice and one in 10 people owning a voice assistant in their homes.[221] Government agencies are at the imagining stage regarding their application in policy and services, e.g., government use. Some government agencies, like in the UK, are beginning to ensure that their web content is 'voice ready' – written clearly and concisely – so that when someone conducts a voice query, they get a coherent answer.[222]

In the US, cities like Las Vegas use Alexa skills to help residents practice for their driver's licence exam and with simple tasks such as renewing a driver's licence.[223] Noting all the 'big brother' privacy concerns, you could also imagine government being able to issue traffic (or terrorism) push alerts, or even conduct public consultations. As the technology gets better, it could improve customer experiences. An example could be the device reminding (and even helping) to complete interactions such as tax returns.

Unlike Alexa and Google Home, cognitive assistants like IPSoft's Amelia have faces and feel far more like interaction with a person.[224] This so-called 'digital labour' can take on a wide variety of service desk roles.

For example, Amelia can take a new employee through the necessary actions when starting a new role and also complete transactions such as to apply for parental leave. This transforms your experience from trying to find the right information on an intranet, interpret, ask questions, and fill in forms to talking to someone who has access to systems and the right processes and gets what you need done there and then. This technology could easily replace swathes of corporate services and shared services support roles as well as drive up compliance and employee efficiency.

Their use and a growing reliance in government on their potential to improve engagement and service quality can be challenged though. Peter Shergold's concern about the failure of 'Nadia', the virtual assistant of the National Disability Insurance Scheme (NDIS), to deliver on 'her' promise of engagement and efficiency has been challenged by one of the co-developers of the solution, who believes this new channel has been successful.[225]

Every day, tens of thousands of interactions with government are conducted on the phone. Virtual agents could replace or augment the thousands of people employed to answer these calls. Using a mix of cloud-based services, AI, and automation, it could be that the virtual agent answers basic queries to resolve customer requests or hands them off to agents who, by that point, have the information in front of them – potentially including previous interactions, such as where they can see that the person calling has been using the app or chat channels.

The prize for government of so-called 'conversational AI' to mimic conversations with real people through a variety of channels is to meet the demand for self-service whilst offering completely personalised and differentiated experiences.[226]

There are also opportunities for real-time translation and data capture that can then be used to improve other channels, such as the website. The thought of not having to wait, listening to endless jingles, or to have to press the right number option on a handset, is enough for us to get over the potential weirdness of a humanised interaction with this conversational interface.

Further reading:
- *Australian:* Deloitte Tech Trends, 2019, https://www2.deloitte.com/au/en/pages/technology/articles/tech-trends.html
- *Global:* Tim O'Reilly's *WTF?: What's the Future and Why It's Up to Us',* Harper Business, 2017
- *Random:* Joe Toscano's 'The ultimate guide to chatbots', 31 Oct. 2016, https://www.invisionapp.com/blog/guide-to-chatbots

b. Proactive AI

Proactive AI is where the AI uses machine-learning capabilities to be better at automation and begin to provide new services and insights using algorithms and by interpreting human behaviour. It mimics and then augments human behaviours, becoming dynamically self-adaptable and managing.

The rules-based chatbots, cognitive assistants, and virtual call-centre agents are now being supercharged by the power of 'machine learning'. The machine – the underlying software powering the chatbot or assistant – discovers new patterns in the data without any prior information or training, then extracts and stores the pattern. The machine-learning branch of AI is where computers sift through data to recognise patterns and make predictions without being explicitly programmed. Computers use trial and error to learn through mining information to discover patterns in information. Or, as leading AI researcher and expert Toby Walsh puts it:

'Programs are sequences of instructions that a computer follows when solving a problem. [AI means] you won't have to find the new program because the computer can find it for itself, learn to do new tasks and even behave intelligently.'[227]

Machine learning means that computers can learn and then change their own code to improve their performance over time and even share with other computers.

> **Machine learning:** A method of data analysis that automates analytical model building. It is a branch of artificial intelligence based on the idea that systems can learn from data, identify patterns, and make decisions with minimal human intervention (including without being explicitly programmed). (SAS Analytics)
>
> **Machine learning model:** A group of specialised, connected, mathematical functions. Together they represent the steps an intelligent machine will take to arrive at a decision. (Google)

Typically, this a two-step process with the algorithm first trained on known data and then unleashed to solve similar problems with new information. The availability of smaller, cheaper, and more powerful electronics can mimic – and even improve – on human judgement, and are based on an analysis of huge amounts of incoming data, including from sensors, cameras, and mobile devices, all at speeds previously thought unimaginable. This can be done through:

- *Supervised learning:* This kind of algorithm takes a data set which has labels that tell the machine what kind of data it is, deduces the salient features that characterise each label, and learns to recognise those features in new data.
- *Unsupervised learning:* This takes an unlabelled data set, finds similarities and anomalies between different entries within that data set, and categorises them into its own groupings.
- *Reinforcement learning:* This works by trial and error. When the algorithm is fed a data set, it treats the environment like a game and is told whether it has won or lost each time it performs an action. This way, it builds up a picture of the 'moves' that result in success, and those that don't.

'Deep Learning' is a branch of machine learning involving artificial neural networks inspired by the brain's structure and function. These neural networks can be trained to recognise images and spoken words, and translate languages.

The machine updates its neural networks, which consist of different layers for analysing and learning data. For example, if the chatbot doesn't know the answer to, say, a particular type of regulatory compliance, it will refer to a human and then learn and remember the answer to later answer the question itself.

They can use AI to narrow down the query, extract meaning – or your intent – from text, integrate with other systems to access relevant data, and generate text that is readable, stylistically natural, and grammatically correct. And the bot will know if you are being sarcastic, as it understands conversational cadences. It might even tell you off for swearing!

Critically, it allows for more intimate interactions, so it feels real, rather than wooden or structured. The predictive analytics within bots uses statistics, modelling, data mining, and more to generate information proactively, rather than in response to a prompt. If used, say, through messaging apps like Facebook Messenger, the bot can access your vital statistics without having to ask you, as well as infer things. For example, it will know that you're unlikely to ask about retirement plans if it knows that you just graduated from university. People hate, for example, having to repeatedly spell out their names and email addresses.

An example of an intelligent chatbot is the US Citizenship and Immigration Services, which has a virtual assistant called 'Emma' that responds to questions, speaks English and Spanish, and learns through supervised learning.[228]

It's not just about providing the right answer; it's about providing it in a way that encourages engagement. A cognitive assistant can learn, using language analytics, to determine the attitude or emotional state of the person they are speaking to.

The ability of computer systems to improve their performance by exposure to data, but without the need to follow explicitly programmed instructions, is likely to be the most prevalent of cognitive technologies.

The Australian Government is working to ensure that the public service has better predictive capabilities for a range of uses, including identifying terrorist threats that humans previously had to do manually, e.g., using facial recognition to identify patterns which may have been missed.

It would be great to see government digital services use machine learning to suggest (or complete) the next-best transaction people usually need, e.g., to update your Medicare information, and have the system suggest completing claims or the benefit that they might be entitled to.

Policy wonks will get excited of the prospect of speeding up consultations with communities using not just (faster) analysis of written submissions, voice, and image recognition but also increasingly sophisticated emphasis and meaning. Government legal and procurement services will rapidly be disrupted as such technology, e.g., will be able to identify all the people and places mentioned or extract terms and conditions in contracts.

IBM Watson is an example of the 'Rolls Royce' of cognitive insights. It's a diagnostic tool offering the precise ability to retrieve answers from a lot of complex information in order to recommend a course of action, enrich interactions, and anticipate problems. It's been used in the US for medical diagnosis, including cancer detection. Watson is now being enhanced to tell you the logic of its answer (the why), which may help to see the capability used in Australia, because practitioners such as doctors can better understand the rationale behind outputs, giving them greater confidence to use this tool. The narrative of augmenting and providing a second opinion, especially for medical professionals, will be important.

Quantum computing could pave the way for computers to solve complex problems at speeds not currently possible, even with the world's fastest computers. Academics, including 2018 Australian of the Year Professor Michelle Simmons, are seeking to put theory into action through harnessing the many practical applications of quantum science.

Governments such as NSW have been investing in and supporting universities and industry groups to have the necessary infrastructure and research facilities to speed up computation to tackle important data-heavy problems and power cognitive insights, e.g., weather prediction, travel, and detection of medical conditions.

Cognitive insight uses include the integration of AI and machine learning into existing platforms. This is sometimes known as 'narrow AI' because it doesn't need to replicate a human, as it is limited to performing the tasks it has been designed for commercial applications to undertake.

Parts of the Australian Government could be revolutionised as the power of machine learning goes mainstream. We explore this in detail in the next chapter, as machine learning will fundamentally change the work undertaken, worker's roles, and the workplace for public servants.

Will citizens accept interacting with bots and cognitive assistants that keep learning to get better and better and the decisions and data flowing from them? The answer is probably yes, if it leads to faster, better, and cheaper interactions with government. That said, we see three immediate specific considerations, aside from the obvious, that concern data use, costs of implementation, and regulation.

The first is that whilst government is meant to be rules based, we all know that individual judgement plays a huge role. Can a machine really replace years of experience, the sensitivities to discern the right thing to do in a situation? Too rigid an application of rules or biases from learning from past datasets can create problems.

Second, people, especially those as naturally social as Australians, really do value talking to other people. The intimacy of a conversation with a government official can provide some of the only contact elderly or vulnerable people have. These will also be the very people who already need digital assistance, either from an understanding, infrastructure, or use perspective.

Third, the rules and regulations around the answers bots and assistants give will need to be considered. How do you, for example, program or learn the duty of care aspects or how to really handle an emotional person? Toby Walsh's book *2062: The World that AI Made* debates what is fair, the need for transparency, and the challenge of decision-making by machines because they can't be held accountable in the way humans are, where their values can be identified.[229]

Citizens will also become increasingly aware of and challenged over who owns data and what government agencies do with it. Citizens could ask for the right for their data not to be used in machine learning unless they are somehow rewarded for the value generated (beyond the public good).

Finally, as Toby Walsh sets out, computers have the advantage to make better decisions because they have more memory capacity, faster speeds, unlimited power supply, no need for rest, and are not forgetful or limited by how they share knowledge compared to humans.[230]

Further reading:
- *Australian*: Australia's Centre for Quantum Computation & Communication Technology, http://www.cqc2t.org
- *Global*: Philipp Gerbert and Frank Rueß's 'The Next Decade in Quantum Computing – and How to play, 14 Nov. 2018, BCG, https://www.bcg.com/en-au/publications/2018/next-decade-quantum-computing-how-play.aspx

- *Random*: Deloitte: Cognitive technologies, A technical primer, https://www2.deloitte.com/insights/us/en/focus/cognitive-technologies/technical-primer.html

c. *Personal AI: mimicking human intelligence*

Personal AI (or 'true AI') will acquire human-like thought processing and thinking capabilities to mimic human intelligence.

The capabilities of current AI and deep learning often get confused with the so-called Holy Grail: to 'build a genuinely intelligent system – a machine that can conceive new ideas, demonstrate an awareness of its own existence, and carry on coherent conversations'.[231]

Once – if – achieved, this would then direct its intelligence inward and become far superior in intelligence than humans. This is the realm of science fiction writers, and it is decades off. It is a distraction when it comes to the debate and considerations of the type of digital transformation covered in this book.

Government leaders need to understand the difference between where technology is now and the potential in the long, long term and have a perspective on this. This is particularly true with the likes of the late Professor Stephen Hawking and fellow scientists openly talking about what 'would be the biggest event in human history' that would usher in the 'singularity' – at the moment in time when AI and other technologies would have become so advanced that humanity undergoes a dramatic and irreversible change – through the invention of super intelligence and through a dramatic technological disruption to civilisation.[232]

This 'true' AI might be a way off, but we can envisage a future whereby people have the kind of personal AIs mentioned above. The smartphone in your pocket or smart speaker at home already knows, and will continue to learn, more about you and your preferences than your closest friends or spouse. It is not hard to imagine a world where Siri on your iPhone is not only recommending restaurants you'd like but engaging on your behalf to book the restaurant and talking to the restaurant employee directly on the phone to make the booking, or perhaps to the restaurant bot. Google famously demonstrated this with its AI making a hair appointment in 2018, and then updated the demo to show the AI identifying itself because the likeness to a human seemed a little creepy.[233]

One potential future is where citizens have their own AI assistants, such as Siri or Alexa, which they enable to access their personal information such as credit card numbers, etc., and then instruct to communicate and transact with other AIs.

For example, you could tell (or be prompted by) your AI to programmatically contact Service NSW's AI and sort out an updated address on your driver's licence. There could thus be a situation where interactions are being handled between AIs rather than between citizens themselves.

Further reading:
- *Australian:* Toby Walsh, *2062: The World that AI Made*, La Trobe University Press, 2018
- *Global:* 'Future Proof: How today's artificial intelligence solutions are taking government services to the next frontier', Accenture, https://www.accenture.com/us-en/insight-future-proof?sr_source=lift_amplify&c=glb_futureproofhowtexacttarget_10058081&n=emc_1117&emc=21945031:emc-111717
- *Random:* Martin Ford, *Rise of the Robots: Technology and the Threat of a Jobless Future*, Basic Books, 2015

Automating trust: blockchain

It was almost a running joke in 2017 that blockchain was the answer to everything that needs fixing in government. For some, the advent of blockchains is becoming a seminal moment similar to the way the iPhone turned phones into platforms and the Internet made computers more relevant.

Blockchain cryptology replaces third-party intermediaries as the keeper of trust; participants within blockchain run complex algorithms to certify the integrity of the whole.[234] Bitcoin exchanges don't go through a bank but, rather, is a transaction that is posted to a public ledger (the blockchain) that is distributed across all other bitcoin owners in the world. The blockchain contains a list of every transaction ever, and is open to everyone. These databases are updated six times an hour and the 'blockchain creates trust by relying on mutual peer-to-peer accounting ...

Blockchain: is a form of distributed ledger technology (DLT) that connects different parties over the Internet to provide a secure and trustworthy record of their transactions (both financial and non-financial), without giving control to a third party. (CSIRO).

[the] system itself runs on thousands of citizen computers (mining) to secure the coins'.[235]

The benefit of blockchain is that you can prove where information has come from and gone to. Trust is not established through a third party but with clever code and mass consensus, using a network. It's beginning to fulfil its potential to open up new economic activity in areas such as financial services and in supply chains.[236]

A whole bunch of start-up fintechs (financial technology companies that are finding new ways to deliver financial services)[237] in Australia are catching this wave. They are trying to disrupt banks (and take a share of their profits) through providing record keeping while removing the need for them as intermediaries. The new Myanmar stock exchange is powered by blockchain. Blockchains can be used for food-provenance and supply-chain tracking, with benefits including quickly finding and addressing sources of contamination around the world and ensuring authenticity, e.g., that the Australian wagyu beef marketed in China really is from Australia.[238]

According to Data61, blockchain could be used as a common reference point to bring together different levels of government (local, state, and federal) to host government lists (registries) of data that is open to anyone to access and use.[239] There is huge potential for more reliable integration across government services, improved mobility and business consistency across states, and better regulatory oversight when blockchains record operational information in regulated industries.[240] In the Republic of Georgia they now use blockchain for their land registry as part of an effort to reduce corruption.[241] The UK Government's Department for Work and Pensions has been testing a blockchain pilot in order to reduce fraud and errors in welfare payments, as well as to track how they are spent.[242]

The sense in Australia is that the Government is seeing how the fintechs get on before considering using the technology in identity management, licensing, and supply-chain/procurement transparency. The Federal government has funded a PowerLedger trial in Freemantle, Western Australia (WA), to create a blockchain-powered distributed energy and water system.[243] This project focuses on how cities can effectively use blockchain technologies to moderate energy and water usage.

The furore about bitcoin trading has also sharpened the sense of a need to work out the regulatory position for blockchains, especially as no one 'owns' them. So, even if government doesn't immediately adopt the use of blockchain –

a few people interviewed for this book stated that they felt that 'it's a technology looking for a problem' – that they will still need to cover the regulatory points.

At the national level, Australia's DTA is positioning with caution and some distance from the current discussion about blockchain's contribution to the public sector. The chief concern is the absence of standards across different examples of blockchain applications, which suggests pragmatic responses; at least which suggests checking out other, better-developed technology alternatives which are more robust and well established.[244]

Further reading:

- *Australian:* CSIRO, 2017, 'Distributed Ledgers: Scenarios for the Australian economy over the coming decades', https://www.data61.csiro.au/~/media/D61/Files/Blockchain-reports/Blockchain-Scenarios-HTML.html
- *Global:* Don Tapscott & Alex Tapscott, *Blockchain Revolution: How the Technology Behind Bitcoin Is Changing Money, Business, and the World,* Portfolio, 2016
- *Random:* Gian Volpicelli, 'Does blockchain offer hype or hope?', *The Observer,* 10 Mar. 2018, https://www.theguardian.com/technology/2018/mar/10/blockchain-music-imogen-heap-provenance-finance-voting-amir-taaki

Virtual and augmented realities

> Virtual reality (VR): Creates a fully rendered digital environment that replaces the user's real-world environment. (Deloitte)

Virtual reality (VR) and augmented reality (AR) technologies can be used for far more than entertainment. VR is where the real world is blocked out; you wear goggles, sometimes a suit, hold controllers, and fully immerse yourself in a virtual world. With the latency and issues with causing nausea being improved all the time, VR headsets like Oculus (now owned by Facebook) are being used for computer gamers and VR entertainment centres. In Melbourne's Zero Latency centre, you can run around an old warehouse killing zombies with your friends. VR is becoming mainstream. You can even buy VR tickets to virtually attend sporting events and concerts.

The quality improvements mean that government use of VR is transitioning. For example, it is being used in mock-up layouts of public spaces to understand the useability, and for consultation purposes, conducting training for emergency services, and remotely fixing machines. A big game changer will be establishing virtual presence meetings using holodeck or VR, which will cut down the need for Government and stakeholder travel across Australia.

Screens are everywhere now, from phones to e-readers, to laptops, to TVs and Apple watches. Even most public servants have two screens on their desks. AR provides another screen to allow, e.g., simultaneous translation, facial recognition, or the ability to walk down a street overlaid with useful information. Snapchat, which is an app that people use to send images of themselves, for example, and is augmented with animal features, and Pokémon Go, a popular computer game where people walk to collect Pokémons, are early examples of AR.

The Australian Government has begun to test using AR in firefighting helmets so that firefighters have access to building plans when entering. Whilst currently expensive, Microsoft's Hololens promises to augment, e.g., government workers inspecting pipes by telling them the temperature or overlaying site plans.[245] Any kind of training, assistance in technical roles, and supporting meetings will all see quality benefits from AR. These new 'screens will enable us to "read" everything, not just text'.[246] Unlike VR, the user isn't blocked off from the outside world. The screens will probably be integrated into reading glasses, even if Google Glass didn't take off in 2013, as people found them too creepy. After that it will be AR contact lenses.

> **Augmented reality (AR):** Overlays digitally created content into the user's real-world environment. Features include transparent optics and a viewable environment in which users are aware of their surroundings and themselves. (Deloitte)

Further reading:

- *Australian:* CSIRO, 'New lab immerses users in environment of Augmented Reality', News Release, 15 May 2018, https://www.csiro.au/en/News/News-releases/2018/New-lab-immerses-users-in-environment-of-Agumented-Reality
- *Global:* US Government General Services Administration, Government IT Initiatives, Virtual and Augmented Reality, https://www.gsa.gov/technology/government-it-initiatives/emerging-citizen-technology/virtual-and-augmented-reality
- *Random:* Kevin Kelly, *The Inevitable: Understanding the 12 Technological Forces That Will Shape Our Future*, Viking Press, 2016

Internet of Things (IoT)

Internet of Things (IoT):
The network of physical devices, vehicles, home appliances and items embedded with electronics, software, sensors, and connectivity that enables these things to connect and exchange data, creating opportunities for more direct integration of the physical world into computer-based systems, resulting in efficiency improvements, economic benefits and reduced human exertions. (Australian Computer Society and PWC, 2018)

The IoT smart sensors enable connected products and the collection of data, which will be enhanced by the impact of fifth-generation wireless (5G) because this technology will enable IoT and AI through removing latency, because it is one hundred times faster than 4G, fourth-generation wireless.[247]

Examples of uses by government include to help with environmental management, including embedded sensors that monitor everything from pollution to land management, supplementing or replacing on-site inspections, or to enhance living with connected smart homes for energy use and predictive analytics that tell city administrators which social interventions could be undertaken. A further example is for security, where sensors have been installed in areas at risk from graffiti and which can smell paint to alert a close-circuit television (CCTV) camera and the police to spraying.[248]

This will help to power civic management improvements promised by so-called 'smart cities'. A city can be defined as 'smart' when investments in human and social capital and traditional (transport) and modern (ICT) communication infrastructure fuel sustainable economic development and a high quality of life, with a wise management of natural resources.[249] It collects and uses data to drive its decision-making, and creates networks of partners among governments, businesses, non-profits, community groups, universities, and hospitals to expand and improve its ability to serve its residents.[250]

Further reading:
- *Australian:* PricewaterhouseCoopers Consulting (Australia), Australia's IoT Opportunity: Driving Future Growth: An ACS (Australian Computer Society) Report, 1 May 2018, https://www.pwc.com.au/consulting/assets/publications/acs-pwc-iot-report-web.pdf
- *Global:* Smart Cities Council, https://smartcitiescouncil.com
- *Random:* Samuel Greengard's *The Internet of Things*, The MIT Press, 2015

Digital technology transformation methods

Broadly, digital transformation methods fit into two approaches, waterfall project management and user-centric agile product/service management. These are summarised in figure 05 below.

Figure 05: Traditional project approaches to government IT versus methods advocated by Digital Central Units

Traditional Approaches to Government IT ('eGovernment')	Methods Advocated by Digital Central Units
Waterfall project management requirements-based design, using release cycles for deployment	Agile, iterative design through learning and favours rapid release and continuous deployment
Preference towards buying and customising	Starting position: build bespoke
Government-centric (focused on adhering to internal government standards, processes, and needs)	User-centric (focused on identifying user needs, and tailoring government standards and processes around these needs)
Limited reliance on data in decision-making and design	Heavy reliance on data-driven decision-making and design
Managing legacy contracts with a small number of big IT providers	Building in-house and procuring with a competitive, pluralistic marketplace
Favours proprietary solutions	Favours open-source solutions
Silos ('one use', department/ initiative specific project development, and IT management)	Horizontal, platform models ('multiple use', whole-of-government project development, and IT management)
More risk-averse, process-first, hierarchical organisational culture	Hacker, delivery-first, 'flatter' organisational culture

Credit: Adapted with kind permission from Amanda Clarke.[251]

Waterfall project management

The waterfall project management model is one in which each phase of a product's life cycle takes place in sequence through the phases of conception, initiation, analysis, design, construction, testing, deployment, and maintenance, so that progress flows steadily downwards through these phases, like a waterfall. (Manifesto.co.uk)

In waterfall methodologies, the vast majority of requirements gathering and design work is done before any coding or technical design takes place.

This method is one where government officials want nearly absolute certainty as to what will happen and why. It's a method for the old theory of the business of government described in chapter 1.

In general, these methodologies have stages that deal with what you need to do before a project, during a start-up phase, a planning phase, an execution phase, and a closing phase. They also then have a series of processes for managing work packages, exceptions, reporting, risks, and issues. Typically, requirements gathering involves a business analyst and some technical people filling in documents of requirements, e.g., how many transactions, level of security, number of user log-ons, etc.

This method is closely associated with the PRINCE2 (Projects in Controlled Environments) project management method which the last two generations of public servants will have been trained in or had some exposure to.[252] Typically, the business cases for government (strategic, outline, and final) and the associated stage gates for funding are also aligned.

This makes sense when you know what you are building and managing to a plan, such as building roads or bridges. However, this was the method used by many governments who largely outsourced their IT functions in the 1980s and 1990s, following the new public management reforms rather than building their own in-house capabilities.[253] Public servants didn't always have the expertise to know if needs (technical and user) were being met. The process can be seen as more important than the outcome; e.g., *We delivered on what's in the business case and that's what counts.*

The result is often bigger, complicated builds undertaken by IT departments and vendors over a number of months and years. In turn, these have turned into expensive procurements in which 'many governments signed onto long-term 'legacy' contracts, procuring services that would only meet their short-term needs, or would not meet their needs at all'.[254] The big challenge with waterfall methodology is the length of the feedback loop where you only know at the end if it works, and even if you find out halfway through that it won't work, you can't easily change course.

The alternate view from technology leads is that this is often caused by requirements that actually changed or are still being defined due to the uncertain technology and political environments causing ongoing analysis and increased development.

There are many books, audit reviews, and special reports which outline IT failures where waterfall has been the predominant method. The US Affordable Care Act (also known as 'ObamaCare' health cover (2013) in the US,[255] IBM with the Queensland Health payment system in 2011, and the UK's National Health Service records system in the early 2000s. All caused huge issues for citizens, costs for government, and reputational damage.[256]

Further reading:
- *Australian:* Mark Ludlow, 'IT disasters now a part of modern life', *Australian Financial Review,* 2016, https://www.afr.com/technology/it-disasters-now-part-of-modern-life-20160628-gptyw6
- *Global:* Frank Turley, *Prince2 Training Manual,* van Haren Publishing, 2017
- *Random:* Anthony King & Ivor Crewe, *The Blunders of Our Governments,* 2nd ed., Oneworld Publications, 2014

Agile

Agile has come into vogue for all Australian governments since around 2014, building on the UK government's use since 2010, and prior to that, industry since as early as the 1970s. Agile is associated with design sprints which use design thinking processes to answer critical business questions through design, prototyping, and testing ideas with customers. These are time-constrained (typically five to 10 days) and are delivered by a multi-disciplinary or cross-functional team.

Agile management, or agile project management, is an iterative and incremental method of managing the design and build activities for engineering, information technology, and new product or service development projects in a highly flexible and interactive manner. (AgileGovLeaders)

As the 'Agile Manifesto' – written by 17 independent-minded software practitioners in 2001 – advocates, the highest priority is to satisfy the customer through early and continuous delivery of valuable software.[257] A good way to think about these purposely ambiguous principles is:

- **Individuals and interactions** over processes and tools
- **Working software** over comprehensive documentation
- **Customer collaboration** over contract negotiation
- **Responding to change** over following a plan
- **Design methodologies: design thinking, service design, and user experience**

The design methodologies of design thinking, service design, and lean user experience (UX) have risen in use and popularity in government over the last five years or so. They tend to get conflated with agile.

Design thinking takes a human-centric approach by using empathy to understand end users. It's a collaborative and engaging process to develop ideas, help understand different perspectives, and function as a communication tool.

Service design is focused on designing the experience and delivery of a service to make it scalable with a particular focus on delivering against a particular problem.

UX is about designing the interface of an interaction, such as the screens on a mobile app, and uses feedback from users to create iterations. The focus is on the user experience rather than deliverables, and as such, involves working closely with the end user, including testing prototypes with them.

The main difference with these design methodologies is that they require interaction with real users to ensure what is being built works for them. Other techniques, such as project management, can be taught and delivered without such interactions.

The popularity of these methods stems from its focus on user needs at a time when government is becoming more attuned to serving customer needs and because, when done well, they deliver working digital services faster, better, and (sometimes) cheaper than waterfall or project-focused methods.

They allow for evolving requirements when you know the least about the problem at the start rather than having to know and define everything upfront.

The NSW Digital Team's guide, one of many similar ones from government teams around the world, summarises it nicely:

'The process allows teams to break a large risk into smaller, more manageable risks. Teams tackle the most valuable thing first. Teams can also test assumptions, especially the risky ones, early. This allows them to make data-driven decisions based on rigorous research.'[258]

It is very much a method of transformation associated with the kind of solution-focused new theory of government we speculated about in chapter 1.

Such methods also tend to favour cross-functional teams, which has been a big enabler for removing the complexities associated with big program structures across multiple divisions and suppliers, and instead favours moving quickly, dispensing with the mountains of paperwork and requirement lists symbolic of 'big IT' projects.

Successful agile examples include most of the UK Government Digital Service's 25 best example digital 'exemplars' between 2013 and 2015, including digital visa applications and a prison visit booking system.[259] Figure 06 shows the UK's GDS explanation as to why this method meets user needs.

Figure 06: Comparison of digital development methods

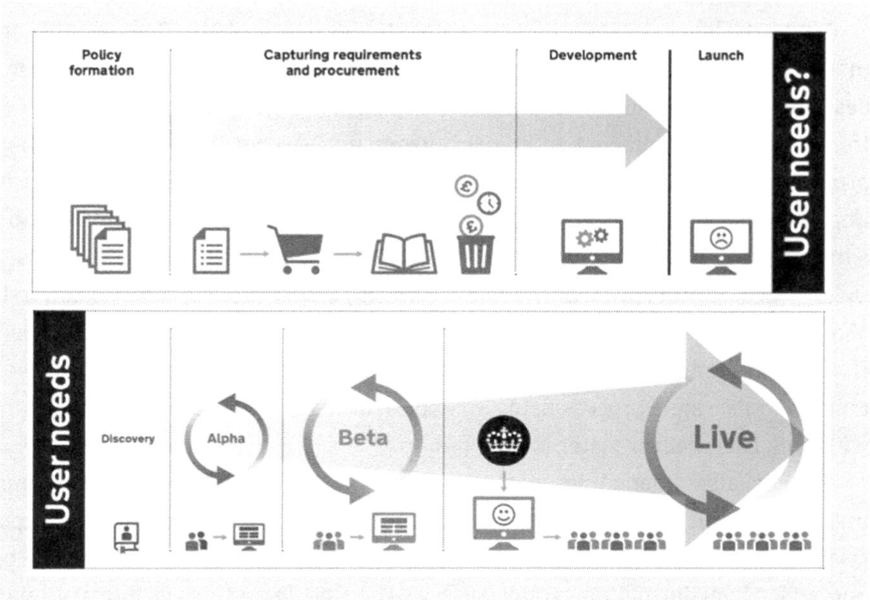

Credit: GDS Service Design Manual reproduced with kind permission of the GDS

The US Department of Veterans Affairs used agile methods to build the US site www.va.gov[260] as a new single point of interaction and information, replacing a system dating back to the 1980s. They fixed the criticism of the way they had previously dealt with returning Iraq war veterans to create a service that met their needs.

The Australian experience of using these methods is still in its infancy. There are green shoots in the work that the Department of Human Services have been doing with the NDIS, the DTA's Digital Marketplace, and new services coming out of Queensland and NSW. Examples include undertaking continuous user research (actually ask and observe rather than guessing, undertaking surveys, or convening focus groups), developing prototypes, and thinking about service design from the users' (rather than government's) perspective.

Increasingly, there are examples of public servants who have been converted and shared their experiences, largely focused on how agile methods have helped them to deliver.

The UK's Public Guardian is a good example of an 'old school' civil servant who has become an advocate, including countering criticisms that agile means less governance: *I've got more control over an agile development, because I see what is being done*, and *We've moved from process to customer outcomes*.[261]

David Hazlehurst, when he was a Deputy Secretary at the Department for Industry in the Federal Government Austrade, was also a convert. As a self-described 'policy wonk', he outlined at a national conference how he changed from feeling disconnected from users from his base in Canberra and using project management techniques to conducting user research with those impacted and using design methods. This included setting up a new 'BizLab', which uses a new eight-phase process of: Problem Codification; Empathise; Define; Idea; Prototype; Test; Activate; and Ongoing Refinement.[262] Hazlehurst challenged his peers to 'be the pragmatists seeking to make a change rather than just keeping their heads down, to seek out the air cover to be innovative, trust the more agile process using an experienced and co-located team to begin with, and then deliver faster for the public'.[263]

This is also happening in the junior ranks of government. Bottom-up initiatives, such as cross-government communities of practice or meet-ups relating to interest areas such as coding, service design, and user experience, and wider transformation groups such as the One Team Gov, an international community of policymakers, service designers, digital people and others working to reform government and make public services better,[264] have all sprung up free of traditional operating structures to build capability and momentum around digital transformation. Australia currently has comparatively few of these going on.

However, adoption of such methods is not without criticism. For example, where the discovery of user needs and problem definition stages and alpha prototype development spend too long analysing, do not design for scale and service integration and, above all, often six to eight months in do not have a sense of what needs to be built, when nor how much it will cost much to the annoyance of senior leaders.

However, the sentiment from interviewees reveals that the focus on user, rapid iteration, and frequent change represents a huge shift and encounters resistance in the public service. The often separate IT departments have resisted agile because they dislike the lack of processes, procedural requirements and associated governance and see the notion of 'failing fast' as being pointless.

All of that is before one gets into the cultural clash between agile/design focused practitioners who sometimes come in from private sector with the attitude that 'it can't really be that hard' to apply the methods that work for (new) businesses into government. The techniques can be seen as the 'province of chatty teenagers' or 'geeks in jeans' who are slacking about, can't write anything other than mountains of post-it notes, and who lack the pragmatism to get things done in a political environment.

The distinctly millennial feel of the method, complete with a whole new language of 'scrum masters', 'epics', 'user stories', 'personas' and so on, and the tendency to ride rough-shod over policy and legal considerations, has all been off-putting to public servants who have done perfectly well career-wise using waterfall. The tendency not to articulate how such projects meet government's (political) needs is a particular irritant.

This new way of working threatens the old adage 'Nobody ever got fired for buying IBM', and as we explore in the next chapter, represents a big shift in the accountabilities, risk, and culture of delivery in the public service.

Further reading:
- *Australian:* Australia Government: Agile and User Centred, https://guides. service.gov.au/digital-service-standard/3-agile-and-user-centred
- *Global:* Agile vs Waterfall comparing project management methodologies, https://manifesto.co.uk/agile-vs-waterfall-comparing-project-management-methodologies

- *Random:* The Agile Manifesto, https://www.agilealliance.org/agile101/the-agile-manifesto

Overview of Digital Central Units around the world

Leading the charge of the digital revolution in recent times have been new Digital Central Units. This is the catch-all term for organisations of groups of public servants within government departments or agencies at central/federal government or at state level who have (varied) responsibilities and remit to drive forward digital transformation in these organisations. Examples include the UK's Government Digital Service (GDS), Australia's DTA, and the US Digital Service, the Canadian Digital Service, and about 20 or so around the world, from Australia to Denmark, from Italy to Peru.

Broadly, their functions have been to:

- Set standards focused on user-centric design (see above section on agile delivery)
- Advise on and build services that use new digital technologies
- Become centres of excellence for digital capabilities (people, process, and technologies)
- Develop whole-of-government shared platforms
- Drive the delivery of exemplar or high-profile projects
- Provide spend controls
- Furnish digital procurement assurance and services

These units have worked with and inspired digital, technology, innovation,[265] policy, and transformation teams within government agencies, departments, and bodies around the world to consider, advocate for, and to use digital methods. Most publish guidance, tools, and methods on designing and delivering digital government, as well as open data sets and code. Apolitical have published a fantastic summary page of these from around the world.[266]

The appendix in this chapter provides an analysis of a selection of these units, including what they do, and brief commentary of their progress.[267] It is notable that the countries widely seen to be leaders in digital government (Denmark, Singapore, and the UK) have sizeable resources – for example, Singapore has a digital transformation office and a technology infrastructure division, both under their Prime Minister's Office – which far outstrip the resources dedicated to any Digital Central Unit in Australia.

Government Digital Service (GDS), UK

The UK's GDS was one of the first of such units. From 2012 to 2013, it had a remit to drive digital change in government, including through direct development of digital products, setting standards, and generally beating the drum for digital transformation. This was in the context of a burning platform where the old ways of working, including big IT spend, couldn't continue with 20–25% budget cuts across government as the UK government focused on reducing its national deficit.

GDS didn't mandate the use of digital services, unlike, say, the path that Denmark and Singapore, who are often touted as world leaders in digital government, chose. Rather, they took the approach that they would build 'digital services so good that people prefer to use them'[268] and to go beyond 'the tyranny of low expectations and redesign services'.[269] The book *Digital Transformation at Scale: Why the Strategy Is Delivery* provides an excellent overview from the historical perspective of four former GDS leaders of how they went about, with the strong political backing of the now Lord Francis Maude as their Minister, revolutionising delivering change in government to be digital.[270]

Changes to the way government works included the introduction of digital service standards which are broadly based on designing for user needs using agile methods and multi-disciplinary/cross-functional teams, and by rapidly delivering first prototypes and then services that could be put in front of users, rather than papers in front of colleagues.[271]

GOV.UK consolidated thousands of websites into one, and the 25 exemplar services developed with agencies, including to streamline the visit visa process and make it easier to book a prison visit, showed that digital could make a big a difference.

At a time when the UK was desperately trying to save money (although underplayed in the GDS narrative and the many, many blog posts published) with their hands-on spend controls, they stopped outsourcing multi-million British pounds of IT spend and saved millions. They did this through a mix of re-architecting and breaking down contracts so that outsourcing was more likely to succeed, developing whole-of-government procurement contracts to leverage economies of scale, building services themselves, and driving hard around open standards and a technology code of practice so that reusable components were developed, according to one GDS Team Lead we interviewed. The latter included:

> **The GOV.UK Verify.** https://www.signin.service.gov.uk/verify-services, appears to have cracked the nut of providing a trusted identity system for government, removing the need for identity documents to be sent back and forth.

> **GOV.UK Notify.** https://www.notifications.service.gov.uk/, permits any government agency (national and local) to send emails, text messages, and letters to its users.

> **GOV.UK Pay.** https://www.payments.service.gov.uk/, is a free, secure online payment service for government and public sector organisations to take payments and issue refunds.

Procurement was diversified away from being largely the domain of big IT and outsourcing companies through the G-Cloud digital marketplace, https://www.digitalmarketplace.service.gov.uk. This has since created an industry of small digital businesses to supply government and the wider economy. The UK now exports this industry through the 'Global Digital Marketplace' initiative.[272]

Like any revolution, there are critics of the GDS's 'centralist digital onslaught'. Amanda Clarke has produced an excellent academic summary as to whether such units work.[273] This is hard, given the limited timeframe that these units around the world have been in existence. Each had different rationales for being set up, and few had defined success criteria. In the case of GDS, the successes listed above are recognised, along with the main finding that it was the capabilities developed within government, including with operational delivery agencies, that has had the lasting legacy (so far).

Clarke also covers the consequences. Driving through such revolutionary change saw battles fought about everything from how government answered phones to business case design, to technology standards, and even what was acceptable to wear as a government official and display in the workplace (hanging bunting and stickers on laptops were favourites).

This annoyed a lot of public servants, particularly as it often came with an overzealous tone regarding agile and aligning to user needs, which often did not align to the realities that any agencies faced, including tight and declining budgets and complex, changing government policy. One of the authors (Simon) remembers being told his digital service would fail one of the digital service standards for not having content in multiple languages. That was despite government policy being that to apply for that type of visa, they had to demonstrate a certain level of English. However, the use of the GOV.UK design system was far quicker than his team attempting to do it themselves, and GDS's assurance that the Digital Service Standards were being met meant for a better quality and user-centric service having been developed.

Subsequent leadership have struck a more conciliatory tone. Combined with changes in political support (and the small matter of Britain leaving the European Union), there is a sense from public servants in the UK that the GDS has lost its way and is no longer able to drive effective digital change. You could conclude that the GDS has done its job in sparking the digital revolution across government and building those capabilities for it to endure.

The alternative view, as Mike Bracken, the former GDS leader, has suggested, is that those traditional mandarins are now winning out against being disrupted.[274] Whitehall isn't built to share, and the straight lines and silos it's built on are deeply resistant to change.

There is something antithetical, he argues, between the Westminster and digital worlds, which is diluting GDS's ability to impact change. They are now in a situation where they are writing large transformation strategies rather than being in delivery mode and seeing their teams transferred to other government departments.[275]

The Digital Transformation Agency (DTA), Australia

The UK experience heavily influenced what the federal government in Australia has tried to do.

The Government's engagement with the digital dimension of change and reform in government, and in wider policy issues too, has rolled through many cycles over the years, starting with the National Office for the Information Economy (NOIE), then the Australian Government Information Management Office (AGIMO), as earlier manifestations of central units setting IT policy and standards, but with few legislative or budgetary teeth.

More recently, the Digital Transformation Office (DTO) was set up with considerable fanfare with the former GDS Director and experienced technology leader Paul Shetler, imported from the UK, along with four other former GDS team members.

Shetler lasted 18 months, with a lot of Canberra mandarins fairly clearly rejecting the bold vision for transformation and disrupter label given to him. As he subsequently explained to a Senate inquiry, 'It's extremely difficult to get an incredibly bureaucratised, incredibly Balkanised bureaucracy to decide it wants to transform itself'.[276]

For example, Shetler says that rather than comply to provide performance data for the DTA's new digital (public) dashboard, 'the APS would rather not embarrass a colleague than report on it'.[277] Two years on, the digital dashboards have very little data on them, compared to the UK's, which have been going for five years and have a thousand services reported in real time.[278]

With rapidly evaporating political support, interest, or capability – the Hon. Malcolm Turnbull, who hired him, became Prime Minister within six months, but then lost the leadership of the Liberal Party and the prime ministership – and access to the kind of digital talent available in London, the DTA's embrace of 'the strategy is delivery' mantra[279] was harder to believe.

For example, plans for a single government website were shot down[280] and exemplars were developed in isolation from departments. Many public servants just didn't see the need to change their digital presence and, with that, to change their ways of working which, bar the odd technology program blowout, seemed to be working fine.

With over 27 years of economic growth and no debt mountain to reduce, or desire to create new industries amongst the political class, motivation for the digital 'project' seemed low and declining at the national level. Even in the face of evidence that the government could save $20 billion,[281] the interest seems limited and fails obviously to align to political priorities.

The point about improving government services – the same services that constituents complain about at MPs' surgeries the length and breadth of the country – somehow gets lost in the departmental silos. Even when Australia ranks lower than its global peers, such as 13th in the Institute of Digital Government,[282] there is little reaction.

If the UAE, which scored higher than Australia on e-participation and digital inclusion, beat Australia at any kind of sport, there would be a national outcry. As one public service middle manager said to us, 'We've grown lazy and complacent as a nation ... there's no burning platform for change, so nobody I work with really cares [about digital transformation].' It is perhaps telling at the time of writing that the Minister for Digital Transformation no longer attends the Cabinet.

After two years of being incubated, the DTO had its remit expanded and became an agency in its own right, outside of the Prime Minister and Cabinet, as the DTA in October 2017. Becoming an agency in its own right had been advocated by Shetler and others who had advised Ministers that to become the down-under version of the UK's GDS, the DTA needed more clout. The new remit included more budget and people to review digital projects from any department as part of creating one portfolio overview for government, the bringing together of the procurement functions from the Department of Finance, and new data and cyber functions added to the portfolio.

A new Deputy Secretary with government experience was brought in with a more policy-focused mandate and a brief for the DTA to repair relationships across government. Shetler stepped into the new role of Chief Digital Officer, Australian Government, but without the support, funding, and focus to build anything, so he quickly left. He shunned the traditional style of 'going quietly', instead giving a series of press interviews citing a difference in philosophy with the Minister responsible and has become a regular critic of how digital transformation is being undertaken by the Australian government.

Three CEOs later, the DTA is finding how it can best add value. Peter Alexander, the Australian Government's Chief Digital Officer since late 2017, explains that the DTA exists to:

'Firstly, catalyse cross-government change using the tools of data, technology and service design. Secondly, build the capabilities of the APS to operate in a digital world including procurement and platforms. Thirdly, to define how digital transformation changes how government operates, delivers services and supports a participatory democracy.'[283]

There has since been a great deal of reported activity, including a portfolio review of all digital projects over $5 million across government. Senate Estimate hearings have, however, seen frustrations aired as to why the DTA has struggled to escalate or intervene when projects on its portfolio watch list have been failing, such as biometrics.[284]

A platforms strategy and a new national digital transformation strategy were launched.[285] The latter was published in late 2018, as this book was being finalised. It declared that all Commonwealth services would be available through digital channels and with a goal to make Australia a top-three digital nation by 2025. Whilst it is good to see the details of the ambition written down the substance around platforms, digitising services and building capabilities is, as one well informed Deputy Secretary pointed out to us, 'largely similar to the previous documents ... the DTA seem to have moved away from "the strategy is delivery" to "the strategy is to state the problem and not how to solve them"'.

This has particularly been the view of agencies who have had their projects reviewed by the DTA and who have then been frustrated that there is limited help forthcoming – unlike the GDS model in the UK – to provide capacity or capability uplifts. These are in development with the platform's strategy and the work with the APS to develop digital skills curriculums and courses, but are not of immediate use.

The topic of digital transformation has all but disappeared from contemporary political rhetoric at the national level. A recent former Federal Government Minister told us that 'at a national level, this conversation is dead ... there is no interest from the mandarin class in this.' With a high employee turnover, it is unclear if those aspirations are, or have a chance of, being met. The views expressed at Senate Estimates – and in private by politicians and public servants across the political spectrum – suggest they are not. This may result in the government deciding to end the experiment that began under Turnbull's watch, having concluded that such an insurgency model hasn't had the desired impact.

Overall, as explored in more detail in the next chapter, such units have been, and will continue to be, valuable and provide a necessary central function, much like a Department of Cabinet or Treasury. However, getting 'there' won't be achieved simply by relying on their role, however well delivered.

New South Wales

The NSW Government have initially taken a lower-key approach, without the fanfare of the DTA and the GDS. There hasn't been until the second half of 2018 a deliberate digital government (central) unit that you can easily align with the DTA or GDS as counterparts, although that is changing rapidly.

As noted earlier in this chapter, the government created a 'one-stop shop' for government services called 'Service NSW' which has been going since 2013. Today, there is one main website and mobile app, a single shop front that handles more than 2,000 transactions across 15 agencies. Measures of satisfaction from people using the platform are consistently high.

The NSW Government published in May 2017 an overarching and refreshingly simple digital strategy called digital.nsw, designing for a digital future (see section below for more on digital strategies p. 269, many of which were authored or are led by Digital Central Units).

The vision is to transform the lives of the people of NSW by designing policies and services that are smart, simple, and seamless. This set the central direction, vision, and cultural change for how digital services should be customer-experience-centric and powered by data. These should in turn be provided by public servants who have the 'digital on the inside' kit to do so.

Notable examples of digital initiatives since then have included a digital driver's licence scheme, a new digital marketplace for cloud services, and Service NSW rolling out digital initiatives to make it easier for citizens to save money with their cost of living and 'energy switch' services.[286] But a number of these felt like they were being done as pilots, in isolation, or without a narrative as to why they were important, and what they would lead to.

Since late 2018, with the experienced new Chief Digital and Information Officer Greg Wells and Executive Director for Digital Government and Policy Pia Andrews, NSW had a distinct and ambitious Digital Central Unit acting as the driver and focal point for not only digital but whole-of-government transformation. Indeed, conversations with Pia and Greg, as well as their then Departmental Secretary Martin Hoffman, about this book have supported the development of many of the arguments put forward.[287]

NSW has accelerated and openly communicated their centrally driven digital transformation approach, including having:

- launched a Digital Design System to provide consistent standards, templates, and ways of working to digital teams across government;
- launched a Policy Lab, to bring human-centred design, multidisciplinary teams, and test-driven approaches to government policy development;
- begun to experiment with 'rules as code', looking at how policy, regulation, and legislation can be turned into computer code, codified and test driven to make service transactions seamless and rule changes more efficient and responsive;

- established an evidence-driven backlog to continuously prioritise all government investment and efforts on improving citizen experience with government, a so-called 'CX (customer experience) Pipeline';
- with the support of the NSW Treasury and the Chief Information Officers (CIOs) from each agency cluster, proposed a digital investment fund to address how the funding mechanisms for agile budgeting for digital delivery needs to transition away from waterfall-style business cases and towards cross-sector and outcome-focused investments;
- brought together the Digital Ministers from each State, Territory, and Federal level to begin to discuss how services across jurisdictions and departments can better share and collaborate on digital agendas; and
- launched a cross agency and cross-sector program of work around 'life journeys' to explore a holistic user experience, through complex journeys such as a birth or death, rather than around government constructs or individual transactions with agencies. In three months, the research led to prototyping of well-evidenced opportunities. (This is not the first time that life or citizen journeys have been used as a frame for digital innovation of service models, but it remains a potentially powerful way to organise and integrate the resources and services across government, and include input from other non-government payers as well).[288]

As this book was completed, the current NSW Government won a third term in the State election (March 2019) and brought in a major reorganisation of the state public sector. One of the most significant pieces of reform is the establishment of a Department for Customer Service, headed by its own Cabinet-level Minister (currently the Hon. Victor Dominello).

The new Department combines all of the government's digital and IT functions, Service NSW, the Data Analytics Centre, and the 'nudge' or behavioural insights unit.

It will be instructive to watch the new department's evolution as a focal point within the public sector for a more or less explicit strategy to transform not just the digital dimension of the public sector but, at some level, the way the public sector as a whole operates.

Rather than centre on digital transformation, which will be a major focus over the next four years, the new department creates a new piece of government machinery to drive a 'government transformation' process, through and with the pervasive application of digital tools, platforms, and culture.

It is a development in line with one of the main conclusions we have drawn from this work, that governments need to focus less on the digital transformation of government and more on the transformation of government itself as the main game.

Victoria

The Victorian approach has been deliberately low-key, with a focus on 'showing, not telling', and bringing public servants on a journey focused on collaboration rather than control. This team is based within the Department of Premier and Cabinet and does not have the distinct identity of a Digital Central Unit, nor a specific digital strategy in the way that the DTA or NSW's team has (or indeed their global equivalents). But it has undertaken similar activities, such as developing and setting frameworks, policies, and guidelines to support a developing digital community across Victorian government agencies, as well as a wider remit on cyber security.289

This team have been exploring the value of taking a whole-of-government shared-platforms approach.

'Engage Victoria' is an enhanced digital public participation and analytics platform, a cross-government engagement platform that any government department can use to run policy and community engagement in a software as a service and annual fee arrangement.[290] This has reduced individual procurements and associated costs for similar services and increased the speed at which consultations can be run and organised.

The new vic.gov.au website was launched in early 2019 and uses open-source software to provide government agencies with the ability to design and link into a common format and user-friendly website service. It provides Victorians with one entry point into government (a single digital presence) and seeks to emulate the kind of successes GOV.UK has had, including rationalising content, reducing costs by up to 50%, and designing government information increasingly around user journeys, not government organisations.[291]

Again, following in the footsteps of GOV.UK and some of the work undertaken at national level, the Victorian government launched an API developer portal, along with API standards and a centralised platform.[292] The Victorian version has focused on opening up data that will be of use to businesses to help create jobs and growth, such as location-based data, and ensuring that it's up to date in a format that can be used more easily.

The question for Victoria is how far this quiet and collaborative way of building out projects and platforms will get in transforming the way government services are delivered. But as the old fable of the tortoise and hare reminds us, slow and steady can win the race.

Since the beginning of the more self-conscious effort to engage the technology revolution to the work of government and the public sector, eGovernment, or 'government 2.0' or digital government, has been struggling to work out whether the 'e' or the 'digital' is necessary. It has often been taken as a sign of sophistication to argue that 'surely, it's not "e" or "digital" that matters; it's just "government". The argument switches between enthusiasm for a degree of separateness, to signal that the intrusion of technology heralds a change, something different, and which therefore needs its own focus and identity, and a concern to bring what can then rapidly turn into a fringe or exotic concern on the edges of the 'real' business of government into its mainstream.

The role of digital transformation units in government, like GDS and DTA and the others that we've reviewed, raises the same dilemma.

Our view is that these units need to go through several stages of evolution to be useful.

In the first stage, their separateness is essential, providing a way to signal a desire for change and reform and collecting together the necessary and necessarily scarce resources and expertise in one place. That provides the firepower and sustained organisational focus for what inevitably will be a difficult assault on the change-resistant structures and culture of the core public sector.

In a second stage, these units need to evolve a different way of working with agencies across the public sector. Maintaining the focus on the rigor and intensity of the reform agenda suggests a certain level of separateness is both necessary and useful. But the operating model has to be much more collaborative and co-equal where the central transformation team plays a coach or support role.

And in a third stage, these units need to become less direct in their interventions and support for a momentum of change and innovation that by then should be well established and, to a great extent, self-reinforcing. Here, the role becomes more akin to a review, a standards and quality role which, among other things, helps to hold together the larger transformation puzzle to which the individual contributions or pieces from the agencies themselves fit and make sense.

Further reading:

- *Australian:* NSW Government Digital Design System, https://www.digital. nsw.gov.au/digital-design-system
- *Global:* Global Government Forum, 'The Rise and Fall of GDS Lessons for Digital Government', https://www.globalgovernmentforum.com/the-rise-and-fall-of-gds-lessons-for-digital-government
- Andrew Greenway et al.'s *Digital Transformation at Scale: Why the Strategy Is Delivery*
- *Random:* Amanda Clarke's *Digital Government Units: Origins, Orthodoxy and Critical Considerations for Public Management Theory and Practice*

Three important messages

These are the important messages to take away from this chapter.

First, the array of technologies and tools we've described represent the toolkit of any public servant or those working with government to do the work of digital transformation. As well as the traditional tools and techniques of policy analysis and good administrative practice (records management, good filing and tracking systems, the right way to prepare and prosecute a Cabinet submission), these will increasingly be technologies that public servants will be expected to know about and feel comfortable using.

Second, even if technology isn't the purpose of digital transformation, there is no transformation without it. And the technology churns and changes with a speed and intensity unlikely to diminish.

Third, all of these technologies carry big implications for the work of the public sector and for the way the public sector works. There are implications, especially for the speed of work that is both required and assumed, the ability to rapidly connect many different voices and perspectives into the work, and deliberations of government and new challenges to technique and culture arising from the security and other risks associated with the shift to digital.

It is to that third message that the next chapter turns.

Appendix: Profiles of selected Digital Central Units

These units have been important vehicles to advocate for digital transformation, to create cross-government capabilities such as platforms, procurement changes and standards, and to deliver digital changes.

Where they have built the capacity of public servants, such as the exemplar program of 25 projects in the UK, or sparked agencies to build these digital teams and change their expectations and ways of thinking relating to digital transformation, this is where they have been the most effective.

However, there is only so far you can get with centrally based teams of about 100 to 200 people and supporting cross-government strategies. Many of these are also under-powered, under-valued or under-funded, which leaves them vulnerable when their sponsors change to having their wings clipped, especially if they have been disruptive.

Our point in this book is that much of what these digital central teams do should become commonplace across all agencies. Or, put another way, much like you'd expect the Treasury to be leaders in terms of financial management and practices, this doesn't mean that public servants in other agencies aren't doing financial functions. Of course they are. Digital transformation needs to become the new normal and not be seen as having been driven or led by a group in the centre.

Government Digital Service,
Cabinet Office, UK Government, 2011–

Formed in 2011 to implement the 'Digital by Default' strategy, reporting to the Minister for the Cabinet Office. The exemplar program of 25 services across different government agencies that we re-designed/built between 2013 and 2015 helped to demonstrate the power of user-centric design and digital services that were built by multi-disciplinary product-delivery teams, increasingly formed of digitally capable public servants.

Platforms including the award-winning single-entry-point website for government, GOV.UK; notifications; digital marketplace and G-Cloud procurement platforms; digital identity; payments; and also tools and standards such as the Digital Service Standards and design toolkits have been imitated and admired by countless digital teams around the world, both in government and in other sectors.

Resourcing: 653 staff; $195 million annual budget

Website: https://gds.blog.gov.uk/

Digital Transformation Agency,
Federal Government, Australia, 2015–

Formed as a stand-alone agency in 2015 to assist the Government in guiding, overseeing, and driving its digital and ICT transformation agendas with an ambition to improve people's experience of government services. This means improving skills in government and helping agencies create services that are simple, clear, and fast.

Successes include developing whole-of-government digital platforms and transformation strategies and launching the digital marketplace in 2016, which has opened up hundreds of millions of dollars of government spend to small businesses.

Resourcing: 200 staff; $35 million annual budget plus projects budget

Website: https://www.dta.gov.au/

digital.nsw.
NSW Government. Australia. 2016–

Responsible for whole-of-government digital and ICT strategy, innovation, policy lab, assurance, ICT infrastructure, cyber, spatial services, procurement, and digital services accelerator. The focus is on supporting government agencies to deliver great government services and developing the tools and reusable components for creating user-centred digital services.

Successes include developing a clear strategy for the whole-of-government digital agenda, the launch of a digital design system and leadership of the Council of Australia Digital Leaders Forum.

Resourcing: 80 staff; $20 million annual budget plus projects budget

Website: https://www.digital.nsw.gov.au/

Queensland Government Chief Information Office.
Department of Housing and Public Works. Queensland. Australia. 2016–

The Queensland Government invests around $1.5 billion a year in information and communication technology (ICT).

Responsible for ensuring the Queensland government's ICT investments of approximately $1.5 billion annually, including through developing policy, service delivery for communities working with departments across government, and seeking value for money. This team provides strategy, policies, and standards, developing proposals for major whole-of-government investments and working with industry partners.

Note the Queensland Government were the only one among the organisations and individuals from whom we requested information or an interview to decline.

Website: https://www.qgcio.qld.gov.au/

Department of Premier & Cabinet,
Digital, Design and Innovation Branch, Victoria, Australia, 2016–

Responsible for whole-of-government digital platforms and web transformation, driving digital transformation strategy across government, and setting standards, policies, and governance frameworks for shared ICT services and also the state's cyber security strategy.

Delivery examples include Engage Victoria, which is an enhanced, digital, public participation and analytics platform, a cross-government engagement platform, a single digital presence www.vic.gov.au website, and API standards, centralised platform, and developer portal.

Resourcing: 98 full-time staff; approximately $35 million annual budget

Website: https://www.vic.gov.au/digital-standards

Office of Digital Government,
Department of Premier and Cabinet, Western Australia, Australia, 2018–

Provides leadership for digital reform within the public sector to improve service delivery to the WA community. Previously known as the Office of the Government Chief Information Officer before it became a discrete business unit in July 2018. Responsibility for Digital Group services, cyber security standards, building data analytics, procurement reforms, policy including reducing the digital divide and any digital disadvantage and legislation, and delivering specific projects such as WA.gov.au, which was launched in early 2018.

Website: https://www.wa.gov.au/organisation/office-of-digital-government

US Digital Service.
Federal Government. US. 2015–

Sits within the White House Office and Management Budget to work with federal agencies on information technology. It seeks to improve and simplify digital service, and to deliver better government services through technology and design. Also responsible for rethinking how the US Government brings digital technical top talent into the civic service. Part of the efforts to restore credibility to the US government following the issues with the 'Obamacare' (Affordable Care Act) health website not working after it was launched. Example project delivery is the College Scorecard, which helps students and their families make more informed decisions about college selection.

Website: https://www.usds.gov/

18F. Technology Transformation Services.
Federal Acquisition Service. General Services Administration.
Federal Government. US. 2014–

Collaborates with other US agencies at the Federal, State and local levels of government to fix technical problems, build products, and improve how government serves the public through technology. Formed in 2014 by a group of Presidential (Obama) Innovation Fellows to extend their efforts to improve and modernise government technology through a team of about 120 designers, software engineers, strategists, and product managers. 18F partners with other federal agencies to build, buy, and share digital services. 18F support has seen agencies move paper processes online, such as land permits, increased data access such as open data, saved on cloud hosting, and implemented new acquisition techniques.

Website: https://18f.gsa.gov/

Canadian Digital Service.
Treasury, Federal Government, Canada, 2017–

The Canadian Digital Service partners with government departments and agencies to design and build simple and reliable technology. Partners with government agencies to deliver solutions, build capacity, and provide advice.

Appears to be replicating and learning from the experiences of the US and UK teams, including through hiring former leaders from these Units, adopting similar digital service standards and taking a similar exemplar set of projects through discovery, alpha, and beta stages. Similar challenge of joining existing ICT-focused strategies and newer digital-focused teams together.

Website: https://digital.canada.ca/ and strategy https://www.canada.ca/en/government/system/digital-government/digital-operations-strategic-plan-2018-2022.html

Service and System Transformation Branch,
Department of Internal Affairs, New Zealand Government, 2015–

This team has a remit to drive digital transformation across government through the role of Chief Digital Officer for Government. Functions include setting digital policy and standards, improving investments, establishing and managing services, developing capability, and system assurance (assuring digital government outcomes). Digital.govt.nz aims to be the online source of information, tools, and guidance to support digital transformation across the public sector.

Website: https://www.digital.govt.nz/home/about-digital-govt-nz/

Danish Agency for Digitisation,
Ministry of Finance Denmark, 2011–

Responsible for the implementation of the government's digital ambitions and the use of digital welfare technology in the public sector in a country where digital transactions with government are mandatory for 85% of the population of six million people.

The Agency has dedicated whole divisions: Centre for Infrastructure Development (building the next-generation platforms for identity, security, and communications); Division for Digital Overview and Communication (building 'my overview' to provide citizens with an improved digital overview of their own information and current cases with the public authorities); and Division for Analysis and Policy (leads broad digitisation policy by conducting analyses of case handling processes and service delivery in order to use digitisation as a tool for more cost-efficient processes and better service to citizens, including the use of AI).

Wider strategic focus is on managing the interdependencies between central, regional, and local governments so that they appear as one unit from the user's perspective, and is creating the foundation for the Danish public sector of the future.

This team runs Borger.dk, a common public-sector portal providing a single point of access to the authorities' digital self-service solutions and information about public authorities and services. Based on a common identity platform called NemID.

Websites: https://en.digst.dk/about-us/

https://en.digst.dk/policy-and-strategy/digital-strategy/

Smart Nation and Digital Transformation Office & Government Technology Agency of Singapore.
Prime Minister's Office Smart Nation: 'Digital Government Blueprint'.
Singapore

Like the other global leader (Denmark), Singapore invests significant resources with two teams that could be classified as Digital Central Units, one centred on setting the strategy and focus and the other on digital infrastructure within the Prime Minister's Office. Strong focus on what digital government means in terms of Singapore's national competitiveness and becoming a 'smart nation'. This builds on the first digital teams and strategy from 2000.

Their vision is to create a government that is 'Digital to the Core, and Serves with Heart'. A Digital Government builds stakeholder-centric services that cater to citizens' and businesses' needs, meaning that transacting with a digital government becomes easy, seamless, and secure. A specific focus on the need for public servants to be able to continually up-skill themselves, adapt to new challenges, and work more effectively across agencies as well as with their citizens and businesses.

The Government Technology Agency is focused on whole-of-government capabilities in application development, cyber security, data science, ICT infrastructure, and sensor & IoT (the only country to explicitly reference this capability).

Websites: https://www.tech.gov.sg/ and

https://www.smartnation.sg/docs/default-source/default-document-library/dgb_booklet_june2018.pdf

gob.pe,
Prime Minister's Office, Peru, 2016–

Works across the Peruvian government to support a vision to create a state that is closer to citizens and have everything online by 2030. Peru has adopted its approach from the UK's Government Digital Service, but with an even stronger mandate, with it enshrined in law that all public entities have to find a 'digital leader' to coordinate everything related with digital government projects. This team has a particular focus on anti-corruption, including during procurement processes for government contracts and to create digital services where transparency and digital payments design out the possibility of corruption.

Website: https://www.gob.pe/ (In Spanish; use Google Translate for English version)

Digital Transformation Team,
Department of Public Function, Italy, 2017–

Team set up to build the 'operating system' of the country, a series of fundamental components on top of which to build simpler and more efficient services for citizens and businesses through innovative digital products. Projects include developing cloud infrastructure, API ecosystem, data analytics services, digital identity, and a regulation as code project (similar to the New Zealand and Australian examples described above). The team is led by a Government Commissioner for the Digital Agenda. The inaugural Commissioner, Diego Piacentini, provides a reflective assessment of the performance and delivery of the Italian Digital Team within its first two years of existence in this report: https://teamdigitale.governo.it/en/report.htm.

Website: https://teamdigitale.governo.it/en/

Chapter 4

Changing the Work of the Public Sector and the Way the Public Sector Works

Introduction and overview

This is the last piece of the puzzle. But like all last pieces of most puzzles, it may be that it's the most important, if only because it helps to make sense of the puzzle itself.

In many ways, this book has been about this chapter. How, exactly, should the work of the public service, and the work of public servants, change if digital transformation is actually happening? Transformation doesn't happen until it changes the way people work, and the work they do. It certainly has to change the way they behave.

That's what this chapter is all about.

The reason this is the last main chapter of the book, and the fourth 'point' of our digital transformation diamond, is that it isn't easy to answer these fundamental questions without first being clear about the cumulative impact of the other three points.

Our argument is that, as a consequence of the impact of digital transformation on the role and purpose of government, as well as its response to the big changes and shifts in politics, economics, culture, and technology, the work of the public service is already changing, which means that the way the public service increasingly will work into the future is also changing. We've looked in earlier chapters at the why and the what of digital transformation. Now, we need to look briefly at the how.

We want to draw some conclusions about how a new theory of the business for government and the public sector, which we call 'new public work', changes the work of government (e.g., moving from programs and process to people and place), what work public servants do (on policy, service design, regulation, including, for example, how humans and machines will work together), how public work is organised (including the notion of 'government as a platform'), and what kinds of capabilities and working styles are increasingly characterising the public service.

The new work of the public service, and the wider public sector, is a mixture of some enduring capabilities and functions that have always characterised what we describe as 'good public work' and of some new capabilities and functions that the public service is only just beginning to engage.

Like all transitions from an old to a new way of doing things in any institutional setting, there are already instances of public servants and government agencies working in new and creative ways. Transitions like this rarely happen in one go. These early signs of the future need to be identified, nurtured, and connected as a powerful contribution to the larger transition process.

This is how the chapter is organised:

- **The changing work of the public sector** introduces the idea of the 'new public work'
- **Changing the way the public sector works – part 1** looks at shifts from programs and process to people and place, from expertise 'inside' to collective intelligence, and from relatively closed to relatively open
- **Changing the way the public sector works – part 2** looks in more detail at some of the ways in which digital transformation introduces new ways of working, including the importance of new practices of leadership and an emerging set of capabilities and skills that public servants will need
- **Three big implications,** which draw some conclusions around power and authority, the use of information and knowledge, and the interaction of integrity, legitimacy, and trust

The changing work of the public sector

Australia has a lot of governments. Their work at national, state, and local levels is done by a workforce of close to two million public servants, 243,000 of them at the federal level. There are, as well, a range of contractors and partners who work closely with government, including as part of the upwards of $6 billion the Federal Government spend on information technology (IT) contracts.[293]

In many respects, the work of the public sector will be exactly the same as it always has been, in recognisable areas of work we will continue to recognise: developing and delivering policy and services, writing legislation and implementing regulations, maintaining good public records, running Cabinet meetings and processes, and conducting defence and diplomacy activities, for example.

The hallmarks of that work will vary little – an obsession with rigour, independence, fairness and equity, accountability and good administrative process, transparency, the highest standards of ethics and incorruptibility, and a responsibility to serve governments of different political stripes.

We might add some more characteristics to the list, not without some contention perhaps from those who might claim that, especially in more recent times, these are attributes more honoured by their absence. For example, we could fairly assume that good public work should engage a sense of the long term and protect the public or common interest.

The more that shift take us into a new operating model for the public service as part of a new theory of the business for the way we govern, the more we need to not just hang on to but cherish and strengthen these characteristics of a good public service. Digital transformation should also provide at least some of the platforms, tools, and cultural capabilities that make it easier for public servants to discharge the obligations those characteristics imply just at the time when their exemplary performance will be at something of a premium.

From public power to problem solving

The work of the public service is changing to reflect a declining obsession with the accumulation and careful curation of public power and authority and a rising interest in the art of the practice of complex problem solving.

What does that shift imply about the nature of the work of the public service?

One change could be that we would expect the public service to be relatively less closed and careful and more open and outgoing. It's the kind of shift that others in other sectors are noticing too, but in terms that contrast a previous obsession with centralised control and power with a gradual and perhaps inevitable transfer of authority outwards and downwards.

This is a 'quiet revolution' epitomised by self-managing teams, often with digital, design, or innovation in their labels, whose members determine, plan, and manage their day-to-day activities and duties under reduced or lighter supervision. It's a shift from dictated standards and one-size-fits-all solutions to strengthening the capacity of people to solve problems for themselves, often in unique and unexpected ways. This is how most digital teams work. (See the subsequent section, *Different ways of working: capabilities and work styles.*)

The bigger implication is drawn in stark terms in this UK analysis:

'The enablement mindset represents a radical shift in authority, accountability and agency from those at the top to those lower down the system. It argues for humility about what can be achieved when power is aggregated and challenges us to raise our expectations about what can be achieved through collaboration and cooperation.'[294]

It's a powerful narrative, but it isn't always clear that these shifts of power and authority consistently and widely characterise the daily work of most public servants.

It's not that we're arguing that the public sector has not in the past been exploratory and bold in pursuit of solutions to big public risks and opportunities. In fact, we'd agree with people like Mariana Mazzucato that we need to rediscover the instinct for bold, open experiment allied to an appetite for careful and creative risk taking that has characterised the public service in the past.

But over the past 50 years or more, the mission of the public sector has often been experienced as an obsession with the accumulation and deployment of public power and authority for largely internal, institutional imperatives. When difficult decisions had to be taken, the overriding concern too often in the public sector has been how best to protect that power and authority, either on its own account or on behalf of defensive or uncertain politicians.

The practical consequence is that problems – big opportunities and big risks – are not dealt with effectively because that would demand a relaxation or even an abandonment of processes and organisational behaviours whose purpose is to preserve and grow power and authority.

If your prime concern is with the accumulation of power and authority to preserve the role and position of the institution you are part of, then it is going to be hard to let go of any of that in the name of more effective problem solving if you think that will diminish the stocks of both on which you have come to rely for authority and status. For example, if your status and remuneration come from the number of team members in your command, or the budget you control, it is hard not to be influenced by that if faced with, say, automation options, or a mixture of design and digital capability, which could provide effective problem solving but diminish your power and authority.

The changing speed, intensity, and connectedness of a world digitally transformed is putting a premium on the expenditure in search of lasting solutions to the problems we want to fix, of more of the currency of political and bureaucratic capital that many public servants are either used to or comfortable with.

Less cathedral, more bazaar

Another way to describe the changing work of the public service is to recognise the need to replace the traditional concern with what goes on inside the institution(s) with a proper and growing obsession with what's going on outside.

A good way to explain that shift is to use Eric Raymond's famous essay, which he wrote in 1997, to explain the power and potential of the nascent but already potent open-source software movement.[295]

It's an iconic contribution to the literature on the technology revolution of the last 30 years. It's also a piece of writing whose potential as a way of understanding the role and work implications for the public sector from wholesale digital transformation is both apt and underestimated. There is much we can learn about the changing work of the public sector from this well-known exposition of the underlying philosophy and deeply changed practice of software development.

Raymond explains, even as its early success was being both enthusiastically recognised and, by some at least, stoutly resisted, the evident impact of the open-source approach to software development. Using what has become a celebrated analogy, Raymond contrasted the old way of proprietary software development – relatively closed, linear, hierarchical, and obsessed with preserving the carefully accumulated and fiercely defended power of the big software houses. He described the latter as the 'cathedral', with the then relatively new, Linus Torvalds-inspired open-source software movement – relatively open, connected and collaborative and, distributed in terms of power, authority, rewards and recognition – as the 'bazaar'.

Raymond's point was not just that open source was the cool new kid on the software development block. His point was that this cool new kid could often, and regularly did, run rings around the staid, stodgy, cumbersome 'old kids' in terms of speed and quality. The simple fact was that the new kid often got the job done faster, better, and delivered a great deal more value and impact.

Adopting the theory of the business framework we've been using, we could say that Raymond was demonstrating that the advent of the open software movement, itself a function of big shifts in the surrounding conditions of technology, economics, and to some extent politics and society too, fundamentally challenged many of the assumptions on which an old theory of the (software development) business was constructed.

He argued that the assumptions on which the 'cathedral' had been built were not only unhelpful but profoundly at odds with the changing nature of the game. The world had changed, but the assumptions on which traditional software development had been based had not. They weren't just out of date. They were completely at odds with the new ethic of rapid, distributed problem solving which a changing world demanded and at which the 'bazaar' palpably excelled.

If you take the analogy all the way back to its two ideas, it isn't hard to understand the difference. What would come into your mind as core characteristics of a cathedral? Large, imposing, static, and inflexible (the whole point was stability and authority), obsessed with hierarchical power and, at all costs, preserving the authority and control of the institution it represented.

And what about a bazaar? Loose, flexible, messy, and apparently often out of control, or at least not controlled by a central authority, running on a network and ecosystem of requisite speed and scale for its densely connected structure, capable of getting things done very fast, so long as those connections and often informal and highly fluid relationships were allowed to work.

Cathedrals assume that their power and authority is what matters most, and bazaars assume that things are fixed much more quickly if the buyers and sellers are allowed a relatively unfettered space to connect and create to get better business outcomes and strengthen the community.

One is slow, closed, and steeply hierarchical. The other is fast, open, and distributed. One is interested in power. The other is interested in getting things done and making things work.

And, we would argue, the nature of the work that gets done in each is dramatically different.

Cathedrals spend their time:

- calibrating their authority
- issuing centralised orders and commands
- sometimes hiding scandals
- putting in place slow and tightly controlled communication and performance management systems (what the software world describes as 'waterfall')

Bazaars spend their time:

- listening and responding to subtle, rapid shifts in information and conditions around them and across the network
- forging different types of connection and solidarity with those they need to work with to fix problems and maintain the health and vitality of the bazaar itself
- avoiding too much investment in formulating (or adhering to) formal, complex top-down rules and regulations
- operating in rapid, distributed, and often opportunistic ways (what the software development world describes as 'agile')

It's not that bazaars and open-source software development are anarchic or devoid of structure, power, and authority. They have plenty of all of those, but they are grown, earned, and deployed in very different ways. The guiding assumption is if you focus first and foremost on solving problems and contributing to the network, its institutional health and welfare tends to take care of itself. Power and influence are a function of contribution, not status; or, rather, not of status flowing from positional or institutional authority.

We probably need to avoid the temptation to turn the cathedral/bazaar choice into a simple binary choice. In any functioning city, we need cathedrals and bazaars to operate in both modes when the time, need, and context demand. We need institutions and networks in much the same way as we need strong regulation and rules and multiple players to make markets work. Each relies on the other.

From 'new public management' to 'new public work'

A third and final framework within which to understand the changing work of the public sector recognises that after 30 or 40 years of pre-eminence, many of the practices and much of the theory of new public management no longer help to justify, explain, or predict the work of the public service or the value and impact it should be having.

New public management

New public management (NPM) was a term coined and used in Australia, New Zealand, and the UK primarily during the 1980s, often attributed to the influence of Margaret Thatcher's period of 'neo-liberal' reform, to define a way of running the public service according to a set of assumptions and characteristics that included:

- Seeking to run the public service on a more business-like basis, including the use of tools and practices to improve efficiency and productivity
- A focus on customer service as the central organising framework for much of the work of the public service
- Various experiments with market or quasi-market tools and frameworks, often using some form of price signal or financial incentives, to lift efficiency, service quality, and impact
- A range of techniques to increase the focus on value for money, evaluation for outcomes and impact (as opposed to inputs, outputs, and process), and a range of business or business-like methods for assessing and rewarding executive performance
- The growing use of different forms of contracting and outsourcing to the private sector (business, philanthropy, and NGOs) to achieve service delivery efficiencies and quality improvement
- Introduction of a sharper distinction between policy development (thinking) and service delivery (doing), often reinforced by structural changes in department and agency arrangements and, along the same lines, a clearer separation between purchaser (central budget-holding

agencies) and provider (either other line agencies within the public service or other organisations outside government)

- A range of experiments to test different models of centralised and decentralised structures and organising frameworks, often with a more or less explicit call to lift levels of innovation, entrepreneurship, and flexibility across public service systems and delivery platforms
- The use of differing combinations of 'commissioning' models, which included but were not the same as contestability and contracting[296]

One analysis suggests that new public management emerged in the 1980s as an enthusiastic attempt to correct some of the perceived weaknesses, both of the way government and the public sector worked and how IT should be procured and deployed as a willing, perhaps inescapable part of the revolution.[297]

Linking NPM to the evolution of eGovernment, according to this narrative, the sequence went something like this. The first iteration of eGovernment emerged in close association with new public management's attempt to introduce transformation 'by command'. Top-down strategies to accelerate change witnessed a proliferation of reports and plans that exhorted greater centrally driven change.

One of the side effects of this approach was the concentration of the IT market in which 80% of the government spend on technology in the UK at this period was divided across 11 major suppliers.[298]

In the new public management framework, there is a tendency to privilege performance indicators that reflect a project and deliverable view of the work – largely transactional and short term – rather than creating the space and the mandate to follow more closely the contours of the actual problems or challenges people and communities want to tackle and working patiently, but purposefully, for their deeper and more sustained resolution.

A critique of the early days of NPM-inspired eGovernment emerged in the work of Patrick Dunleavy and Helen Margetts, whose response to some of what they saw as the more egregious failings of the 'transformation on demand' approach of early digital reform arose in the form of 'digital era governance', or DEG.[299]

The guts of DEG included an attempt to reintegrate elements of government operations that had been separated into discrete pieces (e.g., 'better integrating the use of outsourcing, encouraging the increased use of shared services, and simplifying delivery supply chains'), a focus on 'holism' ('organising services around the citizen'), and greater investment in more widespread digitisation of core service platforms and delivery mechanisms.[300]

These early attempts to refocus the discussion about how to use technology to improve services by wrapping them around the needs of citizens and users showed, according to this analysis, 'little evidence of any interaction with either front-line employees or the users of public services'.[301]

According to another analysis NPM's reforms and techniques fell into one or more of seven basic categories: management, performance standards, output controls, decentralisation, competition, private-sector management, and cost reduction.[302]

The underlying premise of NPM, though, is that the work of the public sector is much more like the work of the private sector than previous theories or generations of practitioners allowed.

Against a backdrop of poor economic performance and political ferment in the late 1970s and 1980s, the public sector seemed unable to come up with answers of its own, inviting rising criticism and mounting dissatisfaction.

The solution was to import more of the private sector's ethos of efficiency and productivity, which seemed both necessary and urgent as a basis for root and branch reform of the culture and system of the public sector.

More recently, a critique of NPM has emerged, illustrated by these observations, whose cumulative effect has been growing resistance to its spread and extension:

- The claimed benefits of NPM of efficiency, productivity and service quality hasn't been as successful as either predicted or claimed;
- Treating citizens as customers and reducing the relationship between government and citizens to transactional 'delivery' terms has diminished the moral and political concept of citizenship with wider rights and obligations than NPM seemed willing to accommodate, raising concerns about equality, fairness, and democratic accountability;
- In some cases, NPM-influenced service delivery models have turned in less than impressive results in relation to those citizens and communities whose more complex needs and requirements didn't fit easily into NPM's frameworks for defining, delivering, and measuring public services; a largely transactional management model was unsuited to the more complex social challenges that governments found themselves facing, which required more relational models of interaction and engagement;[303] and

- The NPM drive for private-sector style efficiency and productivity outcomes – things like shared service models and a financial focus on short-term cost reduction – not only failed to deliver promised results but actually made things worse.[304]

Perhaps most basic of all, a critique of NPM has increasingly been that its conception of the merits of the public and private sectors in terms of their comparative strengths and weaknesses left the public sector with a very poor reputation.

The result has been a steady erosion of confidence, capability, performance, and funding across the public sector in a reinforcing set of assumptions and expectations driven largely by ideology, not by empirical testing or analysis. In the name of performance improvement, more stringent financial controls and cost reductions were pursued using new public management tools; performance often declined or became more constrained, which in turn became further 'evidence' for the need for yet more austerity. All at a time where citizens needs have been become more complex and/or the expectations of governments to provide quality services has increased.

For some, the resulting loss of confidence by the public sector was a major unintended consequence of otherwise well-meaning reform in initiatives. For others, this has been a much more sinister and ideological contest to use the forces of austerity and funding cuts to deliberately shrink the size and potential of government and the public sector, and privilege the power and scope of the private sector in the design and delivery of public services.

New public administration

Concurrently, and in response to some of the critiques of NPM, different models have been advanced. New public administration emerged in response to unhappiness with some aspects of a hierarchical and unresponsive public sector struggling with rising and cumulative social and economic changes.

Elements of its approach included:

- Responsiveness: to make the work and culture of the public sector more relevant to the social, economic, political, and technological context
- Client centricity: using a shift in the experience of government actions and solutions by citizens and services users as a measure of success

- Structural changes: especially the growing use of smaller, more flexible, and less hierarchical structures in administration

The intention was to bridge the politics–administration divide, including shifting the skill base of public servants from law, politics, and administration to community engagement, which was meant to help the transition from policy to implementation.

Goals of the new public administration included a shift from values-neutral and management efficiency to values-loaded (justice, freedom, equality, and ethics), a concern for social equity, accepting the need for change and innovation (to maintain relevance and responsiveness to shifting context and conditions), participation, and a client or people orientation.[305]

The new public service, often associated with a discussion of a new public governance, was a direct response to some of the criticisms of both an old unresponsive model of public administration and the excesses, as the critics saw them, of the new public management.

This 2015 analysis from the UN Development Program's Global Centre for Public Service Excellence, starts from the premise that twenty-first century public administration was going through a 'dramatic change' driven by a number of factors which have coalesced into a familiar litany of strategic forces for change[306]:

- Globalisation and the pluralisation of service provision, at least in some cases
- Policy problems becoming increasingly complex, wicked, and global, rather than simple, linear, and national
- Prevailing administration paradigms through which public-sector reforms are designed and implemented are relatively static and don't respond easily to the bigger external social, technological, and economic shifts

Further, the analysis argues that 'the limitations of hierarchy and rigidity associated with the traditional Public Administration approach and the problems of plurality and fragmentation associated with the new public management perspective that emerged in the 1980s' are both out of step with the nature of the problems that government are being asked to fix.

The key point here is the centrality of citizens as co-producers of policies and the delivery of services, an attribute that differs from both the statist approach associated with the old public administration and market-based NPM approaches.[307]

Finally, the report described the 'new public service' framework, which starts with the premise that 'the focus of public management should be citizens, community and civil society'. In this conception, the primary role of public servants is to help citizens articulate and meet their shared interests, rather than to control or steer society.[308] This is different to NPM's approach, in which 'transactions between public managers and customers reflect individual self-interest and are framed by market principles'.[309] It also differs from the old public administration, 'where citizens related to the bureaucracy as clients or constituents and were treated as passive recipients of top-down policymaking and service delivery mechanisms'.[310]

In the old public administration, control and hierarchy rather than plurality and engagement characterised these relationships.[311] It is an important insight that so much of the discussion across these different ways of characterising the work of the public sector comes down to fundamental questions about control, authority, power, and accountability.

We should bear that in mind when we think about the significance of these apparently abstruse debates about the intricacies of public administration theory and practice in the context of what digital transformation bring to the table.

The New Public Service model integrates elements of democratic theory, premised on the notion of an active and involved citizenship in which people 'are capable of looking beyond narrow self-interest to the wider public interest' and the role of public officials 'is to facilitate opportunities for strengthening citizen engagement in finding solutions to societal problems'.[312]

These are ideas and concepts that should resonate deeply with those more familiar with the contemporary discussion about human-centred design and new ways to spur innovation and transformation in the public sector.

In the new public service, public managers 'need to acquire skills that go beyond capacity for controlling or steering society in pursuit of policy solutions to focus more on brokering, negotiating and resolving complex problems in partnership with citizens'.[313] Or, as we might describe it now, a focus on co-design and co-production.

'In seeking to address wider societal needs and develop solutions that are consistent with the public interest', the report continues, 'governments will need to be open and accessible, accountable and responsive, and operate to serve citizens.' There will be implications for prevailing forms of accountability which need 'to extend beyond the formal accountability of public servants to elected officials in the management and delivery of budgets and programmes to accommodate a wider set of accountability relationships with citizens and communities'.[314]

Finally, the NPS approach also reasserts the importance of a public service ethos, emphasising the values and motivations of public servants dedicated to the wider public good.[315]

A final variation on these different approaches for public administration is something which has been described as public value management. The following is from the abstract of a paper setting out the significance of this frame, again using the contrast with old public administration and new public management to situate its potential significance:

'The aim of this article is to clarify the nature of the management style most suited to the emergence of networked governance. The paradigms of traditional public administration and new public management sit uncomfortably with networked governance.[316]

Gerry Stoker goes on to say:

'In contrast, it is argued the public value management paradigm bases its practice in the systems of dialogue and exchange that characterize networked governance. Building successful relationships is the key to networked governance and the core objective of the management needed to support it.'[317]

As with the other reframing examples, the implicit embrace of big questions of power, authority and control are evident.[318]

All of these different ways to frame the role and purpose of public administration have several things in common.[319] They seek to add a values component to the calculations about public administration's purpose and practice. They insist that efficiency and effectiveness are not enough but need also to include responsiveness to shifting context and conditions and an explicit commitment to ideas like justice, equality, and democracy. And they explore a much richer notion of ideas like participation, engagement, and responsiveness with and to the people and communities, the quality and opportunity of whose lives are ultimately at stake.

But what they all also reinforce is an implicit search for a new theory of the business. New public management has run its course. The variations we've briefly reviewed here suggest some common themes from which a new theory of the business might be fashioned.

We'd argue that the new theory is still not clear. Part of the frustration and perhaps morale-sapping reality of contemporary public service may be a function of this continuing lack of clarity and certainty about what kind of frame makes sense for the next phase of public work.

We'd also argue that digital transformation is an underplayed dimension of this struggle and has a much greater part to play as the cause of, and a central part of the response to, the theoretical and operational disruption from which a new theory will emerge.

New public work

One way of pulling together some of the elements from which a new theory of the business is emerging is a set of ideas which we have called the 'new public work'.[320]

The new public work is characterised by these ideas:

- *The public sector is a key actor to confront the risks and opportunities of a changing world.* It draws on and encourages renewed interest in the intrinsic value of the public realm to the health and welfare of societies and in the potential value of the public sector as an important institutional actor in confronting the big risks and opportunities of a rapidly changing world.[321]
- *It recognises that government is required to go beyond transactional elements to solve for complex problems related to modern life.* Government has transactional elements, for sure, but it also embraces more complex relational and institutional obligations to society; that insight has also come from a rising concern that these more complex relational dimensions of modern life give rise to many of the more difficult problems to which, on their own, governments and the

public sector seem increasingly incapable of finding convincing and sustainable solutions.

- *The essence of public work is collective and highly distributed in multi-disciplinary teams and is no longer 'ivory tower'-based.* Public work calls on a range and mix of skills, expertise, and experience that cannot be expected to come from any single sector, least of all from within government itself.
- *Public work also invests in new ways to think about and test possible futures based on progressive and formative thinking, drawing on wide input and open methods of research and engagement.* That combines with a sense of the public good that frames policy and public investment fuelled by a considerable effort to understand the changing needs of all types of communities.

This work confronts big, complex public challenges, issues that affect our lives in common and a shifting sense of the common or public good – for example, climate change, making our cities more liveable and sustainable, reforming our learning and skills systems for a new, largely digital and dramatically changing economy, and connecting health and social care systems into new models of care and community that are affordable, accessible, and effective.

The new public work reflects and reinforces a common set of attributes and practices. It feeds off rising stocks of trust and legitimacy, primarily by improving engagement, participation, and collaboration with individuals seeking agency and influence. It also adopts an approach that open-sources the problem, not just the technology. It seeks to grow the number of people and communities with problem-solving capabilities that match their local needs and circumstances, rather than seeking to scale the impact of centrally mandated 'solutions' and services. (This is very similar to the way the new public service and new public governance models frame the challenge.)

As well, the new public work is public by virtue of its reach, scope, and its impact on our shared spaces, as well as by the degree to which it can be held to account through transparency and openness. It is not a function of the organisational type or institutional location of those responsible for its delivery.

Its instinct is to change systems by solving problems. It relies on easier access to information, data, and knowledge, which are shared by default and open by design. It crosses boundaries of geography, expertise, and institutional domains to combine different kinds of expertise, especially from those closest to, and directly experiencing the consequences of, the problems and opportunities that are being worked on. Its work tends to use a hybrid mix of digital and physical networks and collaboration to span boundaries of place and time. It mixes hierarchy and networks to match the conditions, work, and decision-making at different times and in different contexts.

As always, language matters. In the new public work, some of the language of reform shifts from undertaking projects and redesigning programs to tackling and funding problems. The point is not to make the project a success; the point is to work out if the project does anything to fix the problem, including whether the project has changed the nature of the problem 'in flight'.

The new public work is the work that needs to be done by lots of very different actors and players on public problems (and opportunities) that demands a mix of creativity and competence within the public sector, but which go well beyond its formal institutional boundaries.

Digital transformation is partly responsible for the emergence of a new set of ideas that frame the changing work of the public sector to which it will be a big part of the response. The new public work implies considerable digital capability and relies on many of its assets and culture of connectedness, speed, and openness to be both effective and sustainable.

As well, the new public work implies a more porous boundary between government and the external context in which it works. It implies, and in many ways is effectively creating, a 'public purpose' sector that subsumes but goes beyond the traditional lines of the public sector itself.

Another distinctive dimension is the different approach to time.

Transactional approaches to public administration tend to be driven by a constrained and relatively short-term sense of time and deadlines. Relational approaches assume that value and solutions that last accept the need for delivery and deadlines, but within a context defined by a view of the long term.

Timescales for current public work are often artificially constrained by an overemphasis on quick and 'measurable' products and outputs, mostly driven by the need to show that something is being done and 'results' can be posted on websites and announced in press releases. There is little doubt that part of the difficulty public servants and their public work partners have in prosecuting the work of deeper transformation is the steady shortening of timelines within which work has to be done to illustrate its 'impact'.

And those tightening timelines, in turn, reflect a more polarised politics in which short-term signs of success are at a political premium for busy and impatient Ministers and their teams. That often comes at the expense of their determination to stick with the issues long enough to find answers that have a chance of shifting the underlying conditions and structures.

In fact, it often seems that the growing insights about the need for patient and persistent work to get to grips with the real causes of many of the complex public challenges that governments are trying to fix are drifting further and further apart from a prevailing culture of short-term, transactional, and highly political responses that many bemoan but few seem able to either shift or transcend.

One of the best treatments of how we engage complex social or public problems is in Stewart Brand's *The Clock of the Long Now*.[322] This is based on his long research and writing about complex social change and its interaction with the rhythms of the Internet and digital technology. (Brand is one of the pioneering philosophers and practitioners of the digital era.)

In his work, Brand looked at the role that time plays in large-scale, complex, social and institutional change. The 'pace layers of change' is a way of understanding how different dimensions of the change process play out with very different rhythms of time, and therefore with very different ways in which they can be varied.

He distinguishes between different layers of change that each have a distinct rhythm of change and impact. He famously noted that 'fast gets all our attention, slow has all the power', a dynamic which itself has to be factored into the change and reform ambitions of the new public work.

This brief rehearsal of the six layers (see figure 07) comes from an analysis of their application to systemic reform in education.

The fastest layer, fashion–art, moves in minutes and months. It is irreverent, engaging, and self-preoccupied. At this layer, a society's culture is set free to experiment, albeit sometimes irresponsibly, learning through creativity and failure.

The barrage of ideas and propositions generated from the fashion layer gets sorted out at the commerce layer. Whether at age-old bazaars or modern-day stock markets and digital crossroads such as Etsy and eBay, commerce brings people together to make sense of new ideas that capture our attention. Commerce tames and harnesses the creative energy of fashion so that society can benefit from it.

In turn, infrastructure changes more slowly than commerce. It is high-cost, high-yield, and delivers delayed payback to society. It provides foundations and platforms for society to operate, among them transportation, communication, energy, and education. It is refreshed and modernised through the innovations from upper layers while being protected and validated through governance and culture.

Moving down a layer, the job of governance is to serve the larger, slower good for society. It provides stability. It preserves what we hold to be necessary and true. As Brand points out, social and political revolutions want quick change, demanding that governance moves faster than it is capable of. The constraints of governance force reflection and pause, which can be paralysing or empowering, depending on where you stand.

Even slower to change, culture is the essential work of people as they gather to make sense of and integrate the many facets of life together on earth. It includes religion, language, and the enduring behaviours and social norms that help to provide constancy across centuries and even millennia.

The slowest-changing layer is nature, with the earth and the human body changing slowly over millennia. Nature's power is immense when unleashed, whether as the processing capacity of the human brain or as the magnitude of earthquakes and hurricanes.

The experience of complex social and institutional change of the sort that digital transformation is shaping and responding to is a function of how well changes at the fashion and commerce layers are accommodated by shifts in infrastructure.

And changes in both those layers, in turn, need to be supported by changes in governance, culture, and nature (in our case, the bedrock of politics, institutional design, and the very human assumptions and expectations that determine what we expect and demand from our institutions and processes of public governance and authority).

Brand makes the point that 'the fast layers innovate; the slow layers stabilise. The whole combines learning with continuity.' So, the experience of change will be forged by what happens in each of the pace layers as well as changes between them.[323]

Figure 07: Pace layering

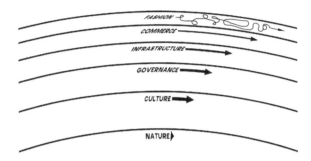

Source: Reproduced with kind permission of Stewart Brand, MIT Press

Whatever the framing, a new theory of the business for a digitally transformed government has to take much better account of the rate at which these different layers change, and particularly of the consequences of their interaction.

In the new public work, there is a greater awareness that problem solving, which is its animating instinct, will be a function of how well the public sector, and the public purpose sector that brings other experience and assets outside of government to the task, can respond to the different timeframes these different layers of change require.

The new public work also invites a more demanding conception of the role of the public sector in larger, mission-driven approaches to innovation and large-scale, complex, social and economic change. That conception comes armed with a reminder that in the past and at its best, the public sector has been a vital, creative, risk-taking investor in big leaps in knowledge, research, and innovation from which others, including those outside government, have benefited.

If for the moment we can take this outline of the new public work as a guide to the way in which the work of the public sector is changing, it begs some important questions about how, as a consequence, the public sector needs to change the way it works.

Changing the way the public sector works (part 1)

We think there are three ways in which the public sector, as part of its role to contribute to, and sometimes to lead, the new public work, will change:

- It will organise its work less around programs and process and more around people and place
- It will assume it has less of an exclusive hold on or access to requisite wisdom and expertise within its own boundaries to solve complex public problems and will become more adept at engaging a complex and evolving collective intelligence inside and outside government
- It will become relatively less closed and elite and relatively more open and democratic

These shifts in culture and practice are powered and enabled by the digital tools and techniques described in chapter 3, which are now more widespread and accessible than ever before.

From programs and process to people and place

Programs and process have always been the currency of good public sector work, and they will continue to be. Both are important to organise, shape, and direct the resources of government, and others, to address specific problems or ambitions. And when you consider the scale, intensity, and longevity that often characterises so much of the work of government and the public sector, these basic organising frameworks are inescapable.

The problem, though, is that while the program and process structures have proven effective at corralling the resources and managing their flow – actually, more accurately, as they have proven adept at managing inputs – they have been shown to be increasingly incapable of following the more complex interactions and interconnections from which the problems they are trying to solve emerge.

Those more complex interactions and interconnections reflect the messier and less tractable contours of people and place in which those problems are incubated and made manifest, and within whose contours they need to be solved.

While programs and processes are good at managing and controlling transactions, they are less able to follow the flow of relationships and connections from which the deeper-seated causes of the problems actually flow.

One illustration comes from the work of Hillary Cottam, in the UK, and her advocacy of a major shift, especially in the health and social care domain (basically, within the familiar constructs of the welfare state), from transactional to relational welfare.

She argues for 'a welfare state defined in principle and practice by human possibility and relationships, rather than the agenda of institutional reform and efficiency'. The social and cultural effect of the market reforms has been to intensify 'a transactional relationship, when what is actually wanted is something more human, caring and time rich'.[324]

The problem is deep and urgent. We have reached the limits of our post-war services and institutions, she argues. 'The welfare state is out of step with modern troubles, modern lives and much of modern public opinion', and that's because 'a set of institutions and services designed for a different era is now threadbare and beyond repair'.[325]

In her early work with the public service design consultancy Participle, Cottam and her colleagues saw first-hand the impact of a mixture of old public administration and new public management when these frameworks landed on the front line.

'Little can be done within the constraints of managerial, bureaucratic welfare systems. Spending time alongside social workers...we saw that 86 per cent of time is system driven - filling in forms for accountability and discussing them with colleagues. Most shockingly, even the 14 per cent of time spent face to face with a family member is not developmental. The dialogue ... is dictated by the forms and their need for data and information. This squeezes out any possibility of the sort of conversation that might be needed to develop a supportive relationship as a first step in fostering change.'[326]

This is a pretty good rendition of the instinct for a new kind of public work which, we're arguing, will become the hallmark of a modern, digital-transformed public service.

Although she's not the only one, Cottam has written especially eloquently about the need to think again about some of the founding assumptions on which we've constructed the welfare state and how poorly those assumptions fit the world in which they are now being asked to work. To adopt our terms, this is a search for a new theory of the business for the welfare state.

A well-known Australian example of the same kinds of instincts at work is Logan Together, one of Australia's largest collective impact projects.[327] The project aims to lift the proportion of children ready to thrive at school and build a strong basis for their later lives. In Logan, about 70% of children under the age of five are developmentally on track for school and beyond. In Australia, the figure is 78%.

Logan Together works across boundaries of community, government, enterprise, and learning to put in place a long-term plan to lift the proportion of Logan children who are ready to thrive at and beyond school.

That's a task that involves a lot of different players, requires a 'long game' of persistence and patience, and assumes the interests and aspirations of Logan children and their families are at the core of the planning, investing, and implementation that is then done in their name.

What these examples illustrate is that, to the extent that the problems each is trying to solve constitute examples of what we are describing here as the new public work, continuing to rely simply on program and process is not only not working but making the problem worse.

In Logan Together's case, for example, the intent is to render the many different streams of help and support that pour into Logan more coherent and consistent when they combine and interact with people's lives.

In another setting, illustrative of the same problem, an initial analysis of programs available to assist troubled families in Swindon, in the UK, found 73 different services on offer in the same town from 24 different departments. A report on that project was unable 'to identify any family that had been successfully transitioned out of social services'. As a result, the team made visual maps with front-line workers of the families' history with these services. In one case, apparently, 18 years of interventions with one family were mapped around the walls.[328]

Continuing to rely on disconnected service delivery systems simply adds more and more transactions to the problem without actually solving it. That can only happen when resources, expertise, and experience, including from those most directly affected and those who are in the front line of serving their needs, come together in more coherent patterns shaped around the lives of actual people in real places.

In other words, context is everything.

The problem is that many public sector programs and processes are designed to be context agnostic. Indeed, that is partly the point. Programs are designed to be 'fair' and, by and large, similarly experienced and consumed by people wherever they are. The whole point is to design the program to be as standardised as possible.

A deep ethic of fairness and equality runs through this concept of public sector work, which consequently presents as highly standardised and rule-driven. It is supposed to be the same for everyone, even though the problems and challenges those programs are trying to solve can't possibly be experienced in the same way for everyone.

We think the work of the public sector, and of the public servants who work in it, will gradually become more place- and people-focused and much less program- and process-focused.

That, in turn, will set up new demands for a range of capabilities that include information and evidence gathering and analysis, communication across more open and connected networks of people and organisations, significant leaps in productivity, and the ability to surround people and place and the organisations who seek to help them with knowledge and support that is 'always on', responsive to different contexts and capable of being managed and tracked at speed, but over long periods of time as well.

These are all capabilities against which the digital transformation investment across government needs to be held to account. It is this kind of new working in the service of the new public work, as we've described and illustrated it here, that these new tools and platforms need to provision and sustain.

From expertise 'inside' to collective intelligence

Collective intelligence lies at the heart of the new public work which, in turn, is at the heart of the purpose and potential of digital transformation.

It's probably an unfair characterisation to claim that, in the past, the public sector worked on the assumption that all that was needed to know to perform its policy and program responsibilities could be found within the sector itself. The public sector has always drawn, to some extent, on the skills and expertise of people and organisations outside government, at least in certain circumstances and where specialist knowledge, for example, might be needed.

More recently too, there has been a small explosion of interest in various forms of consultation and engagement, usually delivered by a mixture of surveys, focus groups and town hall meetings, designed to provide some input to the policy and program design process for people and service users.

But that doesn't change the broad conclusion that, up until recently, there has been a view that the public sector had a privileged and unique position in the ability to access or generate much of the information and knowledge it needed to do its work. It was an approach that was relatively elite, privileged, and closed.

The reasons for this renewed interest in an old phenomenon are clear, even though there are differences from the advent of digital tools and platforms that extend, potentially, the reach, complexity, and impact of collective intelligence.

The nature of the problems which governments and the public sector have to address have become more tangled and intense, with connections and interactions between clashing contexts and conditions that render them now too large and complex for many of the traditional methods and structures we still rely on.

These problems, and the rate and speed with which new knowledge and insights are being shaped, tested, and applied are accelerating. The speed and intensity are increasingly misaligned with the way in which the public sector (or indeed any other sector, for that matter) works.

The result is that an old idea – collective intelligence – is coming in for new and intense scrutiny as one response.

A review by one of the authors (Martin) of Geoff Mulgan's book *Big Mind* discusses Mulgan's observations about the rising significance of collective intelligence for what we are describing here as the new public work.

Mulgan describes collective intelligence as 'the capacity of groups to make good decisions—to choose what to do, and who to do it with—through a combination of human and machine capabilities.' It is important that the explanation combines collective intelligence and AI – the tools and platforms of a new world of ubiquitous data and increasingly sophisticated analysis, much of it automated.

Mulgan argues that 'collective intelligence depends on functional capabilities: distinct abilities to observe, analyse, remember, create, empathize, and judge— each of which can be enhanced by technologies, and each of which also has a cost'.

Intelligence engages a distinct form of complex learning, Mulgan writes: 'The everyday processes of intelligence ... operate at multiple levels that link together in a hierarchy: a first loop using existing models to process data, a second loop of learning that generates new categories and relationships, and a third loop that creates new ways of thinking. These can be combined in triggered hierarchies.'

Mulgan's approach sees collective intelligence 'as assemblies of multiple elements. Discovering which assemblies work best requires continuous shuffling of the elements, since capabilities, infrastructures, and organizational models have to coevolve with environments.'[329]

For our purposes, the rise of collective intelligence as part and parcel of a transition from a relatively elite and closed sense of who has the knowledge and expertise to solve big public problems to one that is more open, connected, and boundaryless, has big implications for the work of the public sector.

New skills are required – data gathering, analysis and patterning, forging new connections between disparate organisations and people in different sectors, and doing often very different types of work.

But this is with the knowledge and insight to contribute to a larger public challenge, new forms of system and collective leadership in which ego and command have to give way to collaboration and persuasion, but without diminishing the necessary obsession with results and impact.

None of these capabilities are even imaginable, much less achievable, without access to the full suite of digital tools and platforms. The value of that transformation, we would argue, lies in its ability not only to furnish those tools and platforms but to develop with them the confidence and skill across a public sector workforce and leadership that can make the most of their potential.

From relatively closed to relatively open: a new toolkit

The final shift we see in the changing work of the public sector combines several elements:

- The growing interest in models of open government, as characterised, for example, in the Open Government Partnership (OGP) to which Australia was a (belated) signatory
- A capability in open data as an increasingly default mode across government and the public sector
- New interest in the tools and culture of design.

The OGP community commits to several practices that, at least prospectively, suggest new skills and capabilities in the public sector workforce.

This is the official definition: 'The Open Government Partnership is a multilateral initiative that aims to secure concrete commitments from governments to promote transparency, empower citizens, fight corruption, and harness new technologies to strengthen governance'.[330]

Launched in 2011 by eight governments, the Partnership is now endorsed by over 90 countries, regions, and cities.

The intention is that governments will 'become sustainably more transparent, more accountable and more responsive to their own citizens, with the ultimate goal of improving the quality of governance, as well as the quality of services that citizens receive.' And, as the Australian website explains, at the heart of open government are the ideas of transparency, participation and accountability.[331]

These are the elements of a working definition:

- Transparency means the public understands the workings of their government.
- Participation means the public can influence the workings of government by engaging with public policy processes and public service providers.
- Accountability means the public can hold the government to account for its policy and service delivery performance.

Australia's second national open government action plan (2018–2020) is built around eight commitments – to strengthen the national anti-corruption framework; improve the sharing, use, and re-use of public sector data; engage States and Territories to better understand information access; engage Australians in the independent Review of the Australian Public Service from 2018; enhance the transparency of political donations and funding; improve public service practices using place-based approaches; enhance public engagement skills in the public service; and expand open contracting and due diligence in procurement.[332] As part of the commitment, the continuing struggle to shift the public sector to a more reflexive default mode of open data will be sustained and accelerated.

It is not a simple or straightforward issue. There are contests within the public sector, and between the public sector and the wider community, about how an open data approach can be prosecuted and how well it is being put into practice.

For example, Data.NSW brings together nearly 4,000 NSW Government datasets in one searchable website, from ferry patronage to vegetation types in particular geographies. This is part of a commitment of the NSW Government to make data more accessible to the public and to industry to stimulate innovative approaches to service delivery. However, as noted in chapter 3, fewer than 10% of those datasets are made available through APIs, with much of the data, which whilst good that it's available, buried in PDFs. The Federal government has a similar website with currently 6,200 APIs, ranging from land titles to rubbish collection, as part of 58,000 data sets. But again, crucial data sets such as legislation is not yet available via APIs.

The growing interest in the more widespread use of design techniques, and the culture and practices of human-centred design for policymaking, as well as for service design and delivery, is, at its core, another step towards a more open and legible approach to government.

'Design and design thinking will permeate the structure and workforce of the public service of the future because people will feel the fit between their tools, techniques and culture and the kinds of risks and opportunities they are grappling with, and, frankly, because they work.'[333]

Being comfortable with large-scale data analysis using the tools and techniques of design to develop policy, programs, and services in more experimental, testable, and prototypical steps, and learning to work in more complex and open communities of practice that spill over traditional organisational and sectoral boundaries will all become part of a new toolkit within the public sector.

None of these replaces the public sector's traditional skills in public administrative processes and capabilities – good recordkeeping, running good Cabinet and other decision-making processes, developing proper processes of accountability and transparency, administering regulation and law, and writing and managing legislation.

But as the new public work gradually asserts its more open and connected foundations, these new tools and capabilities will become more important. And their implications for skills and talent and for new ways of working are inescapable.

Here's a final thought, too, about how to confront the conundrum that sees those in current positions of power and influence resist or undermine portions of these elements, especially of the digital transformation agenda.

In most cases, that resistance reflects perceptions of the loss of the power and influence that have taken a career to accumulate. It isn't the norm to want to trade that personal power and influence away for a sense of the greater good or the health of the larger system. That's never been an easy ask.

But the transformation of the way we govern, and the work of the public sector, driven by a combination of digital and data, and, in many instances, of design, offers the paradoxical prospect of giving away power to become more powerful.

For those public leaders willing to explore the full potential of the new tools and mindset of the digital world, which includes new ways to exploit to the fullest the power of data unlocked and creatively applied to deep problem solving, the prospect emerges of being able to master new patterns of power and influence. It also offers the prospect of a new basis on which to claim and sustain authority, that is, the ability to craft and execute on big agendas of change and reform.

Public servants and other public leaders who want to retain or even augment their ability to wield real influence could find it useful to moderate an exclusive obsession with some of the traditional levers of institutional power, such as the control of people and budgets, and closeness to Ministers and their advisors.

Instead, mixing those skills with mastery of the speed and intensity of new tools of data analytics, of design and different forms of collective and automated intelligence, human and machine, might unlock sources of defensible power that straight-out resistance might undermine or risk losing altogether.

And a final aspect of these transitions: this requires new approaches to reward, through basic tools like performance agreements, and a better approach to experimenting and the risk of failure.

It won't work to call for a more permissive approach to innovation that can learn through constructive and intelligent failure if public servants are held to account, including through mechanisms like audit and the estimates process, according to traditional 'gotcha' means of punitive sanctions.

Changing the work of the public sector (part 2)

These three big themes – from programs and process to people and place, from relatively closed to relatively open, and from an instinct for 'expertise inside' to a more energetic embrace of the tools and practices of collective intelligence – provide one way of framing how changing the work of the public sector changes the way the public sector works.

These next sections contain brief descriptions of some of the practical ways in which, fuelled especially by the consequences of a more determined push to digital, the work of the public sector is changing.

Digital service design and delivery

People need to be able to transact services and access information anytime, anywhere. Like any other service industry, government should design its services in the most user-friendly way. Interacting with government should be as easy as Internet banking or ordering a taxi through an app.

Former Australian Government Communications Minister,
the Hon. Malcolm Turnbull MP[334]

To meet this ambition as well as the goal of Australia to become one of the top three governments in the world in providing digital services to their citizens,[335] the development and delivery of digital services will become a fundamental part the work and capability set for all public servants in one way or the other.

How thoroughly their work shifts and changes will depend on the type of digital transformation being pursued by a government agency or department.[336] Not all digital transformation is the same, it turns out.

We have classified these types as shown in figure 08 based on our experience and research. It might be an interesting exercise to characterise your own agency or organisation according to this taxonomy.

Figure 08: Summary of digital transformation types

	Digital Transformation Type	Activities
1.	'Fake digital': Improving the status quo (basically adding a bit of digital to the way things are done now).	Digitising paper forms, asking customers what they want within the confines of existing business models, and often focused on improving infrastructure, e.g., switching back-end infrastructure to the cloud. Often led by the IT Department. User needs are not prioritised and consideration of data is an afterthought. Limited digital leadership, traditional procurement structures, and siloed behaviours.
2.	'Sticking-plaster digital': Shorter-term technology fixes to patch up current systems or quickly introduce a shiny front end on legacy systems, often with a manual workaround and fragmented under-the-surface processes.	Often, technology focused on where there were very obvious needs, such as security risks and software licences going out of support. Digital awareness may include a digital roadmap and aspirations to hire or develop digital talent. Attitude of minimal spend and user engagement; understanding is limited to user testing. Changes are unlikely to last long and mask underlying, harder structural issues. Data is likely to be unstructured and hard to access.

Digital Transformation Type	Activities
3. 'Digital lite': Introducing a new way of doing things, including the building of products and services with limited testing of/changes to new operating models. Multi-disciplinary and cross-functional teams ways of working have appeared. Works within existing governance structures and tries its best to be organised around user rather than government needs. Incremental, but often badged as 'transformation'. Teams are beginning to undertake the kind of 'new public work' described earlier in this chapter.	Some, usually limited user-experience-led design that is grounded in strategy and aligns the organisation with the way digital teams work. Often focused on bringing transactions or collecting information into digital channels. Products and platforms are being developed. Digital teams are often led by a Chief Digital Officer who is agency/department-based. New data is used to manage/improve the transactions. Incremental but often badged as 'transformation', including in published digital roadmaps and recruitment literature. Other parts of the organisation, such as procurement, finance, including funding models and human resources (HR), find it hard to support this way of working. Existing data is shared only after inter-departmental debates.

Digital Transformation Type	Activities
4. 'Digital Transformation': New operating and 'business' models focused on delivering services based on platforms, and formed using products across systems. Becoming powered by data, cognitive, and AI tools and designed around user needs. This is the stage at which the big switch happens from 'doing digital' to 'being digital' – basically the point at which the starting proposition shifts from *How do we make the way we work now more digital?* to *How would we design the work from the ground up if we assume total and pervasive digital?*, including the possibility that the work is either not necessary anymore or there is a completely different, digital way of achieving the intended purpose or outcome. Teams regularly undertake the kind of 'new public work' described earlier in this chapter.	Products, platforms, and services join together across systems to deliver citizen-centric services with clear whole-of-government funding, commitment, operations, and governance. Clear data-sharing arrangements in place, with privacy protected and appropriate security controls. User experience, data-rich-led machine-learning bases, AIs and cognitive agents are beginning to result in 24/7 enhanced services provided by one or more government-operated platforms. True transformation as organised around user (citizens) rather than government needs. Shifted from digital being on the side of agencies/departments to being at the heart of how the organisation operates, and supported with significant investment. Procurement finance, human resources, and policy teams provide support, and are agile and collaborative.

'Fake digital'

Case study: Government websites

A classic example of 'fake digital' is websites. The Australian Government has lots of them, leading to unnecessary complexity, confusion, and cost. The UK government's GOV. UK became a 'digital lite' project where, for the first time, people could find out what was happening inside government all in one place, and in a clear and consistent format. This resulted in 300 agencies and departments transitioning to GOV.UK. 685 websites closing, including those with hundreds of pages that hadn't been viewed in years. This wasn't without operational issues – it turns out, if you put your contact centre phone number on the front page of your website, your call volumes triple – but six years on, it has been a success. As the first whole-of-government platform, it provided a very visible sign to citizens that things were changing for the better, and acted as a framework for (and perhaps belief in) deeper transformation.

The Australian national version, 'gov.au', has not materialised. Aside from the financial wrangles and personalities involved, the

'Fake digital' sees digital ways of working at the periphery, with largely a business requirements- and analytical-led approach, often using external suppliers (contractors, suppliers, or consultants) to improve the status quo.

This includes digitising paper forms and are sometimes described as lipstick-on-a-pig projects. Other examples, which while necessary and can lay the foundation for 'digital lite' and 'digital', include infrastructure such as new data centres or cloud migration. Policy teams hand off to project managers, who in turn work with the IT department and manage to a plan. Or the IT Department runs the show. Responsibility and accountability are dispersed. Data is an afterthought, so it is hard to access and use. Limited digital leadership, traditional procurement structures, and siloed behaviours are the norm.

It is often run as a large IT program over a number of years, commencing with a business case to access large (capital expenditure heavy) budgets, a project management focus, and large releases. The majority of a government entity won't know it's happening until it is launched, and with something going wrong, it attracts negative press through being late or over-budget, or because it doesn't visibly change what the majority of public servants do.

This type of transformation, Eggers suggests, means that 'we miss a huge opportunity if digital government just entails better versions of what currently exists instead of enabling changes at a much more fundamental level'.[337] The timing of projects tends to be multi-year, and making changes is hard.

'Sticking-plaster digital'

This is where organisations have recognised the value of digital but are largely focused on ensuring the lights stay on. There is a particular focus on extending the life of so-called brownfield legacy systems through software and remedial fixes. Digital awareness may include a digital roadmap and aspirations to hire or develop digital talent.

This is often because there is limited awareness of the types of systems within the organisation, meaning such decisions are the only option to maintain business continuity, including access to data without such forward planning. Often, there has been commercial vendor lock-in through longer-term contracts or simply a mixture of limited digital/technology understanding by leaders and limited funding. Systems data is available but service data and interactions between systems are harder to access.

The challenge here is that such systems which were built decades ago cannot be scaled to take the load and changes of modern digital systems, and it is hard to make changes to standardise rules and processes.

Putting digital 'sticking plasters' over systems that were designed for a world of paper and phones is not transformation, even if you have clever APIs and good-looking front-ends over the top of them. The timing

case of why Departments should give up part of their identity and brand (i.e., power) to make things easier for citizens and businesses wasn't sufficiently made. (Note the existing gov.au is a listing of websites, not a single platform for all government content and services.) The argument was to essentially write from scratch content from a user perspective; e.g., they want to do something like 'Come to study in Australia' that crossed Departmental responsibilities. This fundamentally horrified policy and legal leads and would have required unprecedented collaboration across Departments in Canberra and in other jurisdictions. So, it was killed off. A similar thing happened with Canada.ca.

Citizens who now expect to be able to access information and services anywhere, anytime, through their mobile devices in what is now a 24/7 'always on' unprecedented connected world thus aren't being properly served basic content by the Federal Government. Getting down to one entry point, like GOV.UK, may be hard due to the Commonwealth arrangements but this is a digital transformation in government 'basic' that Australia needs.

of projects tends to be months rather than years, and changes are batched in releases that happen 3–4 times a year.

'Digital lite'

'Digital lite' involves newer digital roles and more of the kind of 'new public work' described earlier in this chapter. In this case either a policy commitment has been made or a particular customer problem has become apparent which spurs action from the Agency's Board, often under the sponsorship of a Minister and Executive Board member(s).

This involves multi-disciplinary teams – more on those later – building digital products which helps a citizen/customer get something done. Obtaining a digital driving licence is an example of a product. Platforms represent the underlying software and hardware that supports the digital experience, e.g., a content management system.

A service brings products and platforms together to create the ability for a citizen/customer to transact and get something done e.g. applying for a new passport. The Australian Federal Government would point to the introduction of SmartGates by the Department of Home Affairs, the virtual assistants who answers enquiries for the Australian Taxation Office and the Department of Human Services (DHS) 98% of Medicare claims are now online and MyTax with prefilled returns as examples of successful delivery.[338] Data is generated and used to improve the service, sometimes in real time.

Changes to connected systems take longer. The digital time to value is much faster, in months rather than years. For new, greenfield services, the time to value can be weeks.

'Digital lite' works within existing governance structures and tries its best to be organised around user rather than government needs. For all the promise of digital government, especially in the UK where they transformed 25 services in 2013–2015, these did not result, for the most part, in re-designing full services around users. These examples tend to represent thin slices, or aspects, of the services provided with manual or paper-based hand-offs to part of the service. For example, for visa processing, the paper identity document still had to be sent in the post.

The products and platforms can be built, bought or adapted. This lends itself to government developing and then delivering these services, and whilst often using private-sector talent and resources, enables more control than the outsourcing popular in the 1990s through to 2010.

It doesn't, however, fit where commodity-based systems are being implemented, like an enterprise relationship system (ERS) or customer relationship management (CRM). There's no point in government replicating what the likes of SAP and Salesforce have spent billions perfecting. Other parts of the organisation, such as procurement, finance, and HR, find it hard to support this way of working.

Digital transformation

What we might describe as 'deep digital' is the manifestation of a new mindset that stops thinking about digital as an add-on and starts thinking about every aspect of the work of the public sector, including how it is organised and framed, as digital from the ground up. This is the point where the majority of leaders understand the need for, and support, this type of transformation. This is where teams regularly undertake the 'new public work'.

It includes a vigorous embrace of the user-centric approach, systems thinking, and power of digital, and increasingly massive amounts of data to fuel AI and cognitive technologies to fully transform how the organisation is structured and how it delivers services.

The majority of examples here are from the private sector, where they have faced a major disruptive change to their basic business and operating models.

Banks or travel agents are great examples. These services are designed around an event such as applying for a mortgage or booking a family holiday. These services are accessible, blend different channels, incorporate different data sources, and are linked together behind the scenes to provide a consistent experience. They represent end-to-end digital transformation. The time to value, where data is available, is much faster, often weeks and months rather than years.

Government agencies have not yet become 'digital' in this full and deep sense, or to quote many a government digital strategy since 2012, 'digital by default'. This would entail nearly every role in an organisation involving digital and technology activities and roles. All of these public servants have the right tools and techniques to work in this way. It would reflect an ethos to make

> This is part of what we would define as 'there' and should be the destination to which all Australian governments should direct their (digital) efforts.

citizens' lives easier through uses of automated decision-making, seamless data exchange, and assisted digital services for those who need help or can't get online for whatever reason (whilst maintaining the core roles of government, like ensuring security and data and service integrity). In the process, the agency becomes open to the possibility that often deeply entrenched ways of working and assumptions about the nature and purpose of the work they do – programs, regulation, policymaking – need to be re-thought.

Figure 09 provides a summary list of the characteristics, or principles, that need to be in place or followed for true digital transformation. (Note that our manifesto captures a number of these characteristics.)

Figure 09. Digital transformation characteristics

- *Committed and clear leadership; e.g., political and public service leaders publicly front 'this will happen' attitude, provide cover for, and drive momentum for delivery*
- *Communications narrative; e.g., clear 'hearts and minds' narrative as to why such transformation is required, focused on showing the thing, not just talking about it*
- *Transformation approaches in place; e.g., realise early value through pragmatic design and learn by doing, working software over long documents, rapid deployments, and taking a minimum viable product (MVP) approach*
- *Agile funding, e.g., a central digital investment fund that can be accessed to fund (small) in-year investments and are distinct from large technology funding mechanisms*
- *Start with user needs (e.g., who is it for, what do they need, and what does the APS need to do?) such as life journeys or events, and have user-feedback cycles*
- *Make data open and use it across the public sector; e.g., common data registries*
- *Open standards; e.g., for sharing and publishing data*
- *Whole-of-government platforms, such as websites, payment, or identity platforms which enable consistent service experiences and become assets*
- *Open source; e.g., re-use of digital service components*
- *Security; e.g., cyber and data privacy standards*
- *Open government; e.g., control the scaling, performance, and learning with clear measures, including numbers that are publicly reported on digital dashboards*
- *Connectivity; e.g., Internet accessibility*

- *Systems-focused, i.e., across government and ecosystems, and not siloed*
- *Assisted digital; e.g., accessibility standards*
- *Capability building; e.g., collaborating in multi-disciplinary and cross-functional teams, and extensive learning opportunities including on-the-job coaching*
- *Sharing capabilities; e.g., whole-of-government platforms*
- *Automation; e.g., justifying why human actions are involved and why automation/AI cannot be used (note that we recognise this last one may be controversial)*

An alternative way of assessing the relative maturity of digital transformation is to assess the relevant digital services organisations. David Eaves and Ben McGuire published a helpful maturity model through the Harvard Kennedy School with input from government digital leaders around the world in late 2018.[339]

This sets out the assessment criteria for political environment, institutional capacity, delivery capability, skills and hiring, user-centred design, and cross-government platforms. The low, medium, high, and future criteria demonstrate a good selection of inputs of how to get 'there'. Figure 11, on page 236, which shows the assessment for cross-government platforms, is a great example.

Digital strategies

Governments will continue to produce strategies which, in varying degrees of clarity, articulate the problem(s) being solved and ideally a set of choices that are funded with a roadmap of delivery.

Currently, whole-of-government digital transformation strategies have *generally* been produced by the Digital Central Units described in chapter 3, who in turn are responsible to coordinate the delivery of various government digital strategies. Most of these strategies have been top-down driven, focused on what actions will be undertaken and showcasing successes rather than setting a framework for agencies to deliver their initiatives in alignment with them.

The appendix at the end of this chapter provides a summary of the strategies from comparator countries to Australia. (That's why there's no China or Estonia in our list.)

There is much that is common to many of these strategy documents, an interesting feature in itself. Each covers similar themes, including, for example, designing to meet citizens' needs and expectations, building the technology infrastructure, making the most of new digital ways of building services, and a nod to developing digital capabilities to enable public servants and government to be more agile and modern.

Most of the focus is on the *what* is changing, rather than the *how*. Those authored by Finance departments tend to focus more on efficiencies, those written by technology teams are technology-focused, and those written by the new Digital Central Units tend to be fairly lightweight so not to offend too many departments or to over-commit.

A few fall victim to shiny-object syndrome, talking about investing in digital technologies without a clear understanding of how they will generate value, or indeed what problem they are trying to solve. Most dance around the subject that a lot of people (citizens and public servants) are fearful of what digital will mean for them and their jobs. The exceptions are the UK's and Queensland's.

None of them are really clear about what kind of government they aim to build or what views they imply about government's role and purpose. This includes making distinct choices as to what not to do and how to organise and build capabilities to get 'there'.

Nearly all of them[340] diffuse the effort, or 'spread the peanut butter too thin', including trying to fix the current state whilst transforming. They often fail to tackle the difference in building new greenfield services and the much harder task of changing existing legacy, or brownfield, services.

The DTA's Digital Transformation Strategy,[341] published in late 2018, sets out how the Federal Government will deliver world-leading digital services for the benefit of all Australians. It's the clearest effort so far, and explains the progress made to date, why there is a need for digital transformation, definitions, and a roadmap of 75-plus projects.

The focus is on delivery by 2025 with the promise that, by then, services will go beyond simply being available online to being organised around user needs and life events, be personalised, and be simple to use. The use of personas and life journeys brings to life what this will mean for real people and businesses. The development of reusable platforms across government is also referenced.

However, there are a number of projects that have been re-announced, much of the ambition is similar to the DTA (then known as the DTO) launch in 2015. There is a feeling that this is a compiled list of everything that's going on in government, rather than reflecting strategic choices (and associated funding) to get 'there' (wherever 'there' might be, in the first place).

The NSW Government Digital Strategy[342] from 2017 brings together digital investment and deployment and policies to 'transform the lives of the people of NSW by designing policies and services that are smart, simple and seamless'. Standards are suitably ambitious to be 'digital by default, designed around user needs, integrated and seamless and accessible'. Technology is seen here as an enabler, along with cyber security, legislation, and delivery capability, so often considered in separate strategies or white papers.

This is effective because too many of these types of documents consider digital in a vacuum, leaving what can feel very much like a shiny front end terminally disconnected from the policy, strategy, and institutional apparatus of governing and the public sector.

The NSW strategy is meant for any public servant – which, in its simplicity, is only 14 pages long, isn't jargon- heavy, and instead sets out commitments including to:

- Use digital ways of conducting business where previously prohibited by outdated legislation
- Co-design services with citizens
- Adopt a digital-by-default starting point
- Partner with industry to develop whole-of-government solutions

Unlike the DTA's strategy, it does set out the *how* in more detail, although any roadmap of projects or commitments isn't included.

Policy and regulation in a world of digital and AI

In many ways, policy and regulation are the stand-out bastion of resistance to 'being digital' as opposed to 'doing digital'.

For many in the policy community, digital means little more than access to the web for research, the (over)use of email, and, occasionally, publishing material for comment and feedback on a range of different digital platforms.

It also reflects a view that digital transformation – all those gadgets and apps and websites and even some of that cool AI and machine-learning stuff – only makes sense in the lesser world of service design and delivery.

It's an attitude that reflects this insight from Nicholas Gruen, who chaired a task force on 'government 2.0' a decade ago and whose long experience as an economist, adviser, and entrepreneur has led him to the conclusion that 'if you're a public servant, go into policy because delivery is both lowly and hazardous. Though delivery can be a worthwhile aspect of a developing professional CV, the road to the top is generally via policy. So that's where the most able and ambitious people go.'[343]

What digital rarely seems to mean for policy people is a willingness to think about how one might do policy work: writing a new defence white paper, recasting child protection policy, developing energy policy, or working out the best way to end homelessness, for example, using the tools, culture, platforms, and techniques that are deep digital at their core.

What, for example, would happen if the first thing policymakers, often working deep and high in the policy and public administration 'stack' and a long way from the world of those whose lives their work will impact, started the policy process not with a bunch of research and a discussion paper which then goes out for comment but with no research or writing at all?

What if policymaking started with the use of digital and non-digital tools (ethnographic research, gatherings of citizens and users, or those likely to be impacted in order to understand the contours of their lives, their aspirations, and their sense of what 'better' might be) to look, listen, and learn first? What if the deep digital instinct is to find new ways to engage and learn and to process the resulting insights as the bedrock analysis, to be joined later by more traditional (and still important) research and analysis?

How comfortable are traditional policymakers with the idea, for example, that instead of coming up with a draft policy and getting some comments on it (often, at least from the perspective of those being asked, mostly to be ignored), they embarked on a series of experiments and prototypes to test different assumptions and approaches? And what does it even mean to prototype a new child-protection policy or a white paper on foreign policy?

It's an interesting observation, and somewhat at odds with this comment from former GDS head Mike Bracken, quoted by Arup's Dan Hill, about the role of strategic design on public purpose or social, systemic change work:

'Policymaking itself in a digital government is potentially radically transformed by user research-driven service design. Policy in this world is largely derived directly from the design, development and delivery practices of digital.'[344]

Mike's right, but his analysis seems to be a little at odds with at least our observed experience. These are the lines of inquiry which point to another dimension of where 'there' is for digital transformation's full impact.

Digital and regulation

A particular aspect of the challenge of digital's full and deep transformation of the policy domain is the work of regulation.

Martin was a member of the independent panel set up a couple of years ago, chaired by former NSW Premier the Hon. Nick Greiner AC, to advise the NSW Government about new thinking and practice in regulatory reform.

In its final report, almost all of whose recommendations were adopted by the Government and have since become the focus of work for the newly established NSW Productivity Commission, the panel made some observations about where and how digital tools and culture should impact the work of regulators.

For example, the Panel agreed that 'much more can be done at all levels of government to harness digital and data capabilities within the regulatory system'. It pointed out that 'greater digital literacy across the population is enabling new ways of implementing and streamlining regulation'. And, partly as a result, 'the ever-increasing data being gathered by businesses and agencies should also be transforming the way governments regulate – much more than we are seeing to date'.[345]

Later in the report, the panel observes that the practice of regulating should change in line with the shifting practice and culture of the people and organisations being regulated:

'Technological advances, growing data availability and access, and increased connectivity are reshaping how business is done and how consumers engage with markets and government. Government is now regulating in a significantly different environment and it needs to incorporate new tools and considerations as it decides when and how to regulate'[346]

And picking up the theme that much of the power of digital derives not from the technology but from a set of cultural assumptions and instincts about individual behaviour and mindset, the panel noted that:

'The most appropriate regulation will not always be developed by regulators working in isolation, but more likely by working in partnership with regulated entities. Co-design and co-development of regulatory models with stakeholders, including the use of regulatory trials and sandboxes, can be an effective policy development tool in complex, uncertain and dynamic environments that demand adaptability from governments.[347]

Much of the regulation that exists today was designed for the industrial, not digital, era.

Whilst governments have been busy thinking how best to respond (and perhaps, if it isn't too unfair, trying to buy some time in the process?), the technology and business communities have focused on finding ways to be innovative, working within the boundaries of regulation to ensure compliance.

Developments, changes, compliance, and monitoring of regulations fundamentally must speed up, without losing anything in terms of judgement and discernment, and adapt to enable digital transformation in the economy and in government. Getting the most from technological change requires an adaptive regulatory approach. New business models using digital technologies may not fit neatly within existing regulatory regimes, and some operate in regulatory grey areas.[348]

Regulators are beginning to adapt to a digital world. Digital has created faster ways of conducting transactions and generating and sharing data, different ways of working and establishing trust, and different challenges to regulate. Regulators face the same challenge as other government services. They need to switch to a proactive, solutions-orientated way of operating. They are working out how to become more customer-centric, use new technologies to automate, and focus on their compliance activities whilst reducing the compliance burden and using data to focus on the highest risks.[349]

Examples of these new ways of working that the Australian government can learn from include:

- Natural language processing and geotagging used by a US health district to identify restaurants flagged for food poisoning in tweets[350]
- State insurers looking at how they use wearable devices to both reduce risks whilst undertaking work and help with recovery

- Use of regulatory sandboxes, which are controlled environments allowing innovators to test products or services without having to follow all the standard regulations
- Risk-weighted regulation, such as where checks on vehicles and food safety inspections are based on ratings from member organisations, social media, and other sources of data

How laws and regulations are written and enacted can act as barriers to digital transformation; they are written for human consumption. Policymakers, private organisations, or individuals can often interpret these differently, which can make it incompatible with digital delivery. Examples include where a signature or witness is required. Governments, including in NSW, have been proactively reviewing legislation to remove such barriers whilst others do so as and when a reason arises.

The New Zealand government have gone a step further in attempting to improve the interpretation of legislation and enhance the creation of digital services by rewriting legislation as code.

According to Pia Andrews, the head of the team who worked on this:

'Legislation-as-code means taking the "rules" or components of legislation — its logic, requirements and exemptions — and laying them out programmatically so that it can be parsed by a machine. If law can be broken down by a machine, then anyone, even those who aren't legally trained, can work with it. It helps to standardise the rules in a consistent language across an entire system, giving a view of services, compliance and all the different rules of government.'[351]

Such machine-readable legislation could speed up interactions and enable policymakers and digital designers to test the impact and whether they are meeting regulations and laws before development takes place.

Susskind describes how rules will be increasingly crafted as in code because laws will be increasingly computed by AI systems applying general standards to specific situations. This would mean they would no longer be written in stature or legislation but, rather, in the code that serves, both to describe what the law is and to enforce it.[352] For example, if your marriage is not registered in a civil registry, you're not legally married. In the future, this will need to be entered in the right digital registry in order to be legitimate.[353]

Regulation and AI

Our laws and regulations are designed for the twentieth century (possibly even the nineteenth century) when these types of technologies didn't exist. Plainly, that will need to change, and quickly, with the need for new standards.

Algorithms are increasingly part of people's everyday lives. We know that, even when we don't know it. These determine what adverts you see on your devices, the cost and level of coverage of your insurance, what you're recommended to watch on streaming services, and if you will go through to the next round on a job application. As machine learning and AI become more commonplace, including in the provision of government services, the ethical management of algorithms and the associated rules and regulations will become a big challenge, and inevitably become a major role of government.[354]

We know from our own interactions that many public servants feel they are 'years off thinking about AI'. This was the view of a Deputy Secretary who said that their agency, which is responsible for issuing licences, are just about getting to grips with putting application forms online, creating APIs, and regulating within the current legal frameworks. If that's the context, thinking about using or regulating for AI is going to feel like a fairly distant priority.

We're seeing the start of this debate played out elsewhere but with worryingly little being done or at least communicated by the Australian government.

There is an opportunity now for regulators and government officials to shape the debate. The response by governments in Australia doesn't seem to match the interest and activity we see from other countries.

Whilst the Victorians have launched an all-Parliamentary group on AI, within their first year they have communicated nothing publicly, other than a short guide on the topic.[355]

In the UK, a House of Lords' report proposed five main principles for an AI code:[356]

- AI should be developed for the common good and benefit of humanity
- AI should operate on principles of intelligibility and fairness
- AI should not be used to diminish the data rights or privacy of individuals, families, or communities
- All citizens have the right to be educated to enable them to flourish mentally, emotionally, and economically alongside AI

- The autonomous power to hurt, destroy, or deceive human beings should never be vested in AI

The French government is focused on creating a regulatory and financial framework to drive the adoption and application of AI. In Singapore, they have an Advisory Council and various other initiatives in this space.[357] Australia needs to respond with similar energy and intent.

Regulators and policy officials should be developing now how they understand and influence, with human oversight, the way algorithms are developed and maintained as part of shoring up the integrity and credibility of a service or product.

Apolitical are right to advocate for a 'regulatory algorithm' which can successfully mitigate the dichotomy of interest between capital interests (represented by the private sector) and the demands for ensuring equity and justice (represented by the public sector) as an essential foundation for the health of the whole system.[358] As we discuss below, these are skills that are in high demand and in short supply.

Professor Genevieve Bell, a former anthropologist at Intel and now a Distinguished Professor at the Australian National University and Director of the Autonomy, Agency and Assurance Institute, challenged delegates at Australia's 2018 Singularity University conference to consider the following challenges when it comes to regulating AI:

- Autonomy: Which version of AI are you regulating? E.g., do Australians want the US or Chinese version of autonomy in our vehicles?
- Control: Who has the agency; which rules are being followed?
- Assurance: How is safety assured and how will we know, including if an AI identifies itself as such?
- Metric: What should be measured, why, and how?

The need for regulatory reform, powered by digital, is here now. For example, in Arkansas, the state used automated decision-making tools powered by an algorithm to calculate the number of hours of Medicaid that severely disabled people could use. But there was a problem: the code was wrong. Many vulnerable people suffered as their hours were wrongfully reduced. This wasn't done with malice, but other cases may have explicit or implicit biases in them.

This means that ways of respecting and protecting the rights of those affected by AI decisions, as though these are being made by humans, need to be accelerated.

Nesta suggests developing certification schemes which assure the quality and fairness of systems without revealing the IP. Essentially, this is a licensing scheme for AI.[359] The issue is part of a bigger challenge, which is to imagine and build whole new governance and regulatory models for the management of data across the public or public-purpose sectors.

The trouble is that these systems can change hundreds of times a second; are often based across international jurisdictions; and can be opaque, so-called black-box systems. The current (default) system of self-regulation seems likely to continue with, perhaps, principles being followed that focus on accountability, visibility, and control to assure that the common public good is being considered.

Maybe those creating and training machines will be obliged to take a version of the Hippocratic oath for doctors, promising to only do good with their skills.[360] How such algorithms are set up, checked, audited, and protected will become vital public service work.

We anticipate, just as the introduction of the General Data Protection Regulation (GDPR) laws in the European Union now mean websites increasingly ask your permission to collect your data, that, soon, if AI is involved in making significant or sensitive decisions about you, you will be informed by the organisation. If you have been refused service or a transaction, there should be a right for 'explainability' as to why that has been the case. This is partly what we mean by the need to make government and the work of the public sector more legible.

Such safeguards should help to address or avert prejudices within the data sets and train the machine to learn not to perpetuate societal inequalities. Something similar will also be required regarding the legal liabilities of decisions made by AIs.

In the end, the best protection will be a function of visibility and contestability. We need to be confident that we will be able to see how algorithms that will possess increasing sway over our lives are being designed, matched by an ability to contest the implications of their biases and assumptions and, where necessary, change them.

What we're talking about here is generally just to be able to operate and regulate today's technology uses. As working AI systems become more sophisticated and move towards independent thought, we will need a raft of ethical and regulatory links into these machines to ensure everything from physical safety to legal compliance.[361]

For some in government, there is a fear that machines and automation will erode their power base. Currently, the number of policies and people you manage plays a huge part in your status (and pay) as a public servant. The more future-looking mandarins will recognise that most of the time they have limited power over the exact decision-making powers, especially of front-line operational staff. AI offers the potential either to enhance traditional command and control responses or provide a new way to be both influential and wield authority for public purpose and common good outcomes.

Data, data everywhere

A mixture of disinterest and avoidance is often the reaction from many public servants when data is on the agenda. It's worse if the guy presenting to you looks like he's never seen sunlight and has used the words *meta, unstructured,* and *APIs* multiple times. (Indeed, one of the authors has watched three senior public servants nod off during a data analytics demonstration).

But if data is the new oil[362] (and there is some debate about whether that analogy is accurate or helpful), then the public sector, and all of those who work in and with it, need to understand how it will drive the engine of government through doing sophisticated analysis across operations and policy.

Data enables digital transformation. What matters is how the data actually gets (safely) used – that whatever gets put into systems needs to be accurate, ideally machine readable, and reusable. Data held by governments, as an authoritative trusted actor, should be treated and managed as if it were a national asset. There are jobs to be done to collate, value, protect, and utilise data, just as much as physical assets, like buildings, are optimised.

At a basic level, good use of data helps avoid repeating information as citizens interact with government (e.g., the service pre-fills your postal address), can tailor services to needs in real time (e.g., the form doesn't ask if you are under 18 because it can tell from your date of birth), and can be used in conjunction with other data to establish correlations ranging from the simplistic (e.g., applicants for a newborn's birth certificate can automatically enrol in Medicare) to the complicated (e.g., determining food health safety inspections based on social media reviews and blocked drains data).

Data science is already becoming mainstream in the public sector and moving out of the preserve of centres such as the NSW Data Analytics Centre (DAC) and the Canadian province of British Columbia's Centre for Data-Driven Innovation.[363] Staffed by data scientists, drawing together more datasets (from across government and the private sector), computing power, and analysts, these centres are the engine rooms for governments to become more problem-solving focused. Recent successes include predicting builder insolvency and building-cladding-fire risk with a far greater accuracy than before, which will save citizens money and possibly lives.[364]

There is, however, a sense among some we've worked with in government that there is a mismatch between the Ferrari ambitions of these new data science capabilities and the P-plate standard of much of the capability available to work with data on a day-to-day basis across government.

The perception is that data science is still the preserve of academic and technical-geeky types. There is also plenty of evidence that many (but not all) politicians and public servants are still scared of data, both in terms of the skills it demands, which many feel they don't have, and the uncomfortable insights it can reveal once you start digging and connecting.

For example, when one of the authors worked in immigration, he used new data analytics capabilities to test previous decisions to determine any applicants' characteristics and subsequent adverse outcomes to transform risk profiles.

Previously, the sheer size of the data sets to be worked on and the analytics required meant this had never been done before. The intention was right, but the challenge was how he might explain to Ministers why previous decisions had turned out, in the light of this new data analysis, to be wrong. The logic of statistical occurrences, data assumptions, and considerations were lost through anxiety and uncertainty about how to manage the practical politics of some of the likely fallout.

The experiments fizzled out. It is an illustration of data's propensity to escape its technical boundaries and become tangled in more human and often intensely political concerns.

If people are worried by the 'What if data is wrong?' question, the best way to improve the quality and reliability of data is not to hide it or make it obscure and difficult to use. It's more efficient and effective to invite a wider and more inclusive engagement by different perspectives inside and outside government to identify and rectify those deficiencies.

Data becomes cleaner the more you work with it and the more you expose it to the view and expertise of plenty of different people. What makes open source more secure is that anyone can find and correct the flaws. As open-source guru Linus Torvalds put it, 'A thousand eyes make all bugs shallow'.[365]

Humans and machines: the impact of AI

Computers are getting dramatically better at performing specialised, routine, and predictable tasks, and it seems very likely that they will soon be poised to outperform many of the people now employed to do these things.

Martin Ford, *Rise of the Robots: Technology and the Threat of a Jobless Future*

This isn't a futurist debate. Every day public servants are already working with and alongside machines.

The nature of public work will be transformed. The activities and tasks that public servants and those engaged in public-purpose work currently undertake, and the new ones relating to administrating and delivering public services, including those described above, flow between the spectrum of machines supporting, augmenting, automating, or replacing (overseeing) them, powered by AI and machine learning.

One way of framing this is illustrated in figure 10 (over page).

Using AI to help people perform tasks faster and better could include speeding up customer enquiry times, spotting fraud such as in procurement or expense transactions, and reminding them to complete more transactions, such as the next-best transaction (e.g., most people who apply for a fishing licence might be reminded/recommended to apply for a shooting licence). These activities will require more data scientists and fewer administrative employees.

Figure 10: Summary spectrum of government transformation examples using AI

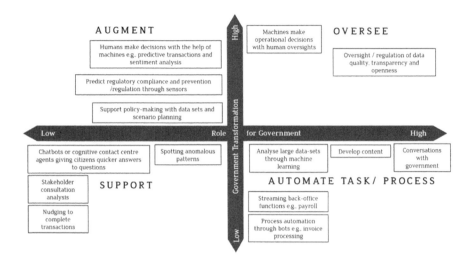

Source: Stewart-Weeks and Cooper (2019)

Using AI to automate typical tasks/processes include:

- Automation of routine, repetitive processes, like sending out tax reminders, processing payments, enforcing regulations or fines
- Streamlining of back-office functions, like payroll
- Analysis and recognition of large data sets
- Content generation, including for budget reports and websites
- Virtual or cognitive contact-centre agents for citizens/back office

Impacts include the creation of more roles, such as bot managers, service and interaction designers, and voice interaction and linguistics designers to manage the intents or meaning of what people are saying; e.g., understanding accents or if someone is being sarcastic. Roles such as executive assistants, call-centre employees, and corporate services could all be reduced, or their capacity increased, e.g., an always open call centre.

Using AI to augment people to make better decisions could include predicting reasons for customer contact; making decisions informed by data sets and scenarios, e.g., on policy leading to solve for better social actions and interventions; predicting work health and safety compliance checks; prevention through sensors (*Is this bridge at risk of falling down?*); and regulation (*Is this factory emitting more than the permitted pollutants?*). This is likely to create a new range of jobs focused on the design, delivery, and management of AI solutions, and then regulators or auditors to check them.

Case Study: Centrelink 'Robo-debt'

The Centrelink Robo-debt scandal in January 2017 saw the automated debt-recovery system match income data reported to Centrelink with data held by the ATO and issuing incorrect debt notices to welfare recipients. The argument about recovering overpaid tax dollars was lost. The newspapers lined up in the slow summer period with stories of personal impact as welfare payments were stopped. The Department of Human Services were swamped with angry phone calls (including, no doubt, from the Prime Minister's office).

Four months, 200,000 letters, and a widespread debate about the perceived brutal use of data and machines later, the program was stopped. The timing before Christmas was obviously a problem. The subsequent Parliamentary inquiry made recommendations that anyone working with the use of data in the public service should know about. These include compliance with privacy procedures; risk assessments, including consultation with stakeholders; checking assumptions in calculations, and having contingency plans in place to handle the inevitable phone calls and requests for re-assessments.

The Senate's inquiry into digital services in 2018 went further, describing it as 'galling' that the 'impact of the program on vulnerable people seemed to be an irrelevant in its design; irrelevant in its evaluation.'*

The example reinforces the need to take a more serious and sustained look at different models of data governance as now an inescapable part of the data revolution at the heart of digital transformation. The challenge, and the framing of solutions, is clear:

'The world is struggling to govern data. The challenge is to reduce abuses of all kinds, enhance accountability and improve ethical standards, while also ensuring that the maximum public and private value can also be derived from data.'**

New models of data trusts might need to be both conceived and experimented with as governments grapple with the new dimensions of data in their digital framing of role, purpose, and performance.

* https://www.aph.gov.au/Parliamentary_Business/Committees/Senate/
Finance_and_Public_Administration/digitaldelivery/Report/co1

** https://www.nesta.org.uk/blog/new-ecosystem-trust/

There will be roles focused on the regulation of data quality, transparency, and openness, as well as a host of human jobs whose roles and functions we can't predict, as we are only just beginning to understand what the machines and their intelligence will be able to do.

We expect that much of the AI low-hanging fruit in government will be as a first line of analysis or decision-making. This could make use of 'commodity AI' which, much like the enterprise management systems and customer relationship management systems that are being installed, will be sold by big brands like Salesforce, Microsoft, IBM, and Amazon Web Services (AWS). Where government uses, for example, virtual agents, it will need to decide how to inform citizens that they are engaging with AI rather than a public servant.

However, unlike these previous kinds of enterprise resource management systems that largely rely on binary, rule-based inputs, the challenge with AI is how these systems deal with context. As one Secretary of a major department said to us:

> 'The challenge of AI will be at a time where people are demanding more personalisation, and we operate [in government] where the rules, regulations, and systems are so complicated and layered on layers where codification is difficult; there is only so far a machine can go in, for example, dealing with a complex Medicare rebate'.

So human judgement will be critical to interpret results, manage harder cases or conversations, and hear appeals and make value-based judgements, which have always been a major part of good public work.

AI will help governments, for sure, by drastically reducing the cost of making predictions. However, as *The Economist* advocates, this won't just happen through waving some kind of magic wand and installing AI like some of the other digital trends or so-called transformations.[366]

To be confident about AI, we need to be confident in the quality of the data, to be able to assure the assumptions on which responses are being built and see how it fits both context and purpose.

William D. Eggers summarises the situation well:

> 'Over time, AI [automation and working with machines] will spawn massive changes in the public sector, transforming how government employees

get work done. It's likely to eliminate some jobs, lead to the redesign of countless others, and create entirely new professions. In the near term, our analysis suggests, large government job losses are unlikely. But cognitive technologies will change the nature of many jobs—both what gets done and how workers go about doing it—freeing up to one quarter of many workers' time to focus on other activities.[367]

We agree with Adrian Turner, CEO of CSIRO's Data61, and Michael Priddis, CEO of an Australian AI start-up called Faethm, that the debate needs to change from being led by 'doomsayers who warn that AI could eradicate jobs, break laws and start wars'[368] to one about positively impacting the way in which government in particular runs a country and provides services.

The Hon. Ed Husic MP, the Shadow Digital Economy Minister up until May 2019, points out that were it possible to have a sensible rather than an alarmist debate, most people would agree that, for example, in a healthcare setting, it makes sense that medical professionals and their support staff spend less time filling and chasing paper, and more time on patient care guided by insights and analysis that can reach new heights of accuracy and speed using AI tools and capabilities.[369]

- Examples of early benefits flowing from automation include:
- Early detection (e.g., automated fraud detection and medical diagnoses planning and scheduling)
- Improved decision-making (e.g., optimised planning and scheduling)
- More accurate predictions (e.g., demand forecasting)
- Reduced costs due to increased efficiency and automation, especially for large-scale processes, creating productivity gains benefiting the wider economy

As explained in chapter 3, a situation where machines assume a 'general intelligence', that is, with the ability of a computer to perform any human task without being explicitly programmed to do so is some way off. Perhaps we'll never end up at the point of singularity.[370]

Whilst there is some truth in the assertion that 'This is not a race against the machines ... this is a race with the machines. Ninety percent of your co-workers will be unseen machines',[371] this is far from inevitable. There are some pretty big challenges, which all require new roles and skills to overcome in public service including:

- **Agreeing definitions, standards, ethics, and regulation** of the use of such technology, including within public services
- **Assuring algorithms** to make decisions that do not entrench the prejudices of the people who designed them, or give apparent legitimacy to the biases embedded in our society, e.g., algorithm managers/auditors who can check so-called black boxes of decision-making
- **New economic and trade roles** focused on understanding how algorithms can be used by Australian companies to achieve desired business goals, accelerate long-term performance, and create differentiation
- **Change management**, including from lower worker morale and collective bargaining/unions
- **Improved medical outcomes** from diagnostic assessments that use machine learning, such as to spot signs of cancer

We think there is still an immaturity of the debate in Australia, although there are people and organisations working hard to change that. But failure to think carefully and invest wisely in these new capabilities, especially as other countries, notably China, move steadily and rapidly forward, could undermine economic growth and deny access to new sources of prosperity.

Governments around the world are rapidly considering the use of AI for economic development and for their own use. The Chinese are basing their economy's 10-year plan around AI, the South Korean, Singaporean and Canadian governments are all launching AI strategies, the UK Government is establishing a Parliamentary Committee to report on AI, and the United Arab Emirates have appointed a Government Minister for AI.[372]

As noted above, Australia is seen as being behind the curve.[373] 'The broader political conversation about AI's economic and security impact is low frequency and low volume.'[374] There is no equivalent government strategy, although one was being developed in 2018.[375]

Government needs to act now, with a mix of funding, policy development, leadership, and as a convener to urgently change the situation where it is ranked the worst prepared for the arrival of AI (the underlying enabler of cognitive technologies).[376]

Cyber and information security

Much like physical security, the misuse of data with criminal intent or through non-compliance of rules will result in ever more focus on prevention, compliance, detection, and response.

Most government entities now either have a Cyber Security Officer or a CIO whose role includes building dedicated teams to ensure that cyber and data security isn't an afterthought. In some cases, part of their role is to inform Departmental leads of threats and attacks that they were previously unaware of and ensuring that these are managed as risks to their organisations. There is an increasing realisation that as Government stores far more data than the private sector, and often keeps it in more vulnerable systems, risk mitigations need to be driven at senior management board level.

Examples of how this is changing the work of public servants to incorporate cyber and data security into what they do include:

- **Prevention:** Much like the work of health and safety legislation, this relates to public servants taking necessary steps within government and encouraging citizens and businesses to protect their data. This includes embedding a sense of shared responsibility through training to take preventive actions and to understand the consequences to protect identities and sensitive information (e.g., when did you last change your laptop password?), designing security measures into new systems (that's why the ATO have a two-step verification process), and setting standards.
- **Compliance:** The role of controls and auditors increasingly using sophisticated AI-enabled software to detect anomalies of workplace behaviours through monitoring.
- **Detection:** This includes using ethical hackers and testing systems for weaknesses and issues.
- **Response:** If it's a question of when, and not if, breaches will occur, then more resilience and scenario testing exercises, communications officers, and crisis teams will be required. This includes quickly returning to business as usual and repairing damage.[377] Not handling the fallout properly, rather than the actual event, can cause the most problems.

However, despite the reminders like the IBM e-census problems in 2016 or the privacy concerns about My Health Record, such activity tends to be reactive.

More needs to be done to ensure the seriousness of this issue gets beyond a narrative about not sharing your computer password, ensuring those software updates go through, and ignoring phishing emails.

If they don't protect our digital systems, govern the use of data, and ensure privacy, the social contract – however implicit or not understood as it is – breaks down between allowing or tolerating use of data to connect systems or make them easier to use and keeping it safe.

Platforms

One of the ways in which the changing work of the public sector will change the way the public sector works is by adopting platform models of policy and service delivery.

Tim O'Reilly is often credited with opening up the discussion about 'government as a platform', using the analogy of the way in which the Apple iPhone transformed the way we use mobile technologies to access data, services, and entertainment.

As he described it: 'Government 2.0 is not a new kind of government; it is government stripped down to its core, rediscovered and reimagined as if for the first time.'[378]

And its implications for government were clear and transformative: 'Apple built a framework that allowed virtually anyone to build applications for the phone, leading to an explosion of creativity, with more than 100,000 applications appearing for the phone in little more than 18 months, and more than 3,000 new ones now appearing every week.'[379]

O'Reilly framed the question: 'How does government become an open platform that allows people inside and outside government to innovate? How do you design a system in which all of the outcomes aren't specified beforehand, but instead evolve through interactions between government and its citizens, as a service provider enabling its user community?'[380]

By 'platform' we mean the products, services, or technologies that serve as (open) foundations for others to build on; in this case we refer to the development and delivery of government services. The authors' layperson's description is that people should never need to understand the structure of government to access public services.

What does 'government as a platform' actually mean? This is perhaps one of the least understood aspects of digital transformation in government. And it is one of those re-framings of government's role, which clearly has democratic and other impacts that can't and shouldn't be left to public servants to decide. It will likely have a major impact on the type of work that the public sector is called on to do well.

Country as a platform

Estonia is the classic example of how government as a platform should be run. If anything, they've gone a step forward with a 'country as a service' concept. This is based on a system of registries that allows all governments to share data across boundaries (the X-road[381]) and can also be used by the private sector, a (compulsory) electronic ID for all citizens, and eEsti.ee, the Estonian State eService portal.

Together, X-road and the digital ID make it possible to digitally sign any contract, access essentially any public service, order prescriptions, file taxes, vote, and so on.[382] The Estonian government claims that its digital infrastructure has led to annual savings of about 2% of GDP and more than 800 years in working time for the public and private sectors.[383]

This is all great stuff. But comparing Australia with a country of 1.3 million people who were able to start from fresh, without legacy issues and a system of government where the people were used to being told what to do, is difficult.

If anything, the continual use of Estonia as an example might be unhelpful because it gives those suspicious of, or resistant to, digital transformation fuel to say how unlike the two countries are, and therefore avoid learning what could be usefully adapted through careful analysis. But it does give an indication of what government as a platform could be, even if the cultural, political, and legacy contexts widely differ.

Government is the platform

Going to the extreme of this platform ideology would mean that government provides the open (digital) platforms, open data, open standards, encouragement for citizen participation, and regulatory/policy frameworks to enable society, businesses, and entrepreneurs to create innovative services using new digital technologies.

O'Reilly's initial conception likened this to government providing infrastructure like roads (or like the National Broadband Network in Australia) that, in turn, non-government actors use to create value in the economy. Examples include where government has provided APIs on open data and encouraged the private sector to create value, such as apps that enable more efficient transport journeys through these new interfaces with government. This relies heavily on an assumption that there is unique value that can be captured by a non-government actor to make it worthwhile for them.

'Tell him he's dreaming' is the best summary response of even the most innovative and digital leaders we have asked about O'Reilly's version of government as a platform. For them, this ambition isn't possible and won't be realised. It would essentially turn upside down the current model of government. It also misunderstands some of the essential and non-negotiable roles that governments play as a direct regulator and policymaker, and occasionally as necessary direct service providers, to intervene in society and the economy. Government has irreducible roles as a player which preclude its embrace, in any simplistic sense, of its role as a platform.

Governments will always have to act directly, as well as to provide the conditions for others to act. And much of the essential work of government and public policy is very non-platform-like; it is intricate and complex work that has to untangle clashing interests, create and protect public values, and apply a public good test to mediate irresolvable problems of access and allocation across inevitably scarce resources and opportunities.

Government providing platforms

The aspiration of a government as a platform as applied in Australia focuses on rethinking how government organises into departments and agencies. Platforms are focused on meeting user needs rather than aligning to organisational structures.

Perhaps the platform concept offers a way to transcend current silo structures, which still reflect the tight control and persistent interests of the professional 'guilds' on the basis of whose work and expertise those structures were conceived and built in the first place.[384]

Tom Loosemore advocates that government should be bold enough to create institutions that are of the Internet, not on the Internet. He argues that these need to be horizontal in nature, making platform-based services and data like identity assurance available to all public service agencies as well as other sectors.[385]

This would mean re-designing or reconfiguring how citizens interact with government from paper-based or paper processes that have been digitised to have a seamless and consistent experience. Loosemore, Richard Pope, and others broadly suggest this would require the following digital infrastructure to provide simple, common, non-business specific services that are needed across government(s):

- Data Registers: reliable lists of information
- Trust and consent: independent oversight from regulators who report to Parliament
- Common platforms: interactions with platforms such as a single log-on to handle payments, digital proof of identities, notifications, and more, requiring telling government only once
- Be easy to connect, using APIs

Each time a user reads content, proves their identity, interacts with services, makes payments, is notified, and accesses data, the experience and its capture would be consistent. Furthermore, this would be a two-way process, with citizens able to expect not to have to re-enter information that they have already provided government, helpful suggestions (e.g., what rebates you can apply for), the opportunity to provide feedback, and, wherever possible, faster (and automated) service times with appropriate levels of human assistance, where needed.

This is broadly what the DTA are advocating at a federal government level, as set out in their whole-of-government platforms strategy published in late 2018.[386] They aim to increase the integrity and consistency of government service delivery and provide a unified and seamless user experience through new shared capabilities built on common technical foundations and shared across agencies/departments.

What's more, because such common platforms provide the underlying digital infrastructure, this means that departments and agencies can spend far less time thinking about these common components and stop reinventing the wheel and get on with providing solutions to meet their user needs in their unique policy and delivery contexts.

Eaves and McGuire summarise well a framework for assessing the relative maturity of cross-government platforms in figure 11.[387] Most Australian states are – in our view – at low to medium. At State level they are being less clear in terms of detail and their ambitions on government providing platforms.

Figure 11: Framework to assess the relative maturity of cross-government platforms

AREA	LOW	MEDIUM	HIGH	FUTURE STATE
Creating Public Registers of Data		A standard for publishing data in a structured way is available, but only a few registers have been published	The standard for publishing data registers is used by most departments, and high-volume registers are published	Public data is published in a structured and API-accessible way by default
Sharing Private Data Registers between Departments	Digital units are aware of platform and data potential, but have no formal plans for development	Data sharing agreements are in place between a few departments, but they are one-offs	A few government departments have created private data registers that they make available to other departments	Data sharing between government departments is governed by standard rules/ agreements and common practice with all departments
Creating Shared Platforms		A few platforms are available in private beta	Some of the most common needs (e.g., identity, payments) are covered by shared platforms that are available to the whole public sector	All common needs are covered by shared platforms and allow for rapid deployment of new services
Developing Platform Governance		A few platforms are available in private beta to a select number of central departments	Platform teams publish their roadmaps and performance and have established a forum for partners to influence their development	A cross-government group of departments decide jointly about the development of new platforms and influences their prioritisation

Reproduced with kind permission of David Eaves and Ben McGuire from the Harvard Kennedy School, Harvard University (2018)

The government in WA have taken a stealth approach. With 500 websites, 80 Departments and senior leaders resistant to creating just one website for government (like GOV.UK), they negotiated to have a search function at the front end. This has the user-centric question 'What can we do for you today?', where citizens and business people can type in and be directed to government information and services.

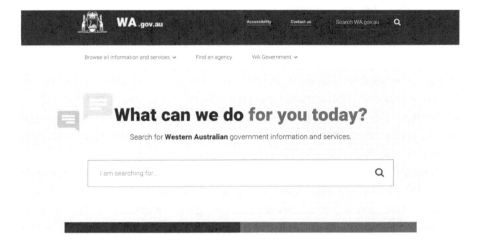

Credit: WA Government

There is an absence of a compelling narrative that might convince Australian citizens about why spending taxpayer money on such national infrastructure is useful and timely. This means, even if the Federal Government can deliver such capability, which will go a long way towards helping to get 'there', there is still a big risk of duplication or missing capabilities at the state level.

It wouldn't subvert the persistent value for experimentation and innovation of a robust and well-functioning federation if the Federal and State/Territory Governments, in an outbreak of common sense and shared purpose, joined forces in terms of investment and capabilities and co-invest and co-develop such public digital infrastructure. The DTA's trusted identity solution – if it works – see explanation in chapter 3 – could become a big part of that infrastructure package, provide a common identity solution across Australia and beyond.

This doesn't mean the DTA should do everything in this space. There's plenty of design and production work to go around, and the effort could be divided between the Federal and State/Territory Governments.

However, the DTA does not have the political or delivery capital to make this argument, and there is seemingly little interest at Ministerial level for doing so, at least at the moment. But it could be done, with examples such as the common electronic conveyancing platform or My Health Record under the Council of Australian Governments serving as cases of building such common infrastructure.

If – and it is a big if, judging by recent experience – such shared platforms are developed and can be adopted, citizens would just see that they are interacting with the Government and not a particular agency. For example, if the service for applying to study in Australia were organised around user needs – the students, in other words – you would not necessarily be able to tell what was from Home Affairs, Foreign Affairs, and Treasury, or from a State or Territory Education Department. That would be a game changer and might see Australia edge a little further away from doing digital to being sensibly and collaboratively digital.

It would reduce the need to brand everything by an individual Department's name (which, by the way, may well point to some of the unspoken brand instincts that betray a much deeper and change-resistant vanity than is often acknowledged). It would put under the microscope the very composition of the Commonwealth of Australia, especially the construct of having three layers of government.

It won't be the first time that the idea of reconstructing the federation using digital and data has been floated, particularly if it means not getting bogged down in shifting the legacy-rich and often burdensome weight of the analogue institutions and associated culture untouched, if radically bypassed.

Digital infrastructure and funding models

How transformation is funded will change to become more focused on creating national public digital infrastructure.

No one government appears to have found or updated its models or methods of providing funding to fit the differences of how the new ways of working that we've described are playing out, although there have been discussions in that direction in NSW. Digital projects tend to be allocated funding either to update or fix something that's coming to the end of its life (e.g., software support is expiring), a high-level policy commitment has been made by a politician and someone has suggested an amount that sounds sensible, or departments/

agencies prepare detailed business cases. When it comes to digital services, these funding methods tend to have a bias from Treasury or Finance teams to prove whether there will be savings or not, and to be very clear about what the benefits will be, based on articulating what the digital service will look like and do, i.e., very detailed requirements that are associated with waterfall project management.

This model doesn't work, and doesn't fit with how 'new public work' should be designed and provisioned. It pre-supposes a clear understanding of the requirements for a business case. It detracts from seeking to really determine what problems are being solved for and underplays the public value as a national asset that having good digital services – or, as we would like to call it, national public digital infrastructure – can have on the competitiveness of the economy.

Pia Andrews, a digital leader with experience with the federal, NSW, and New Zealand governments, summarises well:

'Technology is currently funded as projects with start and end dates, and almost all tech projects across government are bespoke to particular agency requirements or motivations, so we build loads of technologies but very little infrastructure that others can rely upon. If we took all the models we have for funding other forms of public infrastructure (roads, health, education) and saw some types of digital infrastructure as public infrastructure, perhaps they could be built and funded in ways that are more beneficial to the entire economy (and society).'[388]

Furthermore, she argues that the whole business case and associated budgeting processes need to change to become agile, i.e., dynamic, and no longer set and forget documents:

'We need to fund small experiments that inform business cases, rather than starting with big business cases. Ideally we need to not have multi-hundred-million-dollar projects at all because technology projects simply don't cost that anymore.'[389]

This means funding teams, not projects, who work in an iterative fashion and can work in multi-disciplinary ways with governance that supports, not shackles, them to solve problems. The associated procurement processes require the speed and flexibility with which services and expertise can be procured for projects that include rapid, agile learning and experimentation at one end of a spectrum and long-term, multi-jurisdictional, shared infrastructure projects at the other.

Australia should consider digital infrastructure, such as platforms, sensors, telecommunications networks, data centres, and high-powered computers, in much the same way as assets such as roads, hospitals, schools, and railways.

Public digital infrastructure is 'the technology, equipment and systems that provide linkages, networks and pathways to connect people and communities with data, products and services'.[390] It is technical, data, and service infrastructure. Examples include the kind of common platforms explained above, like payments, notifications, identity, single digital entry points, APIs, data registries, and cloud capabilities that can be used by any government agency or, indeed, public sector entity.

In a similar way that dams, pipes, and pumps support the water needs of citizens, digital infrastructure allows information and data to travel around the world and underpin our social and economic lives. Such infrastructure is important for enabling the wider economy, including through, as the NSW Government advocates, solving complex problems, enabling innovation, supporting sustainability, and creating jobs and growth.[391]

Such an approach to national public digital infrastructure would enable:

- A longer-term strategic planning perspective across government (rather than letting departments build adjacent similar digital platforms and services near each other and not join them up) that is adaptable for the rate of technological change
- Valuing digital services as national assets that create value for the country, and are not about saving money or cutting jobs
- Treating, preparing, and managing the data that's held (e.g., in archives) and generated as an asset
- The expectation that, like a road or tunnel, the digital service will require maintenance and optimisation after it has been built
- Government to add digital services to its national balance sheet
- Clearly articulating the 'taxpayer value' of what they will get, the benefits, and why

Leadership

Right now they are squabbling about who pays how much and digitisation as a solution, but there is no real vision in politics or senior executive layers of government.

Anonymous senior government digital leader

Digital transformation of government should be an act of persistent and patient leadership. Having all the strategies, new ways of working, fancy kit labs and incubators, and requisite talent doesn't mean a lot if these digital teams aren't led by professionals who possess the digital skills and credibility that combine imagination, resilience, and a certain quotient of patient guile. Not to mention plenty of luck.

The leadership of digital transformation needs to be distributed and multi-dimensional.

You need leaders at the level of the transformation work itself, people with skill and a mindset that blends vision and imagination with project skills, and the capacity to keep large and complex teams together, focused, and motivated.

And you need organisational and whole-of-service leaders too, with their own blend of imagination and resilience to see the value and virtue of the transformation work at a level of personal engagement that fuels their role. They need to create and hold their own space in which the transformers – designers, builders, technologists, policy people, entrepreneurs, impatient customers, and citizens – can do their work.

Transformation takes time. The public sector works increasingly in an institutional and political regime in which time isn't available or is severely constrained. So, the primary task of the public leadership in a digital age is to counter that unhappy contradiction and take on, often at considerable personal and political cost, the arduous task of opening up and holding the spaces of time and priority setting.

Such leaders tended to come from outside government, with industry experience and the personalities and drive to disrupt the status quo. For example, Mike Bracken had set up *The Guardian* online before he headed up the GDS, and so became known for taking on senior government leaders who were defending the status quo.

Such leaders don't necessarily need to be high-ranking officials. One of the most successful aspects of the GDS in the UK was establishing community-of-practice leaders for disciplines such as user research, service design, development operations, and content.

These people were able to focus on up-skilling people across government, attracting their fellow professionals into government work, and put their skills into building new services and products.

There is a careful balance to be struck here. Too much disruption and the status quo will rally against you. But too much status quo won't. Pushing too hard can come across as arrogant and disrespectful.

A common charge against the GDS and the DTA is that digital types have come in from outside government and think that they can change everything with some kind of magic wand. In doing so, it comes across as a lack of respect for the values and attitudes that public servants expect you to adhere to, or at the very least, try to understand.

Leaders need to be focused first and foremost on working within the new theory of business that we're advocating in this book. They need to conceive of their work as being less about arcane games of power accumulation and more about solving difficult problems whilst managing power and authority as an institutional resource. This is tricky. They need, at the same time, to respect and subvert the institutions they lead, and of which they are also expected to be stewards.

If that sounds like a paradox, it is. It suggests that maintaining the relevance and respect of government as an institution means embracing the unsettling doctrine that accepts *If you want things to stay the same, things will have to change*. Leaders should realise 'the year's big IT projects, planned in minute detail in advance are over ... and grasp the power of modern, Internet-era ways of working, and grant teams that work for them permission to work that way'.[392] As Hillary Hartley, from the Canadian Digital Service, and Janet Hughes, formerly of the GDS, advocate, '[Digital] is about completely changing the way you think and work as a leader, and the way the organisation works',[393] which represents a big challenge.

That means leaders need to reward experimentation, collaboration, and working in the open as well as clear away blockers and flatten power structures. They work best where they can be flexible and operate within an adaptable organisation. Parachuting people in who are just leaders in digital, and who can't or aren't willing to learn how to navigate government, rarely ends well. That should be on every job description relating to digital government.

Different ways of working: capabilities and work styles

If the work of government is staying the same and changing, the ways in which public servants have worked will continue to change. Work will be done using human-centred design, be conducted in the open, the speed and intensity of the design–test–deliver cycle for policy and services will increase, and government's role as convener will be more prominent than ever. And digital will be what everyone does, and how everyone works, not the remit of a special team or 'lab' (whose work may still be necessary and useful, but for different reasons).

Human-centred design

Developing government services that are centred on users (read: citizens/customers/businesses) is central to digital government.

To do that means engaging, observing, and understanding these needs, and then testing versions of the policy and services in a way that replicates their intended use. It means being out of the office and into communities with an empathetic and deeply human approach to how work is undertaken.[394]

This, more and more, is the design toolkit with which public servants will become familiar: user research and ethnography, agile development, iterative prototyping, participation and co-design, stewardship, working across networks, scales, and timeframes.[395]

Up to now, the tools and techniques of human-centred design have been applied largely to service design and delivery. There is no reason why the same tools and mindset shouldn't also increasingly be applied to the work of policymakers.

Many aspects of current models of policymaking are not working well. Some of those we spoke to in preparing this book suggested they were broken. Cycles of policy development and decision took too long and often failed to meet citizen needs, or even put those needs consciously at the heart of the process.

The growing use of policy labs around the world (and there are good examples in Denmark, the UK, the US, and Australia) is being matched by experiments in less linear processes of research, development, consultation, implementation, and review. They are beginning to use agile delivery methods of discovery, alpha/beta cycles of testing, and greater engagement with those experiencing the impact of the policymaking.

In the open

If human-centred design means talking to real people and observing their needs rather than guessing from the distant safety of the office, it means the activities and decisions of public servants will become more open.

This can be as simple as communicating, such as through a blog or social post. The UK's Government Digital Service pioneered – or, for some, Ministerial Special Advisors pushed the boundaries of – public servants publishing stories about what they were doing and why, *during* (and not after the fact, as case studies) the development of new services.[396]

The NSW Government's digital transformation team is adopting a radically open approach to their work, giving very practical expression to the aspiration that, in the future, the revolution will be blogged.[397] For example, they blogged openly about the proposed funding approaches referencing structural changes and millions of dollars of (unannounced and uncommitted) funding in a way that previously would have been subject to a Ministerial announcement.[398]

It also means sharing more data that people can use (e.g., land-use data and the publication of service delivery performance). This is difficult when, traditionally, the public service operates a more closed-door culture.

Public servants in the UK have managed to get data published through a mixture of getting on with it under the radar and introducing some 'sticks' through their digital service assessments. Their digital dashboards showing the real-time performance of currently 800-plus government services has brought a new level of transparency to government.

Speed to value

Most public servants would agree that it often takes a good crisis to transform. Digital tools, techniques, and methods, combined with adopting a new theory of business for government, mean that the speed to value – that is, the speed with which an idea or insight and innovation is turned into a program, service, or response – can be faster than it has ever been.

'Agile' is probably the biggest buzz word of the last five years, and the least understood of these new ways of working.

Agile delivery is not to be confused with agility, which is essentially the ability to change quickly, and pivot when you need to, without losing sight of the end point or compromising your values and principles. Moving to hot-desking, where you can flexibly sit anywhere rather than having your own dedicated desk in an open plan office, doesn't really count.

As explained in chapter 3, agile methods are fundamentally about delivering value as early as possible. That value might equally confirm that something does work and that a prototype or 'minimum viable' service or product could be deployed, or that something doesn't work. The philosophy is one of risk mitigation.

One of the authors – Simon – adopted this way of working for a new service for the UK government called the Immigration Health Surcharge. His digital service team took it from legislated concept to being available globally, integrated within current and legacy visa application systems within eight months. Using waterfall project management would – as the IT department reluctantly admitted – have taken at least 16 months. It wasn't perfect, and was improved using user feedback and data from Google Analytics. But this way ensured a (political) deadline was met, and $400,000 in additional income *per day* for the UK government was achieved.

Convener

Government has a tremendous power to bring together stakeholders and use its levers of influence, as well as the prospect of funding, legislation, or regulation, to tackle problems.

There is a range of methods now for different ways to convene and connect people, including hubs, labs, and incubators, whose purpose is to provide a mix of physical space and focus and collaborative infrastructure, including access to skilled resources and expertise and the necessary technology platforms and tools.

Working styles

> *Digital isn't a list of things to do; it's about how you think, how you behave, what you value, and what drives decisions in your organisation.*[399]

> Janet Hughes, former UK Government Digital Service Director

Working styles within the public service will adapt as the 'what' and 'how' of government changes, as digital transformation becomes more mainstream.

Just like the eras of new public management in the 1980s and 1990s brought a raft of changes – think desktop computers, reporting against targets, and project management charts – and then in the 2000s to more recently the era of customer service – think consistent uniforms, smiling pictures of citizens being served in annual reports, and customer satisfaction surveys – digital government is doing the same. The patterns, rhythms and infrastructure, talent, behaviours and diversity, and leadership are all changing.

Patterns, rhythms, and infrastructure

Digital is all about doing. Eggers describes the digital mindset of 'openness, user-centricity, co-creation, agility and simplicity' as vital attributes for any public servant who requires digital work.[400] Existing patterns and rhythms – broadly, how things get done in the public service – are the opposite: closed, government-centric, developed in silos, cumbersome, and complicated.

Team members work in the same location, surrounded by their work, out in the open, including the dreaded flurry of Post-It notes showing user-research highlights, whiteboards illustrating sketches of new features, and screens showing backlog items on Trello (a web-based list-making application) or a Kanban (work and workflow visualisation tool) wall.

They get together for daily rituals, like stand-ups where each team member is expected to say what they have delivered and where they need help. Show-and-tells are where teams show works in progress, and retrospectives are where team members are open about what worked well and commit to make improvements for the next sprint.

Communication is fast, through instant messages and collaboration tools like Slack. Success is celebrated, including with visible symbols such as stickers on laptops, which, like Scouts' merit badges, highlight the skill of a team member having delivered a product, for example. The flat-team structures, iterative builds of products that are prioritised in sprints, and the external user focus chime against traditional project management, which has hierarchical team structures, detailed plans, and internal organisational user focus.

Little wonder that seasoned public servants sometimes think that the way in which digital teams operate is from another world, one where their work and role, steering groups, lengthy documentation, time for consideration, formality, and risk management aren't valued like they used to be. Why on earth would anyone want to 'fail fast'?

Running agile teams properly takes effort and skill. This implies persistence and agility. This tends to a mean a sensible mix of speed, intensity, flexibility, and collaborative discernment. It is unlikely that such talent just magically transitions in from the IT, Communications, or project teams where they were previously housed.

Often, to outsiders, and those operating functions such as finance, procurement, or HR, this way of working seems like chaos and generates resistance. Whilst most public servants would agree that the delivery mechanism of government has to speed up, they would also argue that you need checks and balances. Developing an app for child welfare has somewhat higher risk levels of getting it wrong than developing an app for a retailer of a newspaper.

Digital teams should invest time in showing and explaining how their patterns and rhythms work to these functional leads. They should not deride these professionals as luddites who 'don't get it' just because they won't sign off expenditure without the appropriate forms being filled in. They can't tell a Deputy Secretary to come down and look at their Kanban wall for an update; some kind of document or prototype demonstration is required. They also need to adjust to the existing governance structures, rather than fighting them, or become smarter about when to do each.

Chief Finance Officers need to know that the often expensive digital teams will deliver something of value, are not seeking to perfect every feature or conduct unnecessary research (often in glamorous places) and be given some idea of when.

The return on investment needs some numbers; it can't be enough to claim the new shiny service 'meets user needs'. For example, in WA, in 2017, the Treasury and the Chief Digital Officer worked together to renegotiate telecommunications contracts from a whole-of-government perspective, with the resulting annual savings of $15 million invested into a citizen-facing digital portal (see page 258).

Chief Strategy Officers need to know that the digital teams are working on problems that relate to Ministerial objectives, and not digital islands or pet projects that won't make much difference. A Chief Operations Officer needs to know how the new service will be scaled and integrated with parts of operations. Business leads need to understand why they are being asked to invest some of their best people as product owners.

Digital teams, overall, with their new working styles, need to avoid being stranded on the shores of a 'counsel of perfection' in which all real-world constraints and obstacles have mysteriously evaporated. Any hint of an attitude that they are 'doing God's work in saving public services' won't be helpful. Humble and helpful will meet their internal user needs and help them to deliver.

Infrastructure means having the right tools and environment to enable digital working. Desks that encourage quiet, individual working in an open plan office where you can't put anything up on the wall for health and safety reasons don't cut it. You need large open spaces or team rooms where multi-disciplinary teams can hold their stand-ups, display their product backlog on the walls, and have screens with real-time information on them. You can have bunting, if you like, as well. The DTO had this with their Surry Hills studio, in Sydney, which was very different to their Canberra offices. It is hard to believe that they are the same organisation.

Some digital teams, like the UK's HMRC (customs and tax) departments, have converted former storage facilities into almost aircraft-hangar-like size locations, where up to 20 product teams have their own dedicated space while benefiting from shared facilities. Like a modern-day factory, these teams deliver new digital services that replace the paper-generating systems that their new accommodation used to store.

Digital teams need the right kit. One of the authors (Simon) remembers that the Home Office had laptops that took 10 minutes to activate and wouldn't let you use collaborative tools like Slack. He used to envy GDS peers who all had shiny Macs that turned on at the flick of a switch, without security constraints. That means persuading people in corporate services that your visual designer will need access to Adobe InDesign, and that, no, you cannot do that kind of design in PowerPoint.

Developing these capabilities – new patterns, new rhythms, new infrastructure – can be done within the public service in Australia. They can be taught to existing public servants and, as new ones are hired, especially a generation of digital natives coming in on graduate programs and people from outside government.

There are two immediate issues holding the public service back, each on which there is a notable lack of political debate.

The first is that the type of digital and data skills, interests, and capabilities have been around for at least the last five years, and the challenges of improving service delivery to citizens and developing usable policy for decades before that.

So why is there a generation who grew up with the Internet now entering the senior public service with little interest in this approach and few digital skills? We're not talking about the change-resistant cohort that exist in any organisation, or those who would have resisted advances such as installing desktop computers or using the Internet at work.

We're talking about people who use Uber, binge on Netflix, and are glued to their iPhones but somehow aren't inclined to learn how these new digital models and technologies that power the rest of their lives might relate to how they do their work. These are often some of the brightest minds, but are not necessarily keen to understand, and confidently use, the new tools and platforms of the digital world in the different context of public work.

They can be critical of cultural custodians who set the tone for their teams on the operational front line, or at headquarters. This seems so strange for people who don't seem to realise 'what they do has fundamentally changed … they are now designing or running digital organisations'.[401]

Perhaps they are playing a protectionist game, learning and following on from those whom they have seen as successful a generation or two ahead of them. They are operating within the old theory of business. Nod along enough to show willingness, but nothing more, or to do anything that would jeopardise the power they have finally tasted and are beginning to relish.

There's a paradox of power and influence at work in the digital transformation process that makes it different from many previous forms of institutional change and reform. Where often those changes present stark win/lose equations to those currently in confident and often complacent possession of the commanding heights of influence and power, the process of digital change transformation can often mean not less power and influence but learning how to engage its new patterns to acquire more.

With the necessary skills and a requisite shift of mindset, public servants and their collaborators can learn how to engage the digital platforms and tools, often aided by access to much more sophisticated tools of data and data analytics, including AI and machine learning, to wield considerable influence.

Those whose resistance to digital might derive from an old-fashioned fear of loss of power or 'relevance deprivation'[402] might, if they stopped to engage the new digital world with a bit more curiosity and willingness to learn, end up with more power and authority than they have now.

In status-driven and hierarchical organisations, questioning those above you is a career-limiting move, and getting heard by a generation who believe you need the years under your belt and the battle scars is often nearly impossible. This situation isn't unique to Australia. Current and former public servants have said to us that this is similar to that in the UK, New Zealand, Canada, and the US.

When was the last time you were in a public sector agency, or worked in one yourself, where there was a palpable sense that 'insurgency' – the willingness to go against the grain, call out the inadequacies of the status quo and try something different, even if it offends current architectures of power and status – was tolerated, or even positively sanctioned, by leaders willing to trade some of their personal and professional capital to offer you that privilege?[403]

It ought not anymore to be acceptable for public sector reform documents, or individual agencies, to espouse concepts like 'user-centricity' or 'insurgency' without fronting up to the scepticism, perhaps even cynicism, with which such terms are rightly treated. We're all too far down the track of hearing, but not necessarily seeing, these ideas play out to assume that the translation of the advice into day-to-day action is as trouble-free as it is sometimes assumed.

Getting into and staying in good, senior public sector roles generally means being good at all the skills: writing, interacting with stakeholders, being good with your Minister and Secretary and Deputy Secretaries, and probably being a decent enough line manager. There is a certain comfort in having your days filled with writing papers about issues.

And, especially in the Federal Government based in Canberra, your level and remuneration will still largely be determined by how many people you have in your command. You are loyal to your department, and working with others requires formal meetings and structures. All the leaders, including those who sit on the executive levels of agencies and departments, tend to be either policy or operational types. There are very few recent examples of visible and celebrated leaders who have made it there through disrupting the status quo, collaborating across boundaries, and pushing digital beyond the IT department or digital team.

If that is what visible success looks like, why, as a rational public servant, would you start trying to get the digital transformation thing going faster, and with new skills – and probably fewer people – if you see that as a fundamental risk to your sense of career and preferment?

Another factor is the digital savviness of Ministers and their willingness to change how they work with the public service. This is the most consistent theme in any of the literature we have reviewed and from the interviews we have undertaken.

A good Minister who understands the potential and impact of digital, ideally in a service delivery agency and/or a central digital unit, so they can provide the authorising environment, is half the battle. Examples include Minister

Dominello in NSW, Francis Maude, former Minister for the Cabinet Office who oversaw the UK's GDS, or the current Secretary of State for Health and Social Care and the former Minister of State for Digital And Culture, Matthew Hancock, in the UK. As one public servant said to us, 'Our Secretary and our Minister get it ... unlike my previous department, I don't spend most of my energy on persuading them'.

Such political will is demonstrated by Minister Dominello in NSW when he says, 'In order to succeed, we must ensure that digital transformation is front and centre of government, and to do this, we need to completely reimagine what it looks like'.[404]

He has translated that will into what he has dubbed the Ten Commandments of digital transformation[405] to focus public servants, the government, and industry on what this means:

- *Thou shall use data*
- *Thou shall make data digital and banish paper*
- *Thou shall make data direct, in real time*
- *Thou shall display data creatively*
- *Thou shall dissect data to generate insights*
- *Thou shall embed a digital approach in thou DNA*
- *Thou shall look towards a 3D digital future*
- *Thou shall defend thy digital platforms (cyber)*
- *Thou shall deliver outcomes from insights*
- *Thou shall not be a dinosaur*

A detailed research report by the MIT Sloan Review into achieving digital maturity found that whilst having the vision from the top and securing leaders to lead it, it also requires committing resources to achieve this vision.[406] That includes chief digital officers who can bring in or develop a team around them.

These senior leaders all need to focus on problems, opportunities, and outcomes rather than specific solutions or programs.[407] This will help see digital as being everyone's tool and responsibility, and not just that of the digital guy. (Sadly, they are usually men, which has to change). And that digital person should have a seat on the executive committee.[408] The talent is lost if they report in to a CIO or Chief Operating Officer.

The new capabilities that are required by public servants are also required by their political masters. There is little to be gained by waxing lyrical, and even inspirational, about being digital and the attributes that you think should characterise the work and delivery of a modern public service if the surrounding organisational and institutional context, including what Ministers and Secretaries or their employees ask for, is untuned or even hostile to those same attributes.

Terry Moran, a former Secretary of the Department of Prime Minister & Cabinet, among other public sector leadership roles over the last 40 years, is unequivocal that developing what he called Public Administration 4.0 is part of the response to digital disruption linked to globalisation.

Being able to pull together that blend of the persistent values of the past with the insistent skills and values of the future is itself rapidly shaping up as a key talent demand for the digital-transformed public service of the future.[409]

There are examples of leaders who are becoming increasingly visible in this space, and whose impact needs to be multiplied, to show the success you can have operating within the new model of government. They are not digital zealots, and combine many of the behaviours, skills, and focus that are required of leaders to help get 'there'.

In the UK, the former Secretary at the Department for the Environment, Fisheries and Food, Clare Moriarty, who was a dyed-in-the-wool, old-school mandarin, has changed her outlook to be passionate in her promotion of digital government, and, in particular, the importance of women being involved in building technology skills.

She is a leader who has met people on the front line and has seen the impact on the services of technology that has either been delayed or doesn't meet needs. These stakeholders simply won't trust government, regardless of who is in power, if the service quality isn't good enough. It doesn't take much to convince them to try a new way of working that delivers, rather than face angry farmers or anglers.[410]

Capabilities and skills

From a range of reports and studies about the public service of the future and the implications of dramatic change for the public sector, including but not exclusively from digital transformation,[411] we have picked some of the common capabilities that we think best summarise what public sector works will need to survive and thrive in a digital future.

- **Data literacy:** Ensuring decisions are data-driven and that data isn't an afterthought
- **User-centricity:** Public services should be focused on solving and servicing users' needs
- **Curiosity:** Seeking out and trying new ideas or ways of working
- **Storytelling:** Explaining change in a way that builds support
- **Insurgency:** Challenging the status quo and working with unusual partners
- **Teamwork:** This will be valued and rewarded and occur more frequently
- **Simulation and experimentation:** Engaging with the front line or walking in the shoes of users
- **Sense-making:** Getting to the deeper meaning or significance of what is being communicated
- **Social intelligence:** Relating to others deeply and directly
- **Adaptive thinking:** Thinking and generating solutions outside of the norm to respond to unexpected and unique situations
- **Cross-cultural competency:** Operating in unfamiliar cultural settings and using differences for innovation
- **New-media literacy:** Leveraging new media forms to communicate persuasively
- **Transdisciplinary:** Understanding concepts across different disciplines to solve complex problems
- **Design mindset:** Designing tasks, processes, and work environments to produce desired outcomes (although the risk is whether that design is used as an isolated technique and out of context of the strategic policy agenda and a systems approach)
- **Cognitive load management:** Filtering important information from the 'noise' and using new tools to expand mental functioning abilities
- **Virtual collaboration:** Working productively with others across virtual distances
- **Leading and managing change:** Roles as agents to make change happen and stick
- **Commercial skills:** This includes skills to undertake commercial transactions, such as commissioning services from the private and voluntary sectors

It's a long list and the intention isn't to suggest every public servant has to manifest all of these attributes. It is likely, though, that across a team, or during different phases of a public sector career, or in different public work contexts, some combination of these will be evident.

There are some big themes emerging from these studies.

For example, the persistent values and capabilities of public work – rigour, impartiality, ethics, fairness, a care for and pursuit of the public or common interest, a concern for the long term – are now mixed with aspirations for a new set of skills that, in the future, will be just as valuable for effective public servants. These include innovation and the ability to think beyond the usual, a capacity for speed and agility, the capacity to lead whole systems and curate complex communities of skills and expertise to achieve big public results (e.g., better health, skills for work, safer and 'smarter' cities, climate adaptation) that can no longer be 'delivered' in a simple or singular production model.

Driven by the pervasive influence of digital transformation, we are witnessing the birth of a new set of traditional skills and capabilities without some mastery of which public servants in the future will feel under-powered and ill-prepared for the new public work in which they will be immersed.

Blending the new and the old

There are some facets of public work that will continue to call on capabilities consistently at the heart of the public service toolkit. For example, the medium may change, especially with the adoption of voice technologies and the use of new media forms, but the ability to write well, expressing ideas, articulating arguments, presenting evidence, and making recommendations, will remain. That might be a well-crafted tweet, summarising user research, or putting together a Cabinet submission. Writing well usually means you can think well, given that writing and thinking are inextricably linked.

New sources of data and the associated emphasis on quantification mean that the demand for good analytical skills will continue. This includes computational capacity and quantitative thinking that can engage large amounts of data and turn them into useful concepts, valuable insights, and data-based reasoning.

Making sense of data and making evidence-based decisions will include getting to the deeper meaning or significance of what is being communicated.

The public service will continue to administer the political will of the government of the day. This includes the type of advice, communications, and support on a daily basis that isn't that far off the *Yes Minister* style of government. It also means keeping good and clear records, be that of Ministerial meetings through to tens of thousands of decisions administered on their behalf every year. There might be more work brought about through the 24/7 news and Twitter cycles, and those decisions may be recorded digitally, but it is essentially a similar set of capabilities.

The accountability of public servants will become more obvious due to the potential speed of delivery and the very visible nature of digital services. What will change is the ability to manage a new set of accountabilities for personal performance in an environment that will generally be faster, more open, and exposed to public and media scrutiny.

Such accountability contributes to the need for resilience. One senior Federal Government leader, who had just completed the first phase of transforming an agency, admitted that digital transformation, and getting it to succeed in government, is like 'being punched in the face 50 times over'. As they pointed out, you just have to 'get on and ignore those defensive punches from people who will never want to change'.

So, resilience means knowing when to listen, when to ignore, when to recharge, and when to get into the ring and fight.

Joined to these are emerging capabilities, which the analysis in this chapter has reinforced. Digital, data, and technology literacy require public servants to possess the competence and confidence to use, interact with, and contribute to improving digital services and products. In the words of the Senate inquiry into digital services, 'Digital work should be considered part of the "core responsibility of the public service".[412]

It does not mean abandoning pens and paper, but it does mean adopting more of a so-called design mindset. It means problem solving when designing tasks, processes, and work environments to produce desired outcomes (solutions), often using digital technology.

It means expressing ideas as working things. We should never have to hear senior leaders in a public service organisation say, 'I don't do technology' as arguably a badge of honour.

Leaders should be able to understand what the terms on a figure like this (figure 12) mean and, broadly, have some perspective on whether their organisation should buy, build, or adapt these.

It doesn't mean they have to learn to code. For us, that would be like saying you need to retrain as a bricklayer in order to renovate your house. But you would do the research to (broadly) understand what it would take to do it yourself, how much to pay someone to do it, how long it should take, to what quality, and what the responsibilities should be for the safe and equitable use.

Figure 12: Skills for a new era

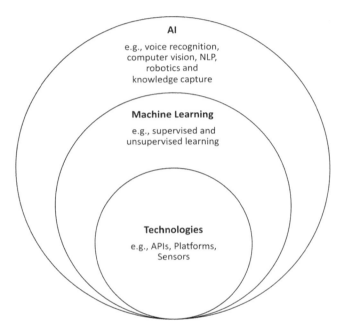

This means, for example, using data: having the confidence as to what data sets are being put into big data analytics, or to know what questions to ask to inform training an AI, and then using evidence to drive decision making, rather than guesswork. They also need to develop the tools to investigate the impacts of others' algorithms in any sector, including being able to investigate the behaviours of decision making, using machines on equality and diversity.

The focus on teams and working in larger, more complex combinations of skill, capability, cross-functions, and expertise are already becoming features of the public service toolkit.

Multi-disciplinary means the ability to work with, and be flexible within, a team comprising different backgrounds, skills, employers, and disciplines. These should ideally reflect their user base. There will be much more nuance in the blend of critical thinking and the enablement and execution required for problem solving.

Example of a digital public service team

A multi-disciplinary team[413] in a modern public sector setting is likely to include this kind of skill mix:

- A senior delivery lead (Senior Executive Service level 1 or 2) responsible for delivery of the new service or change, often with experience in that particular part of the business and/or digital experience
- A product manager who develops and owns the vision for the product, and oversees a development team consisting of the below roles
- Front-end developer(s) who code/configure the screens people see and use, and solve technical problems
- Back-end developer(s) who code/configure the processes that sit behind the scenes, including any data hand-offs with other systems
- User researchers who determine and then test with a variety of real users whether the service meets their needs A service designer who ensures that the full end-to-end service or transaction is designed; i.e., not just the tech bit, and who gets the user through the service; may work with a dedicated content designer who produce the words, images, and graphics
- Product owner(s) often coming from the parts of the entities being impacted, representing their needs, including ensuring policy and legal compliance, and also representing the needs of the end users (such as citizens)
- A delivery manager, often a project manager by training, who is responsible for resourcing, scheduling, and ensuring delivery happens, including managing commercial suppliers

These teams may be assisted by policy leads, business analysts who map processes, cyber security experts (or so-called ethical hackers whose task it is to find chinks in Government's IT armour before the unethical hackers get there), change managers, communications people, and legal advisers.

This is the model of digital delivery advocated by the UK's GDS and which has now spread all over the world, including to Australia's DTA and the governments in NSW and Queensland. It will take time to develop/find people who get to know how to work in government, including the nuances of policy, but who are also adept at product delivery.

The most senior digital person is likely to be a Chief Digital Officer (CDO) or CIO. In turn, they may have dotted-line responsibilities to cross-government versions who, on paper at least, have decision-making and leadership responsibilities focused on ensuring consistency of digital services and the development of whole-of-government solutions. The most progressive organisations have these people on their boards or executive committees.

Figure 13: Sample Chief Digital Officer responsibilities

- Overall, to provide organisational leadership for governance, strategy, and policy for ICT across a government agency, department, or cluster
- Define, communicate, and deliver digital strategy, working with effective partnerships across the organisation, government, and with industry, as well as with Ministers and influential sector leaders
- Chair decision-making bodies for ICT, including making investment decisions/recommendations and providing assurance
- Direct budgetary responsibility of $40m+; line management of Executive Directors and multiple employees
- Possible direct operational responsibility for infrastructure services ranging from physical infrastructure to digital services
- Possible specific responsibilities for procurement, risk, privacy, data, security, and cyber

Source: Adapted by the authors from NSW Government and UK Government job adverts

We anticipate newer roles to start to appear in government, including those relating to algorithm management, more on developing content that works for voice-activated devices, and a host of roles relating to the adoption of AI, blockchain, etc. Some, like Stakeholder Manager, will be rebranded as Ecosystem Manager.

Lessons from the example

Work should be delivered more quickly, but not more than necessary to ensure sufficient time to think clearly about the issues and their implications. Sometimes, a little haste and less speed, and time to deliberate and think, will be the hallmark of good work.

Speed is not the simple or singular answer to everything in organisations, least of all in the public sector. But it will become an increasingly important dimension of the factors that public servants will have to weigh and respond to in their work styles.

Technology and tools mean that the evidence and other considerations to make decisions can be ascertained at a faster speed than previously. That includes iteration – how you incrementally and experimentally develop policies, products, and services – and ensure that you meet user needs through testing, observing, and launching MVPs with them. That means being comfortable sharing things that aren't finished, may not work, or get thrown away.

Speed shouldn't mean that checks and balances are lost. As several Chief Digital Officers have said to us, once you've gone through the effort of setting up and getting your digital capabilities running, you still need to ensure you really know what problem you are solving for; that it is really easy to do the wrong thing in a digital way.[414] As well, it should be said, to do it very quickly.

Storytelling could easily get wrapped up in communications. This misses the point about how important it is to be able to explain change in a compelling way that builds support. For one of the digital services that one of the authors (Simon) worked on in the UK, the commitment and output of the team rapidly changed when we altered the narrative from one about meeting a ministerial target to one about what the National Health Service meant to people. This, in turn, needed to be told within the wider context of change, including the move to digital services, and in this case, an immigration policy designed to recoup the cost of treating foreigners.

Having enhanced emotional intelligence will be vital, because digital government lives and dies by the ability to understand user needs, including hard-to-reach users of government services, to develop high-quality relationships within multi-disciplinary teams, and develop partnerships and alliances with a variety of organisations.

A new piece of government machinery

Let's assume for a moment that the arguments set out in this book, and the framing of the promise of digital transformation, are accepted. As a result, there is broad agreement with the notion that the story is only half told, and as a consequence, the political and bureaucratic stars are aligned to mobilise a shift in tone and intensity for the next phase of the work.

The question arises: Who would do that work? Where in government would responsibility lie for leading and executing this work? Who would get the job? In the Federal Government here, in Australia, there are a number of choices.

One would be to give the work to the existing or an augmented Digital Transformation Agency (DTA). After all, the digital transformation of government is its mandate and purpose, so it would make sense to anchor the work here.

Another option would be to ask the Department of the Prime Minister and Cabinet (PM&C) to take on the task, given its remit at the centre and highest level of the bureaucracy and its sector-wide responsibilities. The scale and intensity of the transformation agenda, as it has been spelled out here, is sufficiently ambitious to warrant that kind of focus and leadership. It also plays directly to the role of the PM&C Secretary as the Head of the Public Service, at least for the moment. (It is likely the APS independent review will make some recommendations about clarifying the role of the head of PM&C and the head of the Australian Public Service Commission (APSC) as overall leaders of the service.)

A third option would be to ask the Australian Public Service Commission (APSC) to take on the work and lead its design and implementation. After all, the Commission carries responsibility for the people and leadership issues across the service, as well as for the legislative and operational base for most of its workforce. And the digital transformation project, as we've conceived it here, will have profound implications for the culture, skills, and capability of the public service, which is the APSC's bread and butter.

Yet another option would be to locate the bulk of responsibility for the work with the Department of Finance, another key central agency which has oversight of the main resource management and planning legislation for the public service, the Public Governance, Performance and Accountability Act 2013.[415] If there's one thing we can be certain about, digital transformation on the scale implied by the full story we're advocating here will have big implications for many of the resource, procurement, and financial management fundamentals that underpin the work of the public sector.

We suspect you could replicate this kind of analysis for pretty much any jurisdiction of government, either around Australia or across the world. And what it reinforces is that, when it comes to settling on the right place to drive a full digital transformation agenda of this sort, there are plenty of institutional places it could live, but nowhere it would be at home.

Given especially the analysis we've set out in this chapter about where all of this lands, in terms of the changing work of the public sector, and how the public sector will have to change the way it works (and already is), we're concluding with some suggestions about where 'home' might be for the transformation agenda, summed up at its simplest with these two insights.

Increasingly, it is becoming clear that we don't just need a Digital Transformation Agency (or Digital Central Unit equivalent) but, for this work, a national Government Transformation Agency.

And the implication is that what we really need is not another machinery of government change. What we need is change of government machinery.

We can get a feel for what might be necessary by looking at a couple of countries where the digital transformation story is generally considered to have progressed pretty well.

Singapore's Government has established a Smart Nation and Digital Government Office as part of the Prime Minister's Office, with the stated ambition 'to enable the government to have a more integrated, responsive strategy and processes for Smart Nation and Digital Government'.[416]

On the other side of the world, the Danish Government has embedded in the national Finance Ministry the Agency for Digitisation. Its description includes the ambition to be 'the engine driving public sector collaboration in the efforts to digital transform the public sector. The Danish digital transformation effort is therefore based on a unique common responsibility to embrace the digital mindset and the vision of a digital public sector.'[417]

What both structures attempt in institutional design is an ambition to put the digital transformation dimension deep into a larger agenda for government transformation. But while both examples are instructive, each still carries a sense of a separate digital agenda – transformational in ambition and reach, for sure – that remains somehow outside of the bigger question of how government itself works and behaves.

A similar example on a different scale comes from the NSW Government in Australia. After the March 2019 election, the new government decided to combine its digital transformation agenda with a 'customer service' strategy and associated machinery changes (a separate Minister, a separate, new departmental structure, and a new Customer Service Cabinet sub-committee through which all significance decisions that impact service to citizens will now have to go); the logic of the arguments we've been presenting in this book suggest the need for something similar.

The logic of the transformation 'diamond' and the emergence of the 'new public work' suggests the need for a new piece of government machinery, which we have called a Government Transformation Agency, or GTA, as a working title.

The GTA would comprise equal measures of:

- Deep, senior, and highly credible mainstream public policy and public administration strategy, research, analytics, and delivery (the sort of expertise and long experience that often still comes armed with reflexive scepticism about all things digital and tech)
- Similarly, deep and eclectic digital and technology strategy, design, and delivery, including a health combination of those with large institutional experience and exposure and those who bring more modern skills in agile working, design, and an ability to experiment and test to learn
- Significant exposure to the changing tasks of platform approaches to better service delivery in and outside of government, with a necessary obsession with experience and the values and impact of digital creativity from the perspective of users and citizens
- Considerable expertise in contemporary approaches to cultural change and organisational reformation, including especially strong exposure to new methods and approaches to using variations on the 'social movement' building expertise of those who have learned how to patiently build hearts-and-minds change and communication strategies
- Finally, an array of financial modelling and analysis, data science, project management, and evaluation skills and experience.

In the federal sphere in Australia, this kind of talent mash-up might be expected to source people from PM&C, the PSC, the DTA, and some of the larger delivery agencies already working on platform plays for whole-of-government reform (especially the Department of Human Services, or Service Australia as it was renamed after the federal election in May 2019).

The GTA would report directly to the Prime Minister and be governed by a mixture of a high-level Cabinet committee and a small group of very senior Secretaries. It could also include several carefully chosen external representatives who bring with them some capacity to prosecute this kind of hybrid institutional reformation.

If we wanted to be more ambitious, we would go further and suggest that the GTA should include representation from State and local government too, perhaps connecting to, and helping to change the mandate of, the Australian Digital Council (the Council of all Ministers who represent digital across the Commonwealth). The GTA model could add considerably to the Council's purpose, 'to establish proposals for better cross-government collaboration on data and digital transformation to drive smarter service delivery and improved policy outcomes.'[418] The intention of the GTA would be, as it is for the Council, to grow Australia's digital capability, but within the context of a larger remit.

Consistent with the framework outlined in this book, the GTA's purpose would be to lead the development of a new 'theory of the business' across all levels of government in Australia and the work of the public sector in the digital era, based on a mission that is consistent with the conditions of, and capabilities required for, the new public work.

It is reasonable to ask why a venture like a GTA would not encounter some of the same barriers to effectiveness that have undermined the full impact of the DTA.

Of course, at one level there are no guarantees that an initiative like the GTA wouldn't suffer a process of institutional resistance and the erosion of its scope. Any kind of transformative change process in any institutional setting is fraught.

But in this case, there are a few conditions that might make a difference.

One is the scale and urgency of the venture itself. If it's right that Australia confronts something of an 'emergency' in its digital transformation agenda so far as it impacts the work and performance of government, there is a chance that timing, and necessity, will provide at least some of the momentum that has been missing. Our collective ability to pull off some of the big changes we discuss here is being severely tested. Our collective unwillingness to fail might provide a measure of insurance against resistance and erosion.

Another factor is the way in which the fuller transformation ambition joins the strategy and delivery pieces in a much more explicit and pragmatic way. How we conceive of the task and write its combined transactional and transformational brief will matter.

And a third factor is the ability to seek out, connect, and therefore amplify the work of those pioneers and entrepreneurs, often working in projects that remain disconnected and unseen, who are busy inventing aspects of the transformed future in the midst of the current conditions. Our call for a 'national mission' to take on this venture at a suitable scale and intensity recognises that we're not starting from a blank sheet. That work is being done, but not fast or widely enough to make the difference it needs to.

The analogy isn't perfect, but the intent of the GTA idea is captured at least in part by the advent, in very different settings, of the notion of setting up a parallel, or 'X', structure outside of, but driven by, the main business it is designed to disrupt.

One example is WooliesX, established by leading Australian retailer Woolworths to combine its digital, e-commerce, data, and customer divisions into a single structure.[419]

Another example, along the same lines but in a very different setting, is NHS-X in the UK. NHS-X was announced as an initiative to 'take forward digital transformation in the NHS, allowing patients and staff to benefit from the latest digital systems and technology'.[420]

The focus of these initiatives is consolidation of digital investments, coupled in the case of WooliesX with data and customer service (not unlike the combination of assets and functions that the NSW Government has drawn together in the new Department of Customer Service) to drive new levels of service and business impact.

For NHS-X, the motivation is similar, driven by a concern that digitally driven change across the NHS has been too slow, 'because responsibility for digital, data and tech has been split across multiple agencies, teams and organisations.' NHS-X will change this by 'bringing together all the levers of policy, implementation and change for the first time.'[421]

What makes these examples interesting is the way in which structural and organisational separation from the main business, combined with integrating a mix of digital, data, policy, strategy, and funding responsibilities, provides a method to accelerate change.

It isn't exactly the same for the GTA, but there is a sense in which it might become something of an 'Gov-X' organisational structure, tying together the same mix of skills and functions that offer more chance that its combined resources and sharper organisational focus might lead to a greater sense of purpose and urgency in designing, and then delivering, new standards of service and engagement with customers and citizens.

The point of the proposal is not to argue in favour of a new piece of organisational infrastructure for its own sake, or as a gesture. Indeed, the proposal is useful in many ways, not because it is something we want to establish precisely in this form, or indeed any time soon, but because it embodies a few principles of institutional change that we think should be at the heart of the digital transformation process.

- We need an urgent confluence of high-level political leadership from Australia (Prime Ministers and Premiers/Chief Ministers, not just Ministers), deep and senior policy and institutional bureaucratic leadership (head of PM&C, head of Premiers Departments), senior technology leadership (CIOs, CDOs, the work of existing digital transformation agencies), and a good number of innovators and entrepreneurs and operational staff who bring deep expertise from experience and front-line delivery.
- Strategy and delivery can't be separated. The trick is to keep high strategy and big ambition tied to design, delivery, and capability.
- Policy and service delivery can't be separated either. The ambition is to get beyond the sense, which often pervades much of the public sector's policy and leadership community, that digital transformation is something done to them, occasionally for them, but rarely with and by them.
- Adoption of the digital transformation principles set out in this chapter
- Serious consideration of our manifesto and associated suggested initiatives set out in chapter 5.

There are two ways you can achieve the outcome we're aiming for with this proposal.

One way is to set up a new piece of machinery with a mandate and a level of deep and sustained political leadership that signals the intention for change at a pitch and intensity that drives performance.

The other way is to give effect to the principles of government transformation, which we've sketched here, and make them work within and across the current structures and systems. But even then, the need for the highest level of highly visible and energetic leadership at political and bureaucratic levels for the intent and ambition implied by this approach is inescapable.

Perhaps this project's real value is to call out the anxiety that we, and others, have that, for too long, the significance and potential impact of the digital transformation project has been hampered by a level of political and bureaucratic leadership and investment of personal and institutional capital that has been variable, to be polite. Completely and dangerously inadequate might be a blunter way to put it.

So, by all means discount the practical considerations implied by a literal reading of this recommendation. But don't discount the importance of the larger message about the need for more and better political and policy leadership, which it implies.

Summary: Three big implications

What this chapter has argued is that big shifts are happening in and around the public sector that will have significant implications for the work of the public sector and the way the public sector works.

Those shifts are driven in large measure by the forces for digital transformation, which are also key to how well government, and others involved in the new public work, respond. As we have pointed out before, digital transformation is a big part of the solution to the challenges it has played a big part in bringing about.

We think there are three big implications for the future direction and impact of that transformation.

The first is a change in the nature and deployment of **public power and authority**.

Public power and authority will always lie at the heart of the work of government and the public sector. Many of the intractable problems and big risks – and some of the equally significant opportunities – of a changing world are making new demands on the formation, curation, and execution of public power and authority. How those powerful assets are conceived, wielded, and held appropriately accountable matters more than ever.

Digital transformation is changing the way those assets are formed, sustained, and deployed. They will increasingly be co-produced and subject to both constraints and amplification from a more complex mix of people and organisations, inside and outside government, from the interaction of whose values, expertise, and experience their value and impact derive.

The second implication is about the way in which **information and knowledge** are created, stored, used, and replenished.

The obvious point from our analysis is that both are becoming irreducibly team sports, relying on the capabilities of a much larger mix of people, a much more interesting mix of hard and soft knowledge, and of formal and informal and experiential knowledge.

Also, the speed, intensity, and legibility associated with information and knowledge creation and flow are all changing dramatically under the pressure of increasingly automated and autonomous digital capabilities

And finally, and in many ways at the bedrock of government's work and the work of the public sector, is the focus on **trust and legitimacy** as the currency of good government.

Digital transformation of government means little in the end if it doesn't mean measurable improvements, in the work that it changes and supports, in all three of these domains – public power, information and knowledge, and trust and legitimacy.

More efficient and convenient transactions in and with the public sector, fuelled by digital tools and platforms, won't count, in our view, as real transformation if there is declining trust in the integrity of government in the first place, and whose legitimacy, as a result, diminishes.

There seems little point investing in faster and more convenient transactions with a public sector that fewer trust and whose work is invested with steadily declining legitimacy. Digital transformation doesn't get 'there' until it embraces this doctrine at its heart.

Three important messages

There are three importance messages from this chapter:

First, digital transformation is already changing the work of the public sector and the way the public sector works. That process needs to go further and faster. If it doesn't feel as if the work of the public sector is changing very much, it's likely that what is happening is more akin to digital embroidery, not transformation.

Second, as much as the work of the public sector is changing, some elements of the new public work, which we are arguing is what digital transformation is both enabling and driving, reinforce enduring values like rigour, fairness, accountability, ethics, and independence. But if the public sector wants to hang on to those values and attributes, and, in the process, retain its relevance and the respect of the political and wider community, it will have to change.

Third, many of the changes in work and working we've covered in this chapter reflect new forms of digital working in particular, especially new ways to design and deliver services. But they also touch on important shifts to some of the traditional work of the public sector – policymaking, writing and enforcing legislation, regulation – which will also need to change to accommodate new methods of digital work.

Appendix: Summary of digital strategies

Digital Transformation Strategy,
Australian Federal Government (2018)

Stated Priorities: Government that is easy to deal with, Government that is informed by citizens, and government that is fit for the digital age; the ambition is to deliver world-leading digital services for the benefit of all Australians. Includes illustrative life journeys to bring to life what this will mean and feel like for Australians by 2025. More than 75 projects are listed from across the federal government, including those in discovery or at alpha stages, more established ones such as digital identity, Digital Service Standards, MyHealth Record, and the Digital Marketplace, and those that will be commenced (eCensus).

https://www.dta.gov.au/our-projects/strategies/digital-transformation-strategy

Digital NSW Designing for a Digital Future,
NSW Government (2017)

The NSW Government Digital Strategy brings together digital investment and deployment and policies to transform the lives of the people of NSW by designing policies and services that are smart, simple, and seamless. Services will be digital by default, designed around user needs, integrated and seamless and accessible. Technology is seen here as an enabler, along with cyber security, legislation, and delivery capability. Commitments in this 14-page document include to:

- Use digital ways to conduct business where previously prohibited by outdated legislation
- Co-design services with citizens
- Adopt a digital-by-default starting point
- Partner with industry to develop whole-of-government solutions

Unlike the DTA's strategy, it does set out the 'how' in more detail, although the roadmap of projects isn't included.

https://www.digital.nsw.gov.au

**Information Technology Strategy 2016–2020
Action Plan, Victoria Government (2016)**

Focused on an ICT vision of Better Information, Easier Engagement, Contemporary Technology, and Capable People. Provides authority, direction, principles, and guidance for the Government's strategic approach to information and data, digital engagement with citizens, effective use of information technology, and the building of capability to use information technology within the public service.

One of the few strategies to lead with a clear position on the 'how' of delivery, with a focus on what capabilities can be enabled by the cloud, including sharing, buying, and, finally, building (by government). Clear standards that are similar to many of the other strategies, including digital by default, co-design and citizen-centric and mobile first. Less detail on the specific projects compared to other documents, but does not claim to be a catchall document for the Victorian public service.

https://www.enterprisesolutions.vic.gov.au/wp-content/uploads/2017/07/Information-Technology-Strategy-2016-to-2020-Action-Plan-2017-2018-PDF.pdf

**Digitalist, Advancing our digital future: The Queensland
Digital Strategy 2017–2021, Australia, Queensland (2018)**

The ambition is to position Queensland as a leader in digital government, now and in the future. Imagery and commitments take account of both cities and rural demographics of the state. Focus is to deliver digital by default for customers of government, but also their workforce, to design and deliver digital services to an exceptional standard. Focus on collaboration with a clear acknowledgement that this Government does not have all the answers, and that also trust and connectivity will be vital components of success. Set of commitments based on digital strategy principles, such as making it easier to provide information to Government, with portals developed for schools and a new state-wide My Account to be released.

https://digitalist.initiatives.qld.gov.au

Digital WA: State ICT Strategy 2016–2020, Western Australia, Australia

The vision is to realise a simple and interconnected Government delivering effective community services focused on:

- Simplifying technology platforms, systems, and standards as part of a unified Government

- Connecting agencies and the community through digital services and system integration

- Informing decision makers, front-line employees and the public with quality data and analysis

Commitments to deliver a digital services portal, marketplace, and digital capabilities for public servants are similar to the other strategies.

The document feels more akin to previous ICT-style strategies, but does have more on the role of government digital services influencing innovation in the wider economy and the importance of this for economic competitiveness. The strategy also includes key performance indicators, such as stability, specific efficiency targets (10%), and capability maturity targets, something that the majority of comparative strategies either do not include or do so as a seemingly afterthought at the end of documents.

https://www.wa.gov.au/sites/default/files/2018-06/Digital%20WA%20State%20ICT%20Strategy.pdf

**Government Transformation Strategy 2017–2020,
UK, 2017**

Very detailed building on the original 'Digital by Default' strategy, which led
to the creation of the Government Digital Service in 2012. Outlines vision to
transform the relationship between citizens and the state through putting
more power in the hands of citizens and being more responsive to their
needs. More detailed commitments than previous versions, including to
transform front- and back-end services (business transformation), growing
the right skills and culture among people and leaders, making better use of
data, and to create, operate, iterate, and embed good use of shared platforms
and reusable business capabilities to speed up transformation.

The most comprehensive of any of the comparative strategies, including
specific commitments for delivery by 2020. The document ends with a vision
of what to build for, beyond that date, including sign posting what the sum
of delivery of these commitments will mean and could lead to, such as
changing how policy is made, benefiting from new technologies like AI, and
a continued commitment to services that meet user needs.

https://www.gov.uk/government/publications/government-transformation-
strategy-2017-to-2020

See the description of the Digital Central Units for references to the Danish,
Canadian, and Singaporean strategies. We recognise that South Australia,
Tasmania, and the Northern Territory also have digital strategies.

Chapter 5

Conclusion: Our Manifesto

The pace and intensity of digital transformation around the world offers a country like Australia a compelling invitation to keep up and stay connected to its leading edge.

But because of our size and relative economic and technology weight in the world, the temptation is to sit back and monitor developments, in areas like AI and data, for example, and then to 'fast follow' when action becomes unavoidable.

It's tempting to compare that strategy with the way aspects of climate change policy and broadband capability over the last decade or so have been engaged in Australia. Often, it seems that policy and investment decisions, and the implications across different sectors for related management and capability reforms, are driven by a view that we should do as little as we need to until we are forced to do more than we want to. That is often backed by arguments that as a 'middle' power, Australia can have little impact on a global scale and that it is therefore both inefficient and inappropriate to attempt anything more ambitious.

In the digital transformation space, we're confronted with similar choices. Stay on the edge and then catch up, reluctantly, when we have to, or pursue the economic and social dividend of staying up with the opportunities of the digital economy by making the necessary investments of money, expertise, and leadership when it is needed. Lead or follow – a perennial political conundrum.

We think Australia's size and place in the world, and especially in our region, whose digital transformation is in many respects leading the world anyway, gives us little choice. We must step up and be bold.

In that sense, we endorse the commitment in the OECD's Declaration on Public Sector Innovation, to which Australia is a signatory, that governments should 'recognise the benefits that can come from enabling experimentation in core systems – such as the use of digital technologies, budgeting, risk management, and reporting – and explore whether and how they can be achieved'.[422]

Sitting back and watching others move further ahead seems an odd choice for a country whose prosperity has typically drawn on a willingness to use leadership, invention, and energy to punch above our weight.

It is why our manifesto for digital transformation, which we set out at the start of this book and we've further detailed in this final chapter, embraces a new 'national mission' to drive exactly that ambition in this increasingly urgent and necessary task.

What we believe

This book is a call to action for a new 'national mission' for the digital transformation of government and the public sector in Australia at scale and speed, and with an intensity that matches its national significance as a vital investment for trust and inclusive prosperity.

The book argues that digital transformation across the public sector is a story missing half its plot.

It should not just be about cost and convenience, although it certainly needs to be about both. It should not just be about improving the customer and citizen experience of dealing with government, although it has to be centrally about that.

As well as these important 'business as usual' improvements to the way we govern, the way we do policy, and the way we design and deliver services, digital transformation should also be an opportunity to think about what 'business as unusual' might look like.

This book is an invitation to see digital transformation as a chance to rethink in quite fundamental ways the assumptions we make about the context, mission, and capabilities of the public sector, or, as we explain it, of public work in all of its variety and complexity. It should be an invitation to rethink the 'theory of the business' that is accepted with energetic creativity.

Below, we have set out 20 propositions that outline a bold vision to refocus and accelerate the digital transformation of government and the public service in Australia.

These propositions reflect what we believe. This book explains where they came from and why we think they're important. In this final chapter, we have expanded them with more explanation about their implications as well as some specific initiatives that could be undertaken.

Some context

Manifestos come is all shapes and sizes. But their purpose and intent tend to be similar. They set out a view of a possible (near) future that offers guidance and inspiration to motivate and sustain those willing to make common cause to achieve their goals.

Manifestos are an invitation, too, to join a larger cause whose ambitions are shared and respected.

The Cluetrain Manifesto

The Cluetrain Manifesto was one of the seminal statements of the early Internet era. Written initially in in 1998 on the Web, and then in 2000 as a book, it offers 95 theses (think Martin Luther, the Reformation, and the church door at Wittenberg Castle in 1517) whose individual and cumulative effect was to turn the potential of the emerging Internet era into a set of values and principles that its authors believed would guide decisions and behaviour in line with the new platform's best and highest aspirations.[423]

The Manifesto contains some powerful insights at the start of what its authors saw as a revolution, not just in marketing and business (which it was) but in a whole way of seeing the world. In that sense, its ambitions and prescriptions are both a valuable model for our work in this final chapter and a pointer to a similar set of ambitions in the context of digital transformation for government to change patterns of thinking and action based on new assumptions.

'A powerful global conversation has begun', the Cluetrain authors announced. 'Through the Internet, people are discovering and inventing new ways to share relevant knowledge with blinding speed. As a direct result, markets are getting smarter, ...and getting smarter faster than most companies.'[424]

They go on to explain that 'these markets are conversations'. But not conversations as most would be familiar. Those taking part in these new world-shaping conversations 'communicate in language that is natural, open, honest, direct, funny and often shocking'. And more, their 'human voice is unmistakably genuine. It can't be faked.'[425]

Manifestos are often ways to almost literally nail your colours to a mast that signals big shifts in underlying beliefs. Here, for example, are the headline versions of the first 10 of the Cluetrain's theses:

1. Markets are conversations.
2. Markets consist of human beings, not demographic sectors.
3. Conversations among human beings *sound* human. They are conducted in a human voice.
4. Whether delivering information, opinions, perspectives, dissenting arguments, or humorous asides, the human voice is typically open, natural, uncontrived.
5. People recognise each other as such from the sound of this voice.
6. The Internet is enabling conversations among human beings that were simply not possible in the era of mass media.
7. Hyperlinks subvert hierarchy.
8. In both *inter* networked markets and among *intra* networked employees, people are speaking to each other in a powerful new way.
9. These networked conversations are enabling powerful new forms of social organization and knowledge exchange to emerge.
10. As a result, markets are getting smarter, more informed, more organised. Participation in a networked market changes people fundamentally.

These headlines reflect ambitions for profound change in culture and practice of the sort we argue here are necessary for the digital transformation project to fulfil its highest ambitions and deepest impact.

The manifesto writers point out that the new digital world was ushering in more than a quicker and easier way to do something familiar – in this case, marketing and business–consumer connections. They were drawing a whole new architecture of human connection and interaction, from which traditional approaches to market engagement needed to rapidly learn, and to which it needed to adapt.

In 2015, a couple of the original authors, Doc Searls and David Weinberger, updated their work and added some 'new clues' about ways in which the original thesis could be adapted to the changes since its original publication.

Their update was prescient to the extent it picked some early warning signs about the likely impact, not so much of the Internet's failure to completely change the way we interact and connect but precisely because its overwhelming success was attracting newly energised 'Marauders' who understood only too well what was happening and viewed it 'as theirs to plunder, extracting our data and money from it, thinking that we are the fools.'[426] Shoshana Zuboff's unnerving investigation of exactly how this ethic of capture has played out in the rise of 'surveillance capitalism' is a more recent, very powerful rendition of this prediction.[427]

The Cluetrain authors explained to their fellow travellers that 'We have grown old together on the Internet. Time is short. We, the People of the Internet, need to remember the glory of its revelation so that we reclaim it now in the name of what it truly is.' 'The Internet is not a thing,' they remind us, 'any more than gravity is a thing. Both pull us together.'[428]

The Copenhagen Letter and Catalog

Another more recent example of a manifesto that has resonance for our work is the Copenhagen Letter and Catalog, drawn up over a couple of big technology conferences in Copenhagen (surprisingly) by a group of several hundred people anxious to define a distinct 'direction of travel' for the relationship between people and technology.[429]

This is an example whose relevance here is partly about form and focus and a way of turning some important ideas and aspirations for the future into accessible prescriptions.

But, like Cluetrain, the original letter and the later catalogue also contain insights whose salience in the context of the digital transformation of government and the public sector becomes more obvious the further you read through the principles.

The catalogue is built on the earlier Copenhagen letter, which was short and to the point:[430]

Copenhagen, 2017

To everyone who shapes technology today:

We live in a world where technology is consuming society, ethics, and our core existence.

It is time to take responsibility for the world we are creating. Time to put humans before business. Time to replace the empty rhetoric of 'building a better world' with a commitment to real action. It is time to organise, and to hold each other accountable.

Tech is not above us. It should be governed by all of us, by our democratic institutions. It should play by the rules of our societies. It should serve our needs, both individual and collective, as much as our wants.

Progress is more than innovation. We are builders at heart. Let us create a new Renaissance. We will open and nourish honest public conversation about the power of technology. We are ready to serve our societies. We will apply the means at our disposal to move our societies and their institutions forward.

Let us build from trust. Let us build for true transparency. We need digital citizens, not mere consumers. We all depend on transparency to understand how technology shapes us, which data we share, and who has access to it. Treating each other as commodities from which to extract maximum economic value is bad, not only for society as a complex, interconnected whole but for each and every one of us.

Design open to scrutiny. We must encourage a continuous, public, and critical reflection on our definition of success as it defines how we build and design for others. We must seek to design with those for whom we are designing. We will not tolerate design for addiction, deception, or control. We must design tools that we would love our loved ones to use. We must question our intent and listen to our hearts.

Let us move from human-centered design to humanity-centered design. We are a community that exerts great influence. We must protect and nurture the potential to do good with it. We must do this with attention to inequality, with humility, and with love. In the end, our reward will be to know that we have done everything in our power to leave our garden patch a little greener than we found it.

Looking back on these manifestos isn't just an interesting piece of historical context. These are bold and imaginative statements of intent and direction for digital transformation which, although emerging in very different contexts, speak in many ways to the same values and priorities we have set out in this book. They bear some study in their own right as part of the current ambition for a deeper and more thorough Australian digital revolution across government and the public sector.

The Digital 9 (D9) Charter

Another relevant is example is that of the D9 nations.

Many of the Digital Central Units described in this book early on recognised that what they were doing was not unique and that there is much to be learned from their global counterparts.

The UK took the lead, convening the Digital Nations 5 in 2014 with Estonia, Israel, New Zealand, and South Korea. Canada and Uruguay joined the group in February 2018, and Mexico and Portugal joined the following November to make the Digital 9, or the D9.

This collaborative network has the shared goal of harnessing digital technology and new ways of working to improve citizens' lives. They have signed up to a charter of cooperation covering commitments to user needs, open standards, collaboration, and wider points on teaching children to code.[431]

This summarises the Charter signed in November 2018:

1. User needs – the design of public services for the citizen
2. Open standards – a commitment to credible royalty-free open standards to promote interoperability
3. Open source – future government systems, tradecraft, standards and manuals are created as open source and are shareable between members

4. Open markets – in government procurement, create true competition for companies regardless of size. Encourage and support a start-up culture and promote growth through open markets

5. Open government (transparency) – be a member of the Open Government Partnership and use open licences to produce and consume open data

6. Connectivity – enable an online population through comprehensive and high-quality digital infrastructure

7. Teach children to code – commitment to offer children the opportunity to learn to code and build the next generation of skills

8. Assisted digital – a commitment to support all its citizens to access digital services

9. Commitment to share and learn – all members commit to work together to help solve each other's issues wherever they can

Aside from annual conferences, this has translated in the sharing of tools, techniques, and even code, e.g., New Zealand's Govt.nz is based on the code from GOV.UK. (It is interesting that Australia's application was apparently rejected because the DTA were judged not to be meeting the required standards, and states such as NSW have been told they are unable to join on their own.)

Our manifesto: what we believe

This book is a call to action, building on what we have done so far, for a new 'national mission' for the digital transformation of government and the public sector in Australia at scale and speed and with an intensity that matches the its national significance for trust and inclusive prosperity.

A new theory of the business for governing and the work of the public sector (chapter 1)

1. Progress with digital transformation in government and the public sector in Australia has stalled, jeopardising its full promise and potential. Australia's progress to this point suggests that while we've often hit the target in some of the digitally based transactional and operational improvements to the way we deliver, we are in danger of missing the point. Far from keeping up, we are falling behind, and there is little

chance we will meet the stated ambition to become a top-three digital government, compared to our global peers.

2. We need to shift our focus from technology modernisation to meeting citizen (customer) expectations of the performance of government in a digital age. The prize is the restoration of trust and legitimacy in government and the ability to harness the power and creativity of the public sector for inclusive prosperity.

3. We define digital transformation as a way of seeing and rethinking the entire business of governing, government, and the work of the public service, including to better serve citizens and customers, in a democratic society and across all levels of government. It is a lens through which to reconsider the nature of that work, its enduring foundations, and its disruption in a very different and rapidly changing (digital) world.

4. The 'theory of the business' for governing and public work is changing. At the heart of the new theory of the business for digitally transformed public work is a mission that is less concerned with the accumulation and management of public power and authority and more concerned with the assembly of collective intelligence to collaboratively solve problems. That is a hugely exciting prospect for public servants. The point of digital transformation is to help the public sector discover, embed, and then live that new theory. Unless it's cast in that light, digital transformation progress will remain stalled.

A changing world (chapter 2)

5. Digital transformation only makes sense if it also helps to make sense of the intersection of a changing world with changing technology, the changing role and purpose of government, and the changing work of the public sector. This should include, but go beyond, making service, policy, and regulation as simple, fast, and convenient as they can and need to be.

6. Australia can't afford to 'wait and see' what happens in the rest of the world. It needs to use digital transformation to urgently rethink the underlying theory of the business – aligning changing assumptions

about context, mission, and capabilities – for success in the digital global economy, for a stronger and more accountable democracy, and to dramatically improve the effectiveness of government and public work in Australia. Nothing less should be expected from a public sector that aspires to global leadership.

Digital technology: Current and future tools, and methods & Digital Central Units (chapter 3)

7. No longer should people need to spend their spare time working out how to complete transactions using complicated and disconnected government websites, filling in long forms, or waiting on hold. Citizens expect to experience the same quality of interactions in their dealings with government as they do in other parts of their digital lives. The technology, funding, and delivery methods are available so that services can be joined up, responsive, and experience-focused around citizen needs and expectations. These include simplicity and convenience, flexibility, renewal, and a proper concern for privacy and safety. Where it is happening, it needs to accelerate and scale with urgency. Where it isn't, it should be.

8. The digital transformation of government is not just about technology. It is relevant for every public servant from the department-based policy makers to people working on the front line. Of course, the technology has to be done exceptionally well, and that is often more complex and demanding than we sometimes assume. But its real value is the way in which it offers the opportunity to rethink the way we govern and do public work, including the opportunity to develop new operating models (assumptions, beliefs, values, and behaviours). If it's not doing that, it's probably not transforming.

9. Digital transformation is no longer the preserve of the digital or tech teams or 'Digital Central Units', vital though they remain to the transformation project. Nor is it sufficient to rely on a few visionary and energetic mandarins prepared to invest some of their personal political and institutional capital to drive a few pockets of great performance that occasionally hit the 'delight' button.

10. Opportunities from the use of new technologies such as artificial intelligence (AI) in the public service needs to be embraced. Realising these opportunities as well as confronting the risks, impact on work and employment implications of AI requires significant attention and Australia needs dedicated (new) institutions to do this to keep up with our peers such as the UK and US. This includes moving towards responsive and personalised services enabling government to help citizens, e.g., telling them where they are entitled to rebates or savings. There should also be a focus on how these can lead to more fulfilling public service jobs and be used to drive clever but fair and truly accountable new ways to solve problems.

11. Making more data open and investing in public servants' capabilities to analyse and interact with data is essential to fulfil the potential of using it to create better services and to solve problems. This must be combined with an instinct for open and legible government and a high degree of ethics, privacy and accountability.

12. The security of data and transactions is at the heart of the relationships between citizens, businesses and government. Cybersecurity has to become a more central and strategic consideration for public service leaders. Appropriate levels of security and privacy controls across every service transaction and relationship in digital government are the basic stakes to play effectively in the transformation process. It's not just a concern for technology leaders and specialists nor a 'tick box' compliance function.

13. Australia's investment in, and curation of, the necessary public digital infrastructure that will enable and amplify the process of digital transformation will have to be increasingly national, integrated and shared. Done properly this will require billions of dollars of investment and new government machinery to make this happen. This will be a major national endeavour, as significant and visible as public physical infrastructure, such as roads and airports, is to the development of Australia.

14. The public service of the future will make much greater use of platform models and the creation of the infrastructure and enabling tools which should be common and shared across different levels of government and, often, with the corporate and non-government sectors too.

Changing the work of the public sector and the way the public sector works (chapter 4)

15. The Council of Australian Governments and every level of government in Australia need to dedicate time and resources to renovating the model of government services to fit the digital era. The work of government and the public sector, and the way governments and the public sector work, are both changing. This is due in large measure to the impact of digital tools, methods and culture that are also a central part of the emergence of the new public work.

16. There is a strong link between the perception and experience by citizens of government's competence and capability in their service transactions and their willingness to invest deeper levels of trust in government itself. Failing to understand the contribution of competence in basic service transactions to trust and confidence risks eroding both.

17. We should not underestimate the considerable effort and resources required to do good transformation work that changes things and sticks. Effective digital government transformation of government and the work of the public sector needs to focus on:

   • Deeply ingraining that customer outcomes which benefit citizens, communities, and businesses as the focus of performance indicators and transformation matter most, not activities and outputs.
   • Remuneration, status and performance management systems should change to focus on the number of customers served or transactions overseen and move away from previous symbols of power such as the number of people they are in 'command' of or budget size.
   • Delivering new value at a faster pace with a 'trial-test-learn' mindset without over-planning or taking an overly purist design approach

but with the appropriate levels of consultation, risk management, and consideration.

- Creating whole-of-government platforms enable consistent experiences and can easily be scaled to respond to rising demand with little additional cost. Examples include websites, payment, and identity platforms. Such a platform approach stops departments' (and potentially state and federal governments') wasteful investments in building multiple versions of the same capability.
- Public servants should, at least once a year, spend in-depth time with the citizens, businesses, institutions, and communities with which they interact to develop better empathy so that policy and decision-making bears some resemblance to the contours of people's lives, their experience of government interactions, and expectations.
- Much more transparency about performance and impact by using publicly available customer service performance dashboards which show the quality of services provided in real time (including prominently in government buildings) and open collaboration and development of (non-security-sensitive) projects.
- Adopting service standards as long as they are pragmatically applied, are not digital-specific, and are focused on meeting customer (citizen) needs.
- Changing funding models to help improve the speed and flexibility with which services and expertise can be procured for projects that include rapid, agile learning and experimentation at one end of a spectrum and long-term, multi-jurisdictional, shared infrastructure projects at the other.

18. The practice of leadership in the public sector should demonstrate the same collaborative, open, human-centred and 'platform' characteristics that increasingly define the public sector in a digital age. Public leaders need to create and holds spaces in their organisations that allow creativity, innovation and agility to flourish, including the need to develop new measures of performance against which to evaluate their teams.

19. Public service learning and capability programs require a massive overhaul to reflect the need to dramatically re-skill the workforce

while blending these with enduring skills of good public work. Tens of thousands of current public servants will rapidly need to learn new skills, such as human-centred design, storytelling, and digital ways of working focused on adaptability, transdisciplinary, and self-organising collaboration, working in the open and driving speed to value. Learning methods such as bite-sized modules on accessible, shared platforms, on-the-job coaching, public service academies, and training courses, as well as through schools, TAFE, and universities, all need to be updated, leveraging the best of global resources and used across Australia. Individual public servants will also share some of the responsibility for developing their own skills.

20. Public servants will need specific help to become more comfortable with sensible risk and intelligent failure associated with problem solving and delivering new value at a faster pace with a 'trial-test-learn' mindset. New ways are needed to reinforce this shift through different rewards built into performance management systems.

Respect and ambition

For those in government and the public sector, it can sometimes seem as if technologists have a poor understanding of the complexities and nuances with which all public work is constrained. That can come across as a mixture of arrogance and disrespect, as if the proponents of digital transformation, or any of the earlier waves of technology's role in government, disregard the essential nature of a representative system of democratic government.

Ministers and citizens can't be ignored (no matter how frustrating that might be) in favour of technocratic and, these days, more automated and 'intelligent' systems that effectively undermine deeply held notions of political and institutional accountability.

We hope we've made it clear from our approach and by virtue of the different paths we have both taken through our engagement with government over many years that we are certainly not advocating some kind of new digital politics. In fact, we think the transformation agenda we're proposing, and the call to action around the manifesto we're issuing with this book, represent an act of deep respect for the complexity and contests of good government and the complexity of public work.

But showing respect doesn't mean a diminished ambition for the transformation agenda around the uses and values of digital thinking and practice. We'd argue it is because both us have learned to respect the work of government that we believe that anything less than the fullest and highest ambition for real and deep digital transformation would itself stand as an act of disrespect.

Initiatives

Manifestos are fine. They can stir the blood and call forth the energy and motivation necessary to sustain big change. And they fuel a sense of what's possible in a future that is compelling and achievable, but right now a little out of reach.

The question in the end, though, is: What is to be done?

We've set out here 10 initiatives that, at different levels of government and across the wider national community working together, are pieces of work that we think will amplify and accelerate the digital transformation project for government and the public sector.

1. The Council of Australian Governments (COAG) should articulate and commit to a clear and practical ambition for Australia to lead the world in the digital transformation of government and the public sector in pursuit of the larger and bolder ambition to transition from the current to a new, more relevant and apt theory of the business for government in the digital era.

    That commitment should come armed with a compelling and accessible analysis of the social, political, and economic benefits for Australia to position itself as a leader in the digital economy, and with a program of work that matches specific and well-targeted objectives with a strategy for collaborative design and delivery and a set of measures against which to monitor progress and test performance, e.g., the real-world impact on customer service for citizens and for businesses.

2. Establish a new national organisation, the Government Transformation Authority (GTA), that draws together all levels of government, the private sector, the start-up community, and the community sector to drive a national mission that establishes Australia as a world leader in digital

transformation of government and the public sector, based on a new theory of the business and associated operating models for governing and the work of the public sector in the digital era.

The national GTA should combine policy, strategy, people and skills, and digital capability and expertise, including many of the functions and responsibilities currently divided between the national and state versions of digital agencies, central agencies (PM&C, Finance, DPC), the Public Service Commission, and aspects of the work of major line agencies in areas like health, human services, education, and tax/revenue.

3. Establish a mission-driven innovation project to pursue global leadership in digital transformation of government and the public sector, with a clear mission, purpose, and a set of goals, targets, and timelines that are ambitious and pragmatic.

4. As part of the new mission, convene conversations across Australia to bring together leading thinkers and practitioners in digital transformation with citizens and businesses to create momentum and energy for a bold plan to shape and implement a new way of working for government and the public sector.

5. Use the national conversation to test and evolve a set of principles for digital transformation that reflect and reinforce the evolution of a new theory of the business that better aligns the contexts, mission, and capabilities of government and the public sector for the digital era. This should include a 'trial, test, and learn' way of working within an appropriate authorising environment.

6. Put a significantly amplified and energised open-government movement and practice at the heart of the emerging theory of the business for a digital-transformed government and public sector. This would include digital performance dashboards for every service provided by governments in Australia and select a named, accountable public service leader to lead them.

7. Create a national Digital Infrastructure Commission and fund to drive the development of shared platform capabilities across Australian

government at all levels so that, increasingly, Australia can call on a stock of digital platforms as national assets, tools, and methods that can be used by multiple services, programs, and initiatives.

This is likely to include considerable investment and focus on AI capabilities. Likely examples, to be developed in a secure cloud environment, include identity verification, single digital presence (websites), payments, notifications, data registers, APIs, and associated components upon which modern, user-centric digital services can easily be built and updated, ideally organised around life journeys.

8. Create a suite of tools and practices for public procurement and business-case development that can be shared across jurisdictions to improve the speed and flexibility with which services and expertise can be funded and procured for projects that include rapid, agile learning and experimentation at one end of a spectrum and long-term, multi-jurisdictional, shared infrastructure projects at the other.

9. Develop new approaches to digital skills development and learning that includes long-term training and education in new skills and knowledge and much more rapid, just-in-time learning that more effectively matches what public servants and Parliamentarians need to learn and enables collective intelligence, and where they can source the necessary learning opportunities in the public, private, or non-profit sectors.

10. Establish a new AI and Data Commission or similar body, drawing on the best examples of similar bodies in Australia and around the world, to accelerate the rate and quality of learning, analysis, and practical implementation of more effective, ethical, and safety approaches to the growing use of data and automation at the heart of new ways of working for government and the public sector.

Some practical questions

One of the practical implications of the shift we advocate in this final chapter, especially through these 10 initiatives, is a list of questions that anyone thinking about digital transformation projects in government should be asking.

For example:

- Is the proposed investment going to result in 'doing digital' (basically, adding digital tools and methods to an existing, unchanged, underlying process or practice) or 'being digital' (where access to digital tools and methods allows the underlying process or practice to be re-designed or replaced)?
- Does the proposed investment introduce new ways of working for the public sector that improve efficiency, lift productivity, or provide the opportunity for more responsive, human-centred service, care, or support?
- How does the investment in digital transformation change the experience of service, care, or support for citizens and businesses? What will they notice, and why is it important?
- How does the proposed investment in digital capability help government to respond more effectively to a major external risk or opportunity?
- Does the investment in new digital capability result in higher trust and a deeper sense of confidence and legitimacy about the role and performance of government and the public sector?
- Will the proposed investment attract, or grow, the right mix of leadership, design, and execution talent and skill to get the work done?

There are inevitably going to be other questions people can think of that turn the desire for transformation into a test of relevance and impact. As with the rest of this book, we're hopeful that others will join the process of thinking through what those might be.

Where would we start?

One of the reasons we wanted to write this book now and to get it out at this stage of the political cycle is that, in NSW and federally, we are in a year of new governments. We hope the book will be both useful and influential in setting new directions for digital transformation, especially nationally.

In that spirit, what would be the top three or four things we would recommend that the incoming Minister with responsibility for this agenda, of whatever political stripe, should do, and in which they should invest their political and fiscal capital to wield the biggest impact?

These are the projects on which we would recommend a new government should concentrate:

- Establish and talk up a national 'mission' to make sure Australian is a leading digital nation driven by a joint federal/state and territory Government Transformation Authority that puts a digital-transformed, new public work at the heart of a new theory of the business for governing and the public sector.
- Concentrate on a limited number of common journeys, from which to eliminate as much friction as possible for citizens and businesses, to improve the experience of interacting with government that saves time and money, reduces emotional pressure and anxiety, and better matches the shape and design of services to the contours and rhythms of the lives of those they are designed to support.
- Invest heavily and rapidly in new, national, public, digital infrastructure that is designed and built using agile and contemporary methods and tools, and which serves national digital objectives for efficiency, productivity, and improved citizen experience.
- Invest in a major modernisation and up-skilling of public-service capabilities that lifts the ability of the sector to think differently about, and design and deliver more effectively, the tools, platforms, and mindset that help the sector to more rapidly absorb the new way of doing public work.

As well as arguing that the story of the digital transformation of government and the public sector is missing the most interesting half of its plot, it's also true that it is a story that doesn't have an ending. In that sense, even though the book is finished, it isn't.

What we would like you to do

The book is associated with the website www.arewethereyetdigital.com where we intend to continue the conversation. In particular, we're keen to get advice about ways in which this manifesto could be improved and, importantly, how its intentions might be translated into practical decisions and achievable pieces of work.

Frequently Used Abbreviations

4IR	Fourth Industrial Revolution
ABC	Australian Broadcasting Corporation
ACSC	Australian Cyber Security Centre
AI	Artificial Intelligence
APSC	Australian Public Service Commission
AR	Augmented Reality
APS	Australian Public Service
ATO	Australian Taxation Office
CDO	Chief Digital Officer
CEO	Chief Executive Officer
CIO	Chief Information Officer
CSIRO	Commonwealth Scientific and Industrial Research Organisation
COAG	Council of Australian Governments
DAC	Data Analytics Centre
DTA	Digital Transformation Agency
DTO	Digital Transformation Office
DHS	Department of Human Services
GDS	Government Digital Service (UK)
GTA	Government Transformation Authority
HR	Human Resources
ICT	Information Communications Technology
IT	Information Technology
IoT	Internet of Things
MIT	Massachusetts Institute of Technology
MVP	Minimum Viable Product
NLP	Natural Language Processing
NGO	Non-Governmental Organisation
NSW	New South Wales
NPM	New Public Management
OECD	Organisation for Economic Co-operation and Development
RPA	Robotic Process Automation
TAFE	Technical and Further Education
UX	User Experience
UK	United Kingdom
US	United States of America
VR	Virtual Reality
WA	Western Australia
WEF	World Economic Forum

Endnotes

Foreword

1   Peter Shergold, 'Public Service 4.0: What Might It Look Like?', Civil Service College, Singapore, Singapore Government, 18 Jan. 2018, https://www.csc.gov.sg/articles/public-service-4.0-what-might-it-look-like'.

Introduction

2   The Hon. Michael Keenan MP, 'Delivering Australia's digital future', rel. 13 June 2018, https://ministers.pmc.gov.au/keenan/2018/delivering-australias-digital-future.

3   Parliament of Australia, 'Digital delivery of government services', 4 Dec. 2017, https://www.aph.gov.au/Parliamentary_Business/Committees/Senate/Finance_and_Public_Administration/digitaldelivery.

4   These are some references that readers can explore in more depth and detail: William D. Eggers, Government 2.0 *Using Technology to Improve Education, Cut Red Tape, Reduce Gridlock, and Enhance Democracy, Rowman & Littlefield, 2004; Beth Simone Noveck, Wiki Government: How Technology Can Make Government Better, Democracy Stronger, and Citizens More Powerful, Brookings Institution Press, 2004; Beth Simone Noveck, Smart Citizens, Smarter State: The Technologies of Expertise and the Future of Governing, Harvard University Press, 2015; bio, Helen Margetts, Professor of Society & the Internet, Oxford Internet Institute, Univ. of Oxford*, https://www.oii.ox.ac.uk/people/helen-margetts/; Alex Benay, *Government Digital: The Quest to Regain Public Trust, Dundurn, 2018; Alan W. Brown, Jerry Fishenden & Mark D. Thompson, Digitizing Government: Understanding and Implementing New Digital Business Models (Busiiness in the Digital Economy)*, Palgrave Macmillan, 2014.

5   Donald A. Schön, *The Reflective Practitioner: How Professionals Think in Action*, Routledge, 1994.

6   Martin Stewart-Weeks and Lindsay Tanner, *Changing Shape: Institutions for a digital age*, 2014.

7   Martin chairs the WPIT Expert Advisory Group which provides advice to the Ministers for Human Services and Finance about aspects of the program's design and implementation. These brief reflections represent personal views.

8   Department for Human Services, Welfare Payment Infrastructure Transformation (WPIT) Programme, last updated 12 Nov. 2018, https://www.humanservices.gov.au/organisations/about-us/welfare-payment-infrastructure-transformation-wpit-programme.

9   Some would argue that spending that kind of money on large infrastructure projects seems the antithesis of agile and modern, even though, in the case of WPIT, there has been considerable use of agile development models and techniques at various stages of the project.

10   Pierre Péladeau and Olaf Acker, Strategy + Business, 'Have we reached "peak" chief digital officer?', 26 Mar. 2019, https://www.strategy-business.com/blog/Have-we-reached-peak-chief-digital-officer?gko=2443a.

11   Péladeau and Acker, 'Have we reached "peak" chief digital officer?'.

12   UK Government (2017), Government Transformation Strategy, Ministerial Forward, https://assets.publishing.service.gov.uk/government/uploads/system/uploads/attachment_data/file/590199/Government_Transformation_Strategy.pdf.

13   The Rt Hon. Ben Gummer, MP, Ministerial Foreword, 'Government Transformation Strategy', UK Government, 2017, https://assets.publishing.service.gov.uk/government/uploads/system/uploads/attachment_data/file/590199/Government_Transformation_Strategy.pdf.

14   Deloitte Access Economics, 'Digital government transformation', 2015, https://www2.deloitte.com/content/dam/Deloitte/au/Documents/Economics/deloitte-au-economics-digital-government-transformation-230715.pdf.

15   Angus Taylor, Nick Cater (ed), 'The Promise of Digital Government: Transforming Public Services, Regulation, and Citizenship', Menzies Research Centre Number 4, Connor Court Publishing Pty Ltd, 2016.

16   Australian Government, Independent Review of the Australian Public Service, https://www.apsreview.gov.au/.

17   Mike Bracken, 'Digital transformation is a leadership problem', Apr. 2019, UCL Institute for Innovation and Public Purpose Blog, University College London, https://link.medium.com/NvjMbVfJMV.

18   Ry Crozier, 'WooliesX predicts ways to connect with customers, iTnews, 15 Apr. 2019, https://www.itnews.com.au/news/wooliesx-predicts-ways-to-connect-with-customers-523682.

19   Hireup, www.hireup.com.au.

Chapter 1

20   The idea of the theory of the business, which will be explained later in the chapter, is taken from work by Peter Drucker. It refers to the assumptions that any organisation makes – corporation, government department, university, or NGO – about the relationship between its mission, its context, and its capabilities. Drucker used the term without limiting the concept of 'business' to a commercial enterprise, but rather in the more general sense of any enterprise or organisation in any sector.

21   Samuel Furphy (ed), *The Seven Dwarfs and the Age of the Mandarins: Australian Government Administration in the Post-War Reconstruction Era*, ANU Press, 2015.

22   Jeremy Heimans & Henry Timms, *New Power: How Anyone Can Persuade, Mobilize and Succeed in Our Chaotic, Connected Age*, Doubleday, 2018.

23   The Hon. Kenneth Madison Hayne AC QC, Royal Commission into Misconduct in the Banking, Superannuation and Financial Services Industry, 1 Feb. 2019, https://financialservices.royalcommission.gov.au/Pages/default.aspx.

24   See Royal Commission into Aged Care Quality and Safety, https://agedcare.royalcommission.gov.au/Pages/default.aspx. See also Royal Commission into Violence, Abuse, Neglect and Exploitation of People with Disability, https://www.ag.gov.au/DisabilityRoyalCommission.

25   Mark Thompson, 'Getting it right this time: Why the strategy is not about delivery for NHSX', *Computer Weekly* online, Mar. 2019, https://www.computerweekly.com/opinion/Getting-it-right-this-time-Why-the-strategy-is-not-about-delivery-for-NHSX.

26   Thompson, 'Getting it right this time'.

27   Peter F. Drucker, 'The Theory of the Business', *Harvard Business Review*, Sep.–Oct. 1994, https://hbr.org/1994/09/the-theory-of-the-business.

28   Harley Dennett, 'Crisis of confidence: a black dog stalks the public service', 17 Oct. 2018, *The Mandarin*, https://www.themandarin.com.au/100087-crisis-of-confidence-a-black-dog-stalks-the-public-service/.

29   Sheila M. Cannon, 'Climate strikes: Greta Thunberg calls for "system change not climate change" – here's what that could look like', 15 Mar. 2019, https://theconversation.com/climate-strikes-greta-thunberg-calls-for-system-change-not-climate-change-heres-what-that-could-look-like-112891.

30   Drucker, 'The Theory of the Business'.

31   See, e.g., Howard Risher, 'Why Is Public-Employee Morale So Bad?', 23 Aug. 2016, *Governing*, https://www.governing.com/gov-institute/voices/col-public-employee-morale-engagement-lessons-private-sector.html. See also Dennett, 'Crisis of confidence: a black dog stalks the public service'. See also 'Public sector morale at "critical levels"', 4 Jul. 2017, *BBC News*, https://www.bbc.com/news/uk-40489256. See also 'Low morale in public sector "caus-

ing more sick days"', 19 Oct. 2018, *Jersey Evening Post*, https://jerseyeveningpost.com/news/2018/10/19/low-morale-in-public-sector-causing-more-sick-days/.

32   This is what public sector organisations should be doing as a matter of course, as part of their strategic and business planning processes; instead, much of that work turns out plans which can feel superficial and lazy, ticking some central agency boxes without manifesting much in the way of deep thinking or careful analysis.

33   Nassim Nicholas Taleb, *The Black Swan: The Impact of the Highly Improbable*, Random House, 2007.

34   Tom Loosemore, 'Winning the Uphill Battle', 2018 State of Digital Transformation, Belfer Center for Science and International Affairs, Harvard Kennedy School, https://www.belfer-center.org/publication/2018-state-digital-transformation#8.

35   Jennifer Guay, '"Government was created for another era": why it must change', *Apolitical*, 2 Oct. 2017, https://apolitical.co/solution_article/government-created-another-era-must-change/.

36   Loosemore, 'Winning the Uphill Battle'.

37   Harley Dennett, 'Crisis of confidence: a black dog stalks the public service', *The Mandarin*, 17 Oct. 2018, https://www.themandarin.com.au/100087-crisis-of-confidence-a-black-dog-stalks-the-public-service/.

38   Rachel Botsman, 'The currency of the new economy is trust', TED Talk, TEDGlobal 2012, https://www.ted.com/talks/rachel_botsman_the_currency_of_the_new_economy_is_trust.

39   Geoff Mulgan, Michelle Eaton & Vincent Straub, 'Collective intelligence design and effective, ethical policing: How AI and collective intelligence could transform policing both at a community and national level', Nesta UK (23 Nov. 2018), https://www.nesta.org.uk/blog/collective-intelligence-design-and-effective-ethical-policing/.

40   In some respects, the trajectory of the open government movement, and the more formal examples of its attempt to influence government through jurisdictional and agency strategies and initiatives like the Open Government Partnership, mirror the story of digital transformation. High ambition and considerable hope that a robust commitment to open government practices would seep into the fundamental structures and culture of the public sector have been stymied by variations on traditional games of institutional resistance and even hostility. Like digital transformation, open government stands as a powerful force for disruption and change, asking large strategic and systemic questions of government and the public sector that have often been answered with strategies that fail to embrace their full implications.

41   Senate Finance and Public Administration Committees, Parliament of Australia, 'Digital delivery of government services', 27 Jun. 2018, https://www.aph.gov.au/Parliamentary_Business/Committees/Senate/Finance_and_Public_Administration/digitaldelivery/Report.

42   Doug Dingwall, 'Labor to push for Senate inquiry into $10b government IT spend and tech wrecks', *The Sydney Morning Herald*, 13 August 2017, https://www.smh.com.au/public-service/labor-to-push-for-senate-inquiry-into-10b-government-it-spend-and-tech-wrecks-20170811-gxu93t.html.

43   Jamie Susskind, *Future Politics: Living Together in a World Transformed by Tech*, Oxford University Press, 2018.

44   Susskind, *Future Politics*.

45   Susskind, *Future Politics*.

46   Rainer Kattel & Ines Mergel, 'Is Estonia the Silicon Valley of digital government?' UCL IIPP Blog, University College London, (28 Sept. 2018), https://medium.com/iipp-blog/is-estonia-the-silicon-valley-of-digital-government-bf15adc8e1ea?source=userActivityShare-cb-c62928feb-1538357232.

47   Elena Bagnera & Danny Buerkli, 'A conversation with Jamie Susskind on the tech revolu-
      tion and the future of politics,' 3 Oct. 2018, *Future Politics*, Centre for Public Impact, https://
      www.centreforpublicimpact.org/conversation-jamie-susskind-tech-revolution-future-
      politics/.

48   Susskind, *Future Politics*.

49   Susskind, *Future Politics*.

50   Susskind, *Future Politics*.

51   Susskind, *Future Politics*.

52   Shoshana Zuboff, *The Age of Surveillance Capitalism: The Fight for a Human Future at the
      New Frontier of Power*, PublicAffairs, 2019.

53   Zuboff, *The Age of Surveillance Capitalism*.

54   Zuboff, *The Age of Surveillance Capitalism*.

55   Zuboff, *The Age of Surveillance Capitalism*.

56   Zuboff, *The Age of Surveillance Capitalism*.

57   Zuboff, *The Age of Surveillance Capitalism*.

58   Jamie Bartlett, *The People Vs Tech: How the internet is killing democracy (and how we save
      it)*, Ebury Press, 2018.

59   Bartlett, *The People Vs Tech*.

60   Bartlett, *The People Vs Tech*.

61   Bartlett, *The People Vs Tech*.

62   Bryan Glick, 'Interview: Government digital chief Mike Bracken – why I quit', *Computer
      Weekly* online, 13 Aug. 2015, https://www.computerweekly.com/news/4500251662/Interview-
      Government-digital-chief-Mike-Bracken-why-I-quit.

63   Glick, 'Interview: Government digital chief Mike Bracken'.

64   Glick, 'Interview: Government digital chief Mike Bracken'.

65   Glick, 'Interview: Government digital chief Mike Bracken'.

66   Glick, 'Interview: Government digital chief Mike Bracken'.

67   Richard Pope, 'Government as a Platform, the hard problems: part 2 – the design of services
      & public policy', blog post, Platform Land, Medium.com, 11 Apr. 2019, https://medium.com/
      platform-land/government-as-a-platform-the-hard-problems-part-2-the-design-of-public-
      facing-services-4b3b2447f379. '...Government as a Platform could change both the nature of
      the services built on top of it, and *how* those services are created. To take full advantage of
      platforms, governments will have to understand the new types of services likely to become
      possible, how it could break some old certainties about who delivers services, and how the
      process can remain accountable.' See also Harvard Kennedy School's Platform Government
      Initiative, led by Richard Pope, open resources for anyone who wants to understand how
      digital platforms will change government and society, https://platformland.org/.

68   Hugh Muir, 'Simon Stevens interview: "The NHS is a social movement and not just a health
      care service"', *The Guardian*, 24 Oct. 2014, https://www.theguardian.com/society/2014/
      oct/24/simon-stevens-interview.

69   Gavin Jackson, 'Bank of England's Andy Haldane goes on tour of the UK', *Financial Times*,
      20 Aug. 2017, https://www.ft.com/content/f87a585a-829b-11e7-a4ce-15b2513cb3ff.

70   See The Australian Centre for Social Innovation (TACSI), Family by Family, https://www.
      tacsi.org.au/work/family-by-family/. See also Logan Together, http://logantogether.org.au/.
      See also Department of Family and Community Services, NSW Government, Childstory,
      https://www.facs.nsw.gov.au/families/childstory.

71   Innovation XChange, DFAT (Dept. of Foreign Affairs and Trade) Innovation Strategy, Final, https://ixc.dfat.gov.au/. See also the DFAT's three-year innovation strategy, 2018–2021, https://d3qlm9hpgjc8os.cloudfront.net/wp-content/uploads/2018/07/03095158/DFAT-Innovation-Strategy-FINAL.pdf.

72   Rutrell Yasin, 'How FDNY uses analytics to find potential fire traps', GCN, 1105 Public Sector Media Group, 1 Aug. 2013, https://gcn.com/articles/2013/08/01/fdny-data-analytics.aspx.

73   The Strategy Group, Project Hive: Redesigning Policy Development in NSW Government, 2017, https://www.thestrategygroup.com.au/project-hive-redesigning-policy-development-in-nsw-government/.

74   Open Banking, Meet the Regulated Providers, 2019, https://www.openbanking.org.uk/customers/regulated-providers/.

75   Lauren Walser, 'A Tale of Two Planners: Jane Jacobs vs. Robert Moses', 14 Apr. 2016, National Trust for Historic Preservation, https://savingplaces.org/stories/a-tale-of-two-planners-jane-jacobs-and-robert-moses#.XLQ6ivZuLD4.

76   Jane Jacobs, *The Death and Life of Great American Cities*, New York: Vintage Books, 1961.

77   Jacobs, *The Death and Life of Great American Cities*.

78   Jacobs, *The Death and Life of Great American Cities*.

79   Jacobs, *The Death and Life of Great American Cities*.

80   Mariana Mazzucato, *The Entrepreneurial State: Debunking Public vs. Private Sector Myths*, Anthem, 2013.

81   Mariana Mazzucato, *The Value of Everything: Making and Taking in the Global Economy*, Penguin, 2018.

82   Jeremy Heimans & Henry Timms, 'Understanding New Power', *Harvard Business Review*, Dec. 2014, https://hbr.org/2014/12/understanding-new-power.

83   The work of the newDemocracy Foundation in Australia, which advocates more experiments with different forms of citizen deliberation, including juries, is a good example. See https://www.newdemocracy.com.au/.

84   OECD, 'Core Skills for Public Sector Innovation', Apr. 2017, https://www.oecd.org/media/oecdorg/satellitesites/opsi/contents/files/OECD_OPSI-core_skills_for_public_sector_innovation-201704.pdf.

85   David Weinberger, *Too Big to Know: Rethinking Knowledge Now That the Facts Aren't the Facts, Experts Are Everywhere, and the Smartest Person in the Room Is the Room*, Basic Books, 2014.

86   GovLab, 'Who We Are', http://www.thegovlab.org/about.html.

Chapter 2

87   We use the idea of a project to describe the collection of initiatives and investments in technology and capability associated with the ambition to apply the tools, platforms, and culture of digital technology to every aspect of the work of government and the public sector.

88   Spotless Data (2017), 'Amara's Law: A [Gartner's] hype cycle perfectly visually illustrates Amara's law', https://spotlessdata.com/blog/amaras-law.

89   The larger challenge of connecting consequences of technology innovation to the human concerns of ethics and equity is the substance of Shoshana Zuboff's exposition of the internal dynamics of what she describes as 'surveillance capitalism', and frames an important set of considerations about the consequences of digital transformation for the work of government and the public sector, which we return to in chapter 4. See https://en.wikipedia.org/wiki/Surveillance_capitalism for an outline of the arguments.

90   Klaus Schwab, 'The Fourth Industrial Revolution: What It Means and How to Respond', *Foreign Affairs*, (U.S.) Council of Foreign Relations, 12 Dec. 2015, https://www.foreignaffairs.com/articles/2015-12-12/fourth-industrial-revolution.

91   Schwab, 'The Fourth Industrial Revolution'.

92   Australian Council of Social Service (ACOSS), Inequality in Australia: A Nation Divided, ACOSS, Australia, 2015.

93   OECD, 'Inequality and Income', 2019, http://www.oecd.org/social/inequality.htm#income.

94   As noted in Wikipedia, the Gini coefficient is designed to represent the income or wealth distribution of a nation's residents, and is the most commonly used measurement of inequality. See https://en.wikipedia.org/wiki/Gini_coefficient.

95   Oxfam, 'An Economy for the 99%', Australian Fact Sheet, Jan. 2017, https://www.oxfam.org.au/wp-content/uploads/2017/01/2017-PA-002-Inequality-Report-V3a.pdf.

96   Oxfam, 'An Economy for the 99%'.

97   Thomas Piketty, *Capital in the Twenty-First Century*, Harvard University Press, 2014.

98   Tim Worstall, 'Why Thomas Piketty's Global Wealth Tax Won't Work', *Forbes* online, 30 Mar. 2014, https://www.forbes.com/sites/timworstall/2014/03/30/why-thomas-pikettys-global-wealth-tax-wont-work/#351542aa1272. See also Robert Kirkby, 'Summary of Piketty: Criticisms', 27 July 2015, http://www.robertdkirkby.com/blog/2015/criticisms-of-piketty/.

99   Susannah Cahalan, '9 charts that prove there's never been a better time to be alive', *New York Post* online, 3 Mar. 2018, https://nypost.com/2018/03/03/9-charts-that-prove-theres-never-been-a-better-time-to-be-alive/.

100   Samantha Hawley & staff, 'Rose McGowan on the global impact of #MeToo, Weinstein's trial and the resulting "cultural reset"', 8 Mar. 2019, *ABC News*, https://www.abc.net.au/news/2019-03-08/rose-mcgowan-speaks-to-the-abc-about-the-impact-of-metoo/10877886.

101   Mariana Mazzucato, 'Mission Oriented Innovation Policy: Challenges and Opportunities', IIPP Working Paper, UCL Institute for Innovation and Public Purpose, University College London, 25 Sep. 2017, https://www.ucl.ac.uk/bartlett/public-purpose/publications/2018/jan/mission-oriented-innovation-policy-challenges-and-opportunities.

102   'Towards the end of poverty', *The Economist*, 1 Jun. 2013, https://www.economist.com/leaders/2013/06/01/towards-the-end-of-poverty.

103   Jacob Morgan, 'What Is the Fourth Industrial Revolution?', *Forbes* online, 19 Feb. 2016, https://www.forbes.com/sites/jacobmorgan/2016/02/19/what-is-the-4th-industrial-revolution/#3dde558f392a.

104   Klaus Schwab, 'The Fourth Industrial Revolution: what it means, how to respond', World Economic Forum, 14 Jan. 2016, https://www.weforum.org/agenda/2016/01/the-fourth-industrial-revolution-what-it-means-and-how-to-respond/.

105   Schwab, 'The Fourth Industrial Revolution'.

106   AlphaBeta Advisors, 'Digital Innovation: Australia's $315b opportunity', commissioned by CSIRO's Data61, Sep. 2018, https://www.data61.csiro.au/en/Our-Work/Future-Cities/Planning-sustainable-infrastructure/Digital-Innovation.

107   AlphaBeta Advisors, 'Digital Innovation'.

108   Geoff Mulgan, 'How can the fourth industrial revolution be made good?', Nesta, 20 Nov. 2017, https://www.nesta.org.uk/blog/how-can-the-fourth-industrial-revolution-be-made-good/.

109   Julian Bajkowski, 'Home Affairs chief Pezzullo decries rise of the "digital industrial complex: Cyber tsar worried about "connectivity without values"', *iTnews*, 14 Mar. 2019, https://www.itnews.com.au/news/home-affairs-chief-pezzullo-decries-rise-of-the-digital-industrial-complex-520539.

110   Mulgan, 'How can the fourth industrial revolution be made good?'.

111   Philip Baker, 'When Frank Lowy and Rupert Murdoch sell, it's time to join them', *Financial Review* online, 13 Dec. 2017, https://www.afr.com/markets/equity-markets/when-frank-lowy-and-rupert-murdoch-sell-its-time-to-join-them-20171213-h03mjh.

112   John Hagel III, John Seely Brown & Lang Davison, 'The Big Shift: Measuring the Forces of Change', *Harvard Business Review*, Jul./Aug. 2009, https://hbr.org/2009/07/the-big-shift-measuring-the-forces-of-change.

113   John Hagel & John Seely Brown, 'Institutional innovation', part of a Deloitte series on innovation, Deloitte Insights, 12 Mar. 2013, https://www2.deloitte.com/insights/us/en/topics/innovation/institutional-innovation.html.

114   Mazzucato, *The Entrepreneurial State*.

115   Mazzucato, *The Entrepreneurial State*.

116   This is the focus of Francis Fukuyama; e.g., see Francis Fukuyama, *Identity: The Demand for Dignity and the Politics of Resentment*, Farrar, Straus and Giroux, 2018.

117   Stefan Hajkowicz, Hannah Cook & Anna Littleboy, 'Our Future World: global megatrends that will change the way we live', CSIRO Futures report, 9 May 2012, https://doi.org/10.4225/08/584ee9706689b, sourced at https://www.csiro.au/en/Do-business/Futures/Reports/Our-Future-World.

118   E.g., see this work from the Centre for Policy Development (Martin is a current Board member), 'Public authority directors' duties and climate change', Jan. 2019, https://cpd.org.au/2019/02/public-authorities/.

119   United Nations, 2015 Revision of World Population Prospects report, http://www.un.org/en/development/desa/news/population/2015-report.html.

120   Australian Institute of Health and Welfare, 'Older Australia at a glance', Sep. 2018, www.aihw.gov.au/reports/older-people/older-australia-at-a-glance/contents/demographics-of-older-australians/australia-s-changing-age-and-gender-profile.

121   World Health Organization, Global Health Observatory (GHO) data, Urban population growth, 2014, https://www.who.int/gho/urban_health/situation_trends/urban_population_growth_text/en/.

122   Edge Foundation, 'Collective Intelligence: A Conversation with Thomas W. Malone', 21 Nov. 2012, https://www.edge.org/conversation/thomas_w__malone-collective-intelligence.

123   Edge Foundation, 'Collective Intelligence: A Conversation with Thomas W. Malone'.

124   Edge Foundation, 'Collective Intelligence: A Conversation with Thomas W. Malone'.

125   IBM Institute for Business Value, 'Collective Intelligence: Capitalizing on the Crowd: Access the untapped knowledge of your networks', https://www-935.ibm.com/services/us/gbs/thoughtleadership/ibv-collective-intelligence.html.

126   New York University Tandon School of Engineering, Collective Intelligence Conference, 5th Edition, June 2017, http://collectiveintelligenceconference.org/.

127   Geoff Mulgan, *Big Mind: How Collective Intelligence Can Change Our World*, Princeton University Press, 2018.

128   Mulgan, *Big Mind*.

129   Mulgan, *Big Mind*.

130   Mulgan, *Big Mind*.

131   Mulgan, *Big Mind*.

132   Mulgan, *Big Mind*.

133   Global Risks Report, 2017, World Economic Forum, http://reports.weforum.org/global-risks-2017.

134   Australian Government, Department of the Prime Minister and Cabinet, Open Government Partnership Australia National Action Plan 2018–2020, https://ogpau.pmc.gov.au/.

135   David Donaldson, 'Tony Shepard: public service capability run down "too far"', The Mandarin, 1 Feb. 2018, https://www.themandarin.com.au/87978-tony-shepherd-public-service-capability-run-far/.

136   Mazzucato, The Value of Everything.

137   Richard N. Haass, 'Liberal World Order, R.I.P.', Project Syndicate, https://www.project-syndicate.org/commentary/end-of-liberal-world-order-by-richard-n--haass-2018-03?barrier=accesspaylog, sourced from https://www.cfr.org/article/liberal-world-order-rip.

138   Haass, 'Liberal World Order, R.I.P.'.

139   Haass, 'Liberal World Order, R.I.P.'.

140   Joseph S. Nye Jr., 'Will the Liberal Order Survive? The History of an Idea', Foreign Affairs, Jan./Feb. 2017, https://www.foreignaffairs.com/articles/2016-12-12/will-liberal-order-survive.

141   Nye, 'Will the Liberal Order Survive?'.

142   Nye, 'Will the Liberal Order Survive?'.

143   Nye, 'Will the Liberal Order Survive?'.

144   Haass, 'Liberal World Order, R.I.P.'. See also Christina Larson, 'China's massive investment in artificial intelligence has an insidious downside', Science, 8 Feb. 2018, http://www.sciencemag.org/news/2018/02/china-s-massive-investment-artificial-intelligence-has-insidious-downside.

145   Australian Government, 2017 Foreign Policy White Paper, Chapter Two: A Contested World, 'An evolving international order', https://www.fpwhitepaper.gov.au/foreign-policy-white-paper/chapter-two-contested-world/evolving-international-order.

146   Jordan Weissman, 'Think We're the Most Entrepreneurial Country in the World? Not So Fast', The Atlantic, 2 Oct. 2012, https://www.theatlantic.com/business/archive/2012/10/think-were-the-most-entrepreneurial-country-in-the-world-not-so-fast/263102/.

147   Jamie Fullerton & Agence France-Presse, 'Xi Jinping says China willing to fight "bloody battle" to regain rightful place in the world, in blistering nationalist speech', The Telegraph, 20 Mar. 2018, https://www.telegraph.co.uk/news/2018/03/20/xi-jinping-says-china-willing-fight-bloody-battle-regain-rightful/.

148   Geoff Wade, 'China's "One Belt, One Road" initiative', Parliament of Australia, https://www.aph.gov.au/About_Parliament/Parliamentary_Departments/Parliamentary_Library/pubs/BriefingBook45p/ChinasRoad.

149   Jane Perlez & Yufan Huang, 'Behind China's $1 Trillion Plan to Shake Up the Economic Order', The New York Times, 13 May 2017, https://www.nytimes.com/2017/05/13/business/china-railway-one-belt-one-road-1-trillion-plan.html.

150   Australian Government, 2017 Foreign Policy White Paper, Chapter two.

151   Sam Roggeveen, 'Lowy poll: Are we losing faith in democracy?', The Interpreter, The Lowy Institute, https://www.lowyinstitute.org/the-interpreter/are-we-losing-faith-democracy.

152   Edelman Trust Management, 2019 Edelman Trust Barometer, 20 Jan. 2019, https://www.edelman.com/trust-barometer.

153   Edelman, 2019 Edelman Trust Barometer.

154   Roggeveen, 'Lowy poll: Are we losing faith in democracy?'.

155   Edelman Trust Management, '2017 Edelman Trust Barometer Reveals Global Implosion', 5 Jan. 2017, https://www.edelman.com/news/2017-edelman-trust-barometer-reveals-global-implosion.

156   Edelman Trust Management, 2018 Edelman Trust Barometer, 21 Jan. 2018, https://www.edelman.com/research/2018-edelman-trust-barometer.

157   Edelman, 2019 Edelman Trust Barometer.

158   Rachel Botsman, *Who Can You Trust? How Technology Brought Us Together and Why It Might Drive Us Apart*, PublicAffairs, 2017.

159   Botsman, *Who Can You Trust?*.

160   Botsman, *Who Can You Trust?*.

161   One view is from the Australian Government Productivity Commission: 'This report contributes to that task by exploring the potential impacts and challenges of digital technology for markets and competition, workers and society, and the way governments operate. With a few exceptions, governments across Australia have, to date, evidenced largely reactive responses to dealing with digital technologies. Despite promising statements, we have also been unremarkable in our adoption of technologies to improve public sector processes and service delivery.' See Australian Government Productivity Commission, 'Digital Disruption: What do governments need to do?', 15 Jun. 2016, https://www.pc.gov.au/research/completed/digital-disruption.

162   Nicholas Confessore, 'Cambridge Analytica and Facebook: The Scandal and the Fallout So Far', *The New York Times*, 4 Apr. 2018), https://www.nytimes.com/2018/04/04/us/politics/cambridge-analytica-scandal-fallout.html.

163   Cameron Stewart, 'Menacing march of the titans', *The Australian*, https://www.theaustralian.com.au/news/inquirer/amazon-apple-google-and-facebook-the-menacing-march-of-the-tech-titans/news-story/aadec443de6b1bfc0b2187abbbec6cab.

164   Stewart, 'Menacing march of the titans'.

165   The Digital Platforms Inquiry from the Australian Competition & Consumer Commission is a major input to this challenge. Its preliminary report from 10 Dec. 2018 provided some predictably controversial contributions to the discussion about the best way for the public realm to engage with the big technology players. See https://www.accc.gov.au/system/files/ACCC%20Digital%20Platforms%20Inquiry%20-%20Preliminary%20Report.pdf. The problem statement was unequivocal: 'In particular, this report identifies concerns with the ability and incentive of key digital platforms to favour their own business interests, through their market power and presence across multiple markets, the digital platforms' impact on the ability of content creators to monetise their content, and the lack of transparency in digital platforms' operations for advertisers, media businesses, and consumers. Consumers' awareness and understanding of the extensive amount of information about them collected by digital platforms, and their concerns regarding the privacy of their data, are critical issues as well. There are also issues with the role of digital platforms in determining what news and information is accessed by Australians, how this information is provided, and its range and reliability.'

166   AlphaBeta, 'The New Work Order: Ensuring young Australians have skills and experience for the jobs of the future, not the past', The Foundation for Young Australians, 2017, http://www.fya.org.au/wp-content/uploads/2015/08/fya-future-of-work-report-final-lr.pdf.

167   Martin Hoffman, 'Martin Hoffman: performance auditing – friend or foe to public sector innovation', *The Mandarin*, 10 Apr. 2018, https://www.themandarin.com.au/90952-martin-hoffman-performance-auditing-friend-or-foe-to-public-sector-innovation/.

168   Stephen Easton, 'Paul Shetler: forget high tech fantasies if you can't answer the phones', *The Mandarin*, 2 Aug. 2018, https://www.themandarin.com.au/82114-shetler-forget-high-tech-fantasies-cant-answer-phones/.

169   This is the Singapore unit that builds 'a strategically agile public service'. See https://www.csf.gov.sg/. See also Ross Dawson, 'Government foresight programs', https://rossdawson.com/futurist/government-foresight/, for a useful review of some other strategic 'futures' units in other governments.

Chapter 3

170   Australian Government: Australian Tax Office, Chapter Nine: The 1990s: Continuing Change, 2018, https://www.ato.gov.au/assets/0/104/300/362/18b29211-4270-42b5-9bd1-0fe9aa2634b5.pdf.

171   Australian Government, Digital Transformation Agency, 'About the Digital Service Standard', 2018, https://www.dta.gov.au/help-and-advice/about-digital-service-standard.

172   Nathan Hurst, '"Design of the Year" is UK government's data website, proving aesthetics aren't everything', *Wired*, 17 Apr. 2013, http://www.wired.co.uk/article/design-of-the-year.

173   Kylie De Courtney, Service NSW's Chief Customer Officer, 'Citizen-First: Service NSW Update', Australian Information Industry Association, 15 May 2019, NSW Navigating Digital Government Summit.

174   Justin Hendry, 'Why Service Victoria doesn't want to be a digital trailblazer', iTnews, 18 May 2018, https://www.itnews.com.au/news/why-service-victoria-doesnt-want-to-be-a-digital-trailblazer-491204.

175   Tom Loosemore, 'We're not 'appy. Not 'appy at all', Government Digital Service (GDS), UK Government, https://gds.blog.gov.uk/2013/03/12/were-not-appy-not-appy-at-all/.

176   See Experience WA smartphone app, Tourism Western Australia, https://www.tourism.wa.gov.au/marketing/How-to-get-involved/Digital-Marketing/Pages/Experience-WA-smartphone-app.aspx#/. See also Northern Territory Fishing Mate app, https://nt.gov.au/marine/recreational-fishing/get-the-free-fishing-mate-app. See also Iview app, Australian Broadcasting Corp., https://www.abc.net.au/app/.

177   Progressive web apps, *Google Developers*, https://developers.google.com/web/progressive-web-apps/.

178   Tom Burton, 'Driving a modernised bureaucracy: Turnbull's lasting legacy', *The Mandarin*, 27 Aug. 2018, https://www.themandarin.com.au/97727-driving-a-modernised-bureaucracy-turnbulls-lasting-legacy/.

179   Simon Wardley, 'Wardley Maps: On playing chess', 8 March 2018, https://medium.com/wardleymaps/on-playing-chess-2634b825dbac.

180   Judith Hurwitz, Marcia Kaufman, Fern Halper & Dan Kirsh, 'What Is Platform as a Service (PaaS) in Cloud Computing?' in *Hybrid Cloud for Dummies*, 2012, Hoboken, NJ: John Wiley & Sons.

181   Interview with Jordan Hatch, Deputy Chief Digital Officer at Austrade, by Simon Cooper, May 2019.

182   Australian Government, The Digital Transformation Agency, Secure Cloud Strategy, 2017, https://dta-www-drupal-20180130215411153400000001.s3.ap-southeast-2.amazonaws.com/s3fs-public/files/cloud/secure-cloud-strategy.pdf.

183   The National Institute of Standards and Technology (NIST), U.S. Department of Commerce, NIST Cloud Computing Program – NCCP, https://www.nist.gov/programs-projects/nist-cloud-computing-program-nccp.

184   Damon Rees, speaking at the Institute of Public Administration Australia, NSW State Conference in June 2017.

185   My School is a resource for parents, educators and the community to find information about Australia's schools, https://www.myschool.edu.au/.

186   See Fuel Check, https://www.fuelcheck.nsw.gov.au/app.

187   The Hon. Minister Dominello, Digital Transformation in Government Industry Event, December 2017.

188   Data Analytics Center, Treasury, NSW Government, https://www.treasury.nsw.gov.au/projects-initiatives/data-analytics-centre.

189 Data-Smart City Solutions, How can data and analytics be used to enhance city operations?, Harvard Kennedy School Ash Center for Democratic Governance and Innovation, A Catalog of Civic Data Use Cases, 19 Jul. 2017, https://datasmart.ash.harvard.edu/news/article/how-can-data-and-analytics-be-used-to-enhance-city-operations-723.

190 McKinsey & Company, 'The opportunity in government productivity' Report, Apr. 2017, https://www.mckinsey.com/industries/public-sector/our-insights/the-opportunity-in-government-productivity.

191 Preventing Hospital Emergency Department Admissions Research Report, AURIN (Australian Urban Research Infrastructure Network), https://aurin.org.au/resources/research-impacts/preventing-hospital-emergency-department-admissions/.

192 See 'Integrate digital health into your platform with My Health Record Developer', https://myhealthrecorddeveloper.digitalhealth.gov.au.

193 Australian Privacy Foundation, 'What we and others think of My Health Record', 2019, https://privacy.org.au/campaigns/myhr/.

194 Nicole Brangwin, 'National security—cybersecurity'. Definition from International Standard: IEC/TS 62443-1-1 ed. 1.0, https://www.aph.gov.au/About_Parliament/Parliamentary_Departments/Parliamentary_Library/pubs/BriefingBook45p/Cybersecurity.

195 The Hon. Dan Tehan MP, National Press Club Address – Silent Dangers – Launch of the Australian Cyber Security Centre's 2017 Threat Report, 10 Oct. 2017, https://ministers.pmc.gov.au/tehan/2017/npc-launch-australian-cyber-security-centre-2017-threat-report.

196 David Crowe, 'Increasing cyber-crime attacks "costing up to $1b a year"', The Sydney Morning Herald, 11 Apr. 2018, https://www.smh.com.au/politics/federal/increasing-cyber-crime-attacks-costing-up-to-1b-a-year-20180410-p4z8ui.html.

197 National Archives of Australia (NAA), The Australia Card, http://www.naa.gov.au/collection/explore/cabinet/by-year/1984-85/australia-card.aspx.

198 Australian Government, Digital Transformation Office, Digital Identity, https://www.dta.gov.au/our-projects/digital-identity.

199 Bryan Glick, 'Gov.uk Verify has "failed users" and its leaders lack accountability, say MPs', Computer Weekly online, 8 May 2019, https://www.computerweekly.com/news/252462967/Govuk-Verify-has-failed-users-and-its-leaders-lack-accountability-say-MPs.

200 Deloitte Media Consumer Survey 2018, Australian media and digital entertainment preferences, https://www2.deloitte.com/au/en/pages/technology-media-and-telecommunications/articles/media-consumer-survey-2017.html

201 Blog, Government Digital Service, UK Government, https://gds.blog.gov.uk/.

202 Richard Mulgan, 'Social media guidelines could prove oppressive for public servants', 30 Aug. 2017, The Sydney Morning Herald, https://www.smh.com.au/public-service/social-media-guidelines-could-prove-oppressive-for-public-servants-20170821-gy0j9y.html.

203 This framework was informed by an interview with Pia Andrews, Executive Director, Digital, Policy and Innovation NSW Government, and a lot of reading and research on the topic of AI during 2018–19.

204 At the time of writing, the Australian government were developing a national AI roadmap led by Data61 as part of CSIRO, following an announcement in the 2018 Federal Government Budget; see https://www.minister.industry.gov.au/ministers/cash/media-releases/funding-advance-new-scientific-and-technological-developments. For more on its economic potential, see CSIRO News Release, 'Australia's $315bn opportunity in digital innovation', 18 Sep. 2018, https://www.csiro.au/en/News/News-releases/2018/Australias-315bn-opportunity.

205 Chris Curran & Anand Rao, Briefing: 'Artificial intelligence', 2 Jan. 2018, PricewaterhouseCoopers, http://usblogs.pwc.com/emerging-technology/briefing-ai/

206 Kevin Kelly, *The Inevitable: Understanding the 12 Technological Forces that will shape our future*, Viking Press, 2016.

207 Hila Mehr, 'Artificial Intelligence for Citizen Services and Government', Harvard Kennedy School Ash Center for Democratic Governance and Innovation, Aug. 2017, https://ash.harvard.edu/files/ash/files/artificial_intelligence_for_citizen_services.pdf.

208 Accenture, 'Future Proof: How today's artificial intelligence solutions are taking government services to the next frontier', https://www.accenture.com/us-en/insight-future-proof?sr_source=lift_amplify&c=glb_futureproofhowtexacttarget_10058081&n=emc_1117&emc=21945031:emc-111717.

209 Laura Sacks & Simon Cooper, 'Transforming government using cognitive technology', 7 Apr. 2017, Deloitte, http://blog.deloitte.com.au/transforming-government-using-cognitive-technology/#_ftn1.

210 Deloitte, 'The new machinery of government: Robotic Process Automation in the Public Sector', 2017, https://www2.deloitte.com/content/dam/Deloitte/uk/Documents/Innovation/deloitte-uk-innovation-the-new-machinery-of-govt.pdf.

211 Deloitte University Press, 'Rewriting the rules for the digital age,' 2017 Deloitte Global Human Capital Trends, https://dupress.deloitte.com/content/dam/dup-us-en/articles/HC-Trends_2017/DUP_Global-Human-capital-trends_2017.pdf.

212 David Schatsky, Craig Muraskin & Ragu Gurumurthy, Cognitive technologies: The real opportunities for business, 26 Jan. 2015, *Deloitte Insights*, Deloitte Review Issue 16, https://dupress.deloitte.com/dup-us-en/deloitte-review/issue-16/cognitive-technologies-business-applications.html.

213 Yolanda Redrup, 'ATO deploys Alex a talking "Siri for tax" digital assistant you can talk to', *Australian Financial Review*, 6 Dec. 2016, https://www.afr.com/technology/ato-deploys-alex-a-talking-siri-for-tax-digital-assistant-you-can-talk-to-or-shout-at-20161205-gt46on.

214 State Government of Victoria, Service Victoria, 'Ask Vicky for Help', https://service.vic.gov.au/.

215 Australian Tax Office, 2019, 'Introducing Alex, our new web assistant', https://beta.ato.gov.au/Tests/Introducing-Alex--our-new-web-assistant. See also Government of Germany, 'Govbot: dialogues with e-government' [in German], https://www.govbot.io/.

216 Australian Associated Press, 'More than 33m calls to Centrelink missed in the last year: Department of Human Services blames call-queuing technology for 500,000 increase in unanswered calls', *The Guardian*, 2 Mar. 2018, https://www.theguardian.com/australia-news/2018/mar/02/more-than-33m-calls-to-centrelink-missed-in-the-last-year.

217 Government of the Island of Jersey, Public Consultations, https://www.gov.je/Pages/default.aspx.

218 PwC Belgium, 'Artificial Intelligence (AI) for all: Government chatbots for personalised digital public services', https://www.pwc.be/en/news-publications/insights/2017/ai-public-sector.html.

219 Mai-Hanh Nguyen, 'How artificial intelligence & machine learning produced robots we can talk to', *Business Insider*, 6 Oct. 2017, http://www.businessinsider.com/what-is-chatbot-talking-ai-robot-chat-simulators-2017-10/?r=AU&IR=T.

220 'Now we're talking: How voice technology is transforming computing', *The Economist*, 7 Jan. 2017, https://www.economist.com/leaders/2017/01/07/how-voice-technology-is-transforming-computing.

221 iProspect, 'The Future is Voice Activated', whitepaper, https://www.iprospect.com/en/au/insights/whitepapers/the-future-is-voice-activated-5a0e6/. See also Deloitte Media Consumer Survey 2018, Australian media and digital entertainment preferences, https://www2.deloitte.com/au/en/pages/technology-media-and-telecommunications/articles/media-consumer-survey.html.

222   Sam Dub & Mark Hurrell, 'Hey GOV.UK, what are you doing about voice?', UK Government Digital Service, 23 Aug. 2018, https://gds.blog.gov.uk/2018/08/23/hey-gov-uk-what-are-you-doing-about-voice/.

223   Zack Quaintance, '7 State or Local Governments Using Amazon Alexa', *Government Technology*, 27 Sept. 2017, http://www.govtech.com/7-State-or-Local-Governments-Using-Amazon-Alexa.html.

224   Amelia, IPsoft, https://www.ipsoft.com/amelia/.

225   Stephen Easton, 'Nadia: the curious case of the digital missing person', 3 Apr. 2019, *The Mandarin*, https://www.themandarin.com.au/106473-nadia-the-curious-case-of-the-digital-missing-person/.

226   Robert Overend & Simon Cooper, 'Conversational AI: Delivering the next wave of customer experiences', 8 May 2019, Deloitte, https://www2.deloitte.com/au/en/blog/consulting-blog/2019/conversational-ai-delivering-next-wave-customer.html.

227   Toby Walsh, 2062: *The World that AI Made*, La Trobe University Press, 2018.

228   U.S. Citizenship and Immigration Services, 'Meet Emma, Our Virtual Assistant', https://www.uscis.gov/emma.

229   CSIRO's Data61 released a paper on the ethics of AI in 2018 and, at the time of writing, was engaging in a wide consultation with the community about its framework and suggested principles. See 'Artificial Intelligence: Australia's Ethics Framework, 2019, https://consult.industry.gov.au/strategic-policy/artificial-intelligence-ethics-framework/.

230   Walsh, 2062: *The World that AI Made*.

231   Martin Ford, *Rise of the Robots: Technology and the Threat of a Jobless Future*, Basic Books, 2015.

232   Stephen Hawking, Stuart Russell, Max Tegmark, Frank Wilczek, 'Stephen Hawking: "Transcendence looks at the implications of artificial intelligence – but are we taking AI seriously enough?"', *The Independent*, 1 May 2014, http://www.independent.co.uk/news/science/stephen-hawking-transcendence-looks-at-the-implications-of-artificial-intelligence-but-are-we-taking-9313474.html.

233   Peter Stratton, 'AI can book a restaurant or a hair appointment, but don't expect a full conversation', *The Conversation*, 18 May 2018, http://theconversation.com/ai-can-book-a-restaurant-or-a-hair-appointment-but-dont-expect-a-full-conversation-96720.

234   Eric Piscini, Joe Guastella, Alex Rozman & Tom Nassim, 'Blockchain: Democratized trust: distributed ledgers and the future of value', *Deloitte Insights*, 24 Feb. 2016, https://dupress.deloitte.com/dup-us-en/focus/tech-trends/2016/blockchain-applications-and-trust-in-a-global-economy.html?id=gx:2el:3dc:dup3039:awa:cons:tt16.

235   Kevin Kelly, *The Inevitable: Understanding the 12 Technological Forces That Will Shape Our Future*, Penguin Books, 2016.

236   Data61, CSIRO, 'Blockchain: what does the future hold for blockchain in Australia?', https://www.data61.csiro.au/en/Our-Work/Safety-and-Security/Secure-Systems-and-Platforms/Blockchain.

237   FinTech Australia, 'What is FinTech?', https://fintechaustralia.org.au/learn/.

238   Paul Sidhu, 'Australian food safety: Could blockchain be the unexpected solution?', 8 Jun. 2017, IBM A/NZ Blog, https://www.ibm.com/blogs/ibm-anz/australian-food-safety-blockchain-unexpected-solution/.

239   Data61, CSIRO, 'Blockchain: what does the future hold for blockchain in Australia?'

240   Data61, CSIRO, 'Blockchain: what does the future hold for blockchain in Australia?'

241   In Georgia, Blockchain Technologies Provide Significant Opportunity to Innovate, Improve Services for Citizens', The World Bank, press release, 8 May 2018, https://www.worldbank.org/

en/news/press-release/2018/05/08/in-georgia-blockchain-technologies-provide-significant-opportunity-to-innovate-improve-services-for-citizens.

242   Conner Forrest, 'UK government using blockchain to track welfare spending', Tech Republic, 14 Jul. 2016, https://www.techrepublic.com/article/uk-government-using-blockchain-to-track-welfare-spending/.

243   Dominic Powell, 'Power Ledger receives part of $8 million government grant for Fremantle blockchain energy project', SmartCompany, 21 Nov. 2017, https://www.smartcompany.com.au/startupsmart/news-analysis/power-ledger-receives-part-8-million-government-grant-fremantle-blockchain-energy-project/.

244   Australian Government, Digital Transformation Agency, Blockchain, https://www.dta.gov.au/help-and-advice/blockchain. See also Joseph Brookes, 'Proceed With Caution: DTA's Blockchain Advice to Government', Insights, Which-50 Media, 14 Feb. 2019, https://which-50.com/proceed-with-caution-dtas-blockchain-advice-to-government/.

245   Microsoft HoloLens Development Edition; see https://www.microsoft.com/en-au/store/d/microsoft-hololens-development-edition/8xf18pqz17ts?activetab=pivot%3aoverviewtab.

246   Kelly, *The Inevitable*.

247   Ray Sharma & Amir Bashir, 'Fifth-Generation Wireless: the backbone beyond smart cities and smart government', in Alex Benay, *Government Digital: The Quest to Regain Public Trust*, Dundurn, 2018.

248   William D. Eggers, John Skowron, Forces of Change: Smart Cities', *Deloitte Insights*, https://www2.deloitte.com/content/dam/insights/us/articles/4421_Forces-of-change-Smart-cities/DI_Forces-of-change-Smart-cities.pdf.

249   Deloitte, 'Building the smart city with data, digital, and design: Smart city 2.0: Examples of the second wave in smart city transformation', https://www2.deloitte.com/us/en/pages/public-sector/articles/smart-city-big-data.html?nc=1#.

250   Deloitte, 'Building the smart city with data, digital, and design'.

251   Amanda Clarke, 'Digital Government Units: Origins, Orthodoxy and Critical Considerations for Public Management Theory and Practice', 12 July 2017, https://ssrn.com/abstract=3001188.

252   Axelos, Global Best Practice, PRINCE2 – Project Management, https://www.axelos.com/best-practice-solutions/prince2.

253   Patrick Dunleavy, Helen Margetts, Simon Bastow & Jane Tinkler, *Digital Era Governance: IT Corporations, the State, and e-Government*, Oxford: Oxford University Press, 2008.

254   Clarke, 'Digital Government Units'.

255   David Auerbach, 'Err Engine Down: What really went wrong with healthcare.gov?', *Slate*, 8 Oct. 2013, http://www.slate.com/articles/business/bitwise/2013/10/what_went_wrong_with_healthcare_gov_the_front_end_and_back_end_never_talked.html.

256   Mark Ludlow, 'IT disasters now part of modern life', *Australian Financial Review*, 21 Dec. 2016, http://www.afr.com/technology/it-disasters-now-part-of-modern-life-20160628-gptyw6.

257   Agile Alliance, 'Manifesto for Agile Software Development', Feb. 2001, https://www.agilealliance.org/agile101/the-agile-manifesto/.

258   NSW Government, Digital NSW Team, 'Agile approach to service delivery', https://www.digital.nsw.gov.au/digital-design-system/guides/plan-project/lead-agile-culture/agile-approach-service-delivery.

259   Government Digital Service, 'GDS transformation programme (2013 to 2015)' policy paper, UK Government, 'https://www.gov.uk/government/publications/gds-transformation-programme-2013-to-2015.

260   Deborah Sills, Kevin Tunks & John O'Leary, 'Scaling Agile for government', 12 June 2017, *Deloitte Insights*, https://www2.deloitte.com/insights/us/en/industry/public-sector/agile-at-scale-in-government.html.

261   James Holloway, 'The Public Guardian on agile development', 26 Sep. 2014, Government Digital Service Blog, UK Government, https://gds.blog.gov.uk/2014/09/26/the-public-guardian-on-agile-development/.

262   David Hazlehurst, Acting Deputy Secretary, Commonwealth Dept. of Industry, Innovation and Science, 'No Digital State Is an Island – Commonwealth thinking about digital transformation', IPAA NSW State Conference, 15 June 2017, Sydney.

263   Hazlehurst, 'No Digital State Is an Island'.

264   One Team Gov, @OneTeamGov, https://twitter.com/oneteamgov?lang=en.

265   Note we have chosen not to cover Innovation Labs or teams which are not usually focused on the business of digital transformation in government, although we acknowledge that they often work closely or alongside what we have defined as Digital Central Units.

266   'The digital government atlas: the world's best tools and resources', 29 Aug. 2018, Apolitical, https://apolitical.co/solution_article/the-digital-government-atlas-the-worlds-best-tools-and-resources/.

267   These have been selected based on the availability of information, and those we judge to have the most relevancy for our readers. We intend, in subsequent updates of this book, to cover more. Please contact us if you'd like your Digital Central Units to be included.

268   Chris Ferguson, (2013) GDS Presentation, http://www.egovforum.bh/Files/SCC600-SF734-07%20Chris%20Ferguson%20Presentation.pdf.

269   Olivia Neal, 'The future of Government Services' in Alex Benay, *Government Digital: The Quest to Regain Public Trust*.

270   Andrew Greenway, Ben Terrett, Mike Bracken & Tom Loosemore, *Digital Transformation at Scale: Why the Strategy Is Delivery*, London Publishing Partnership, 2018.

271   Andrew Greenway, 'The disruptive digital institutions pulling government into the internet era', Apolitical, 30 Apr. 2018, https://apolitical.co/solution_article/the-disruptive-digital-institutions-pulling-government-into-the-internet-era/.

272   Global Digital Marketplace, Government Digital Service, UK Government, https://gds.blog.gov.uk/category/global-digital-marketplace/.

273   Clarke, 'Digital Government Units'.

274   Matt Ross, 'The rise and fall of GDS: lessons for digital government', Global Government Forum, 9 Jul. 2018, https://www.globalgovernmentforum.com/the-rise-and-fall-of-gds-lessons-for-digital-government/.

275   'Government Transformation Strategy, 2017 to 2020', policy paper, 9 Feb. 2017, UK Government, https://www.gov.uk/government/publications/government-transformation-strategy-2017-to-2020.

276   Australia Government (2018). Digital delivery of government, 1.18 services. Oral Evidence from Paul Shetler, Former Digital Transformation Office CEO. Comment ref: https://www.paulshetler.com/transcript-issues-around-centrelink-mobile.

277   Interview with Paul Shetler, former CEO of the Digital Transformation Office, July 2018, by Martin Stewart-Weeks and Simon Cooper.

278   Denham Sadler, 'A dashboard with little digital data', InnovationAus, 17 Sep. 2018, https://www.innovationaus.com/2018/09/A-dashboard-with-little-digital-data.

279   Mike Bracken, 'On Strategy: The strategy is delivery. Again.', 6 Jan. 2013, https://mikebracken.com/blog/the-strategy-is-delivery-again/.

280 Paris Cowan, 'Australia will no longer get a single government website: Why the govt dumped DTO vision', 12 Jan. 2017, iTnews, https://www.itnews.com.au/news/australia-will-no-longer-get-a-single-government-website-447255.

281 Deloitte Access Economics, 'Digital government transformation', 2015, Deloitte, https://www2.deloitte.com/content/dam/Deloitte/au/Documents/Economics/deloitte-au-economics-digital-government-transformation-230715.pdf.

282 International Academy of CIOs, (2017), '2017 WASEDA–IAC International e-Government Rankings' Report, Waseda University, Japan. https://www.waseda.jp/top/en-news/53182.

283 Interview with Peter Alexander, Australian Government Chief Digital Officer, by Simon Cooper, September 2018.

284 Justin Hendry, 'Questions over DTA's govt-wide IT oversight function', 19 Feb. 2019, iTnews, https://www.itnews.com.au/news/questions-over-dtas-govt-wide-it-oversight-function-519503.

285 Australian Government, Digital Transformation Agency, 'Oversights delivers early insights', 10 Nov. 2017, https://www.dta.gov.au/news/oversight-delivers-early-insights. See also its digital transformation strategy, https://www.dta.gov.au/our-projects/strategies/digital-transformation-strategy.

286 Simon Cooper, 'Lessons from Down Under: The Australian Transformation Experience in New South Wales: Digital Government', keynote presentation to the ICIO Connect Conference, Victoria, British Columbia, 3 Oct. 2018, posted 14 Oct. 2018, https://www.linkedin.com/pulse/lessons-from-down-under-digital-government-simon-cooper/.

287 Pia Andrews has a huge global digital transformation following, including nearly 15,000 Twitter users; check out @piawaugh.

288 NSW Government, Digital.nsw Blog, https://www.digital.nsw.gov.au/blog, and interviews with the Digital.NSW Leaders.

289 Victorian Government, Digital Standards for Victoria, https://www.vic.gov.au/digital-standards.

290 Engage Victoria, https://engage.vic.gov.au/.

291 Jithma Beneragama, 'Not just a pretty face: meet the new vic.gov.au', 6 Mar. 2019, Digital Government Victoria, https://medium.com/digital-government-victoria/not-just-a-pretty-face-meet-the-new-vic-gov-au-ab395d6bec40.

292 Kerrie Cruickshank, 'Opening up data to help startups and small business grow', 18 Mar. 2019, https://medium.com/digital-government-victoria/opening-up-data-to-help-startups-and-small-business-grow-6c5abf4526e4.

Chapter 4

293 Allie Coyne, 'The biggest Australian govt IT suppliers, ranked: And which agencies are spending the most money.', iTnews, 6 Dec. 2017, https://www.itnews.com.au/news/the-biggest-australian-govt-it-suppliers-ranked-479272.

294 Adrian Brown, 'Opinion: A quiet revolution in public services has got Whitehall's attention', Civil Service World, 19 Feb. 2019, https://civilserviceworld.com/articles/opinion/opinion-quiet-revolution-public-services-has-got-whitehall's-attention.

295 Eric Steven Raymond, 'The Cathedral and the Bazaar', see http://www.unterstein.net/su/docs/CathBaz.pdf.

296 Gary Sturgess, 'Gary Sturgess: A middle way for contestability', 15 Apr. 2015, The Mandarin, https://www.themandarin.com.au/29563-gary-sturgess-contestability-alternatives-outsourcing/. See also Gary L. Sturgess, 'Double Government: The Art of Commissioning Public Services', 2012, https://www.academia.edu/12013356/Double_Government_The_Art_of_Commissioning_Public_Services

297 Brown, Fishenden, & Thompson, *Digitizing Government*.

298 Comptroller & Auditor General, National Audit Office, 'Digital transformation in government', UK Government, https://www.nao.org.uk/wp-content/uploads/2017/03/Digital-transformation-in-government.pdf.

299 Brown, Fishenden & Thompson, *Digitizing Government*.

300 Patrick Dunleavy, Helen Margetts, Simon Bastow & Jane Tinkler, 'New Public Management Is Dead—Long Live Digital-Era Governance', *Journal of Public Administration Research and Theory*, Volume 16, Issue 3, Jul. 2006, pp. 467–94, orig. published 8 Sep. 2005, Oxford University Press, https://doi.org/10.1093/jopart/mui057.

301 Brown, Fishenden & Thompson, *Digitizing Government*.

302 Christopher Hood, 'A Public Management for All Seasons?' in Per Lægreid, *The Oxford Handbook of Classics in Public Policy and Administration*, Steven J. Balla, Martin Lodge & Edward C. Page (eds), Oxford University Press.

303 Kelly Farrow, Robert Sturrock & Sam Hurley, 'Grand alibis: how declining public sector capability affects services for the disadvantaged, Report, Centre for Policy Development, Dec. 2015, https://cpd.org.au/2015/12/grand-alibis-how-declining-public-sector-capability-affects-services-for-the-disadvantaged-report-december-2015/.

304 'Failure demand: from the horse's mouth, with John Seddon', 23 Jul. 2018, Vanguard Consulting Ltd, https://vanguard-method.net/2018/06/failure-demand-from-the-horses-mouth-with-john-seddon/.

305 Goals of New Public Administration, GKBasic, 2013, http://www.gkbasic.com/2013/06/goals-of-new-public-administration_23.html.

306 'From Old Public Administration to the New Public Service: Implications for Public Sector Reform in Developing Countries', Global Centre for Public Service Excellence, 9 Jun. 2015, United Nations Development Programme, https://www.undp.org/content/undp/en/home/librarypage/capacity-building/global-centre-for-public-service-excellence/PS-Reform.html.

307 Jocelyne Bourgon (former Canadian public service leader) in her 'new synthesis' framework, 'Responsive, responsible and respected government: towards a New Public Administration theory', International Review of Administrative Sciences, 1 Mar. 2007, https://doi.org/10.1177%2F0020852307075686.

308 Robert Denhardt and Janet Denhardt, 'The New Public Service: Serving Rather Than Steering', Public Administration Review 60(6):549 – 559, Nov. 2000.

309 Bourgon, 'Responsive, responsible and respected government'.

310 Bourgon, 'Responsive, responsible and respected government'.

311 Bourgon, 'Responsive, responsible and respected government'.

312 Bourgon, 'Responsive, responsible and respected government'.

313 Bourgon, 'Responsive, responsible and respected government'.

314 Bourgon, 'Responsive, responsible and respected government'.

315 Denhardt and Denhardt, 'The New Public Service'.

316 Gerry Stoker, 'Public Value Management: A New Narrative for Networked Governance?', 1 Mar. 2006, https://doi.org/10.1177%2F0275074005282583.

317 Stoker, 'Public Value Management'.

318 As if these different ways to rethink and reimagine the work and significance of the public sector weren't enough, we could also discuss the idea of 'new public governance', described in a 2014 paper as part of a 'new public administration movement' which 'a response to the challenges of a networked, multisector, no one wholly in charge world and to the shortcomings of previous public administration approaches. In the new approach, values beyond efficiency and effectiveness—and especially democratic values—are prominent.

Government has a special role to play as a guarantor of public values, but citizens as well as businesses and non-profit organizations are also important as active public problem solvers.' See John M. Bryson, Barbara C. Crosby & Laura Bloomberg, 'Public Value Governance: Moving Beyond Traditional Public Administration and the New Public Management', 1 Jun. 2014, Wiley Online Library, https://doi.org/10.1111/puar.12238.

319   There are others, of course, that could feature in this discussion, e.g., the work of Jocelyne Bourgon, the former head of the Canadian civil service, whose 'new synthesis' is another way to frame the work of the public sector in a complex and interconnected world. See Jocelyne Bourgon, *A New Synthesis of Public Administration: Serving in the 21st Century*, Montreal & Quebec: McGill-Queens University Press, 2011, https://www.mqup.ca/new-synthesis-of-public-administration--a-products-9781553393122.php.

320   These ideas about the new public work have been developed over some time, especially by Martin in his work with a range of public-sector clients in Australia and the UK, and with a range of people and organisations, including Nesta, The Australian Centre for Social Innovation, and The Young Foundation, with whom he has worked on new thinking about the role and significance of social innovation in the context of public sector reform.

321   In many ways, this is the realisation that animates much of the work of thinkers and researchers like Mariana Mazzucato, whose work on the 'entrepreneurial state' and the 'value of everything' are garnering, rightly, a lot of interest and attention right now.

322   Stewart Brand, *The Clock of the Long Now: Time and Responsibility*, Basic Books, 2000.

323   It is an interesting reflection on Brand's powerful layering model, in relation to some of the traditionally slower layers of change around especially infrastructure and their contemporary manifestation as platforms, that technology and technique are speeding up their provision. More and more of the basic infrastructure needs implied by a more energetic pace of digital transformation needn't take the three or four years that once they did, hostage to a slow game of infrastructure conception, design, and provision. That suggests that, while we need to work out how best to align the different and often clashing rhythms of the different pace layers, their dynamics are not immune to the same forces of disruption, digital and cultural, with which they are trying to grapple. See Stewart Brand, 'Pace Layering: How Complex Systems Learn and Keep Learning', Journal of Design and Science, 4 Feb. 2018, https://jods.mitpress.mit.edu/pub/issue3-brand.

324   Hilary Cottam, 'Relational welfare', Participle, http://www.participle.net/includes/downloader/MTg0NzMwNzI4NjZkMGQ1MTA4MzAxMGQyZGYzNmJjYjhvy_Bkw5J5tvpI8s7ajaLKNFZZa1R5Vm1Lam05Y2ZibHROWnE5SmFwQkx1dUV5bUMoO G9CTVh2YjNoboVRaytLNjFxSoo5bS9zMTFpdk41eUpzRisrMjl6VEcyeXVxRHFI ZFFEaFE9PQ.

325   Hilary Cottam, *Radical Help: How we can remake the relationships between us and revolutionise the welfare state*, Virago, 2018.

326   Cottam, 'Relational welfare'.

327   See Logan Together, http://logantogether.org.au.

328   Participle (2013), The Life Programme, Participle report, http://www.participle.net/families.

329   Mulgan, *Big Mind*, as cited in the article by Martin Stewart-Weeks, 'The art and practice of intelligence design', https://publicpurpose.com.au/art-practice-intelligence-design/).

330   See Open Government Partnership, https://www.opengovpartnership.org/.

331   See Open Government Partnership Australia, https://ogpau.pmc.gov.au/.

332   Open Government Partnership Australia.

333   Martin Stewart-Weeks & Dominic Campbell, 'Design Matters: The Implications of Design Thinking and Practice for Future Public Service Workforce Skills and Culture' in H. Dick-

inson, C. Needham, C. Mangan & H. Sullivan (eds), *Reimagining the Future Public Service Workforce*, SpringerBriefs in Political Science, Springer, Singapore, 2018.

334 The Hon. Malcolm Turnbull, 'Digital Transformation Office to Deliver 21st Century Government', a speech on 23 Jan. 2015, https://www.malcolmturnbull.com.au/media/digital-trans-formation-office-to-make-it-easier-to-connect.

335 The Hon. Michael Keenan (2018), 'Delivering Australia's digital future', 13 Jun. 2018, Address to the Australian Information Industry Association, National Press Club, Canberra, https://ministers.pmc.gov.au/keenan/2018/delivering-australias-digital-future

336 An example of a more complex digital maturity model is provided by Rick Howard & Andrea Di Maio, 'Introducing the Gartner Digital Government Maturity Model 2.0', Gartner Research, 20 Jul. 2017, https://www.gartner.com/doc/3764382/introducing-gartner-digital-government-maturity We haven't used this because it is too Chief Information Officer-centric and thus misses the point that digital is every team's opportunity (or problem).

337 William D. Eggers, *Delivering on Digital: The Innovators and Technologies That Are Transforming Government*, RosettaBooks, 2016.

338 Australian Government, Digital Transformation Agency, Vision 2025: 'We will deliver world-leading digital services for the benefit of all Australians', https://www.dta.gov.au/our-projects/strategies/digital-transformation-strategy.

339 David Eaves and Ben McGuire, 'Proposing A Maturity Model for Digital Services', in their report '2018 State of Digital Transformation', Oct. 2018, Belfer Center for Science and International Affairs, Harvard Kennedy School of Government, Harvard University, https://www.belfercenter.org/publication/2018-state-digital-transformation.

340 Tanguy Catlin, Laura LaBerge & Shannon Varney, 'Digital strategy: The four fights you have to win', Oct. 2018, McKinsey & Company, https://www.mckinsey.com/business-functions/digital-mckinsey/our-insights/digital-strategy-the-four-fights-you-have-to-win.

341 Australian Government, DTA, Vision 2025.

342 NSW Government, Digital Strategy, Digital.nsw, 28 Feb. 2019, https://www.finance.nsw.gov.au/ict/nsw-digital-government-strategy.

343 Martin Stewart-Weeks, 'Do Bureaucrats care? A take on talent in the public sector', Government and Public Sector Reform, Public Purpose Pty Ltd, 22 Oct. 2017, https://publicpurpose.com.au/bureaucrats-care-take-talent-public-sector/. See also Nicholas Gruen, 'The living and the dead: government's arteries and capillaries have lost symbiosis', 7 Apr. 2017, *The Mandarin*, https://www.themandarin.com.au/77680-governments-organic-structure-the-living-and-the-dead/.

344 Dan Hill, 'Strategic design for public purpose: Why UCL's new MPA must help rebuild design capabilities within government, the public sector, and beyond', UCL IIPP Blog, University College London, 8 Mar. 2019, https://medium.com/iipp-blog/strategic-design-for-public-purpose-33c3899dba5e.

345 The Hon. Nick Greiner, Su McCluskey & Martin Stewart-Weeks, NSW Regulatory Policy Framework, Independent Review, Final Report, Aug. 2017, NSW Government, NSW, https://www.treasury.nsw.gov.au/sites/default/files/2018-02/Independent%20Review%20of%20the%20NSW%20Regulatory%20Policy%20Framework%20final%20report.pdf

346 Greiner, McCluskey & Stewart-Weeks, NSW Regulatory Policy Framework: Independent Review.

347 Greiner, McCluskey & Stewart-Weeks, NSW Regulatory Policy Framework: Independent Review.

348 Australian Government, Productivity Commission, 'Digital Disruption: What do governments need to do?' Productivity Commission Research Paper, Jun. 2016, https://www.pc.gov.au/research/completed/digital-disruption/digital-disruption-research-paper.pdf.

349   Harry Armstrong, Chris Gorst & Jen Rae, 'Renewing Regulation: 'anticipatory regulation' in an age of disruption', Innovation policy report, Nesta, 6 Mar. 2019, https://www.nesta.org. uk/report/renewing-regulation-anticipatory-regulation-in-an-age-of-disruption/

350   William D. Eggers, David Schatsky & Peter Viechnicki, 'AI-augmented government: Using cognitive technologies to redesign public sector work', Deloitte University Press, Deloitte Center for Government Insights, n.d., https://www2.deloitte.com/content/dam/insights/us/ articles/3832_AI-augmented-government/DUP_AI-augmented-government.pdf.

351   Anoush Darabi, 'New Zealand explores machine-readable laws to transform government: Legislation-as-code might be the key to kick-starting digital reform', 11 May 2018, Apolitical, https://apolitical.co/solution_article/new-zealand-explores-machine-readable-laws-to-transform-government/.

352   Jamie Susskind, *Future Politics: Living Together in a World Transformed by Tech*, Oxford University Press, 2018.

353   Susskind, *Future Politics*.

354   Julia Bossman, 'Top 9 ethical issues in artificial intelligence', 21 Oct. 2016, World Economic Forum, https://www.weforum.org/agenda/2016/10/top-10-ethical-issues-in-artificial-intelligence/.

355   Parliament of Victoria news release, 'Artificial Intelligence Group Launched', 7 Mar. 2018, https://www.parliament.vic.gov.au/about/news/4029-artificial-intelligence-group-launched.

356   UK Government House of Lords, Select Committee on Artificial Intelligence, Report of the Session 2017–19 'AI in the UK: ready, willing and able?', 16 Apr. 2018, https://publications. parliament.uk/pa/ld201719/ldselect/ldai/100/100.pdf.

357   Tim Dutton, 'Tim Dutton: An overview of National AI Strategies, Medium, 28 Jun. 2018, https://medium.com/search?q=Tim%20Dutton%20An%20overview%20of%20National%20 AI%20Strategies.

358   Anoush Darabi, 'New York writes new rules to rein in government by algorithm: Opaque software is already being used to sentence criminals and rate schoolteachers', *Apolitical*, 25 Apr. 2018, https://apolitical.co/solution_article/new-york-writes-new-rules-to-rein-in-government-by-algorithm/.

359   Geoff Mulgan, 'A machine intelligence commission for the UK: how to grow informed public trust and maximise the positive impact of smart machines', a paper based on a talk given to the Alan Turing Institute, London, Feb. 2016, Nesta, https://media.nesta.org.uk/ documents/a_machine_intelligence_commission_for_the_uk_-_geoff_mulgan.pdf.

360   Brad Smith & Harry Shum, 'The Future Computed: Artificial Intelligence and its role in society', 17 Jan. 2018, Microsoft Blog, Microsoft, https://blogs.microsoft.com/blog/2018/01/17/ future-computed-artificial-intelligence-role-society/.

361   Stuart Kennedy, 'Gov't ponders AI's governing ethics', 24 Apr. 2018, InnovationAus.com, https://www.innovationaus.com/2018/04/Govt-ponders-AIs-governing-ethics?utm_ medium=email&utm_campaign=Newsletter%20209%2024%20April%202018&utm_ content=Newsletter%20209%2024%20April%202018+CID_31b2101ffd7abb4d821c887a9935d09 3&utm_source=Email%20marketing%20software&utm_term=Govt%20ponders%20AIs%20 governing%20ethics.

362   'The new oil data is the world's most valuable resource', 6 May 2017, *The Australian*, http:// www.theaustralian.com.au/news/inquirer/the-new-oil-data-is-the-worlds-most-valuable-resource/news-story/f386217a9c63ac5ee6e1473413e90bda.

363   Data Management and Research, British Columbia Government, https://www2.gov.bc.ca/ gov/content/data/about-data-management.

364   Dr. Ian Oppermann, Data Analytics Centre, NSW Government, 'Digital Transformation in Practice', 20 Nov. 2017, https://www.nera.org.au/Attachment?Action=Download&Attachment_id=169.

365 'Open Source Myths', Opensource.com, Red Hat, https://opensource.com/open-source-myths.

366 'GrAIt expectations', Special Report, AI in Business, *The Economist*, 31 Mar. 2018, https://shop.economist.com/products/special-report-on-ai-in-business.

367 Eggers, Schatsky & Viechnicki, 'AI-augmented government'.

368 'Battle of the brains: Google leads in the race to dominate artificial intelligence: Tech giants are investing billions in a transformative technology', *The Economist*, 7 Dec. 2017, https://www.economist.com/news/business/21732125-tech-giants-are-investing-billions-transformative-technology-google-leads-race.

369 Interview with the Hon. Ed Husic MP, Shadow Minister for the Digital Economy (2016–2019), Sep. 2018, by Martin Stewart-Weeks and Simon Cooper.

370 Christianna Reedy explains: 'The singularity is that point in time when all the advances in technology, particularly in artificial intelligence (AI), will lead to machines that are smarter than human beings'. See Christianna Reedy, 'Kurzweil Claims That the Singularity Will Happen by 2045: Get ready for humanity 2.0', Future Society, Futurism, 5 Oct. 2017, https://futurism.com/kurzweil-claims-that-the-singularity-will-happen-by-2045/.

371 Kelly, *The Inevitable*.

372 'China Has a New Three-Year Plan to Rule AI', Artificial Intelligence, MIT Technology Review Panel, 15 Dec. 2017, https://www.technologyreview.com/the-download/609791/china-has-a-new-three-year-plan-to-rule-ai/. See also Hannah Miller, André Petheram & Emma Martin-ho-Truswell, 'Want to get serious about artificial intelligence? You'll need an AI strategy', 23 Jan. 2018, Oxford Insights, https://www.oxfordinsights.com/insights/2018/1/23/aistrategies. See also UK Parliament, House of Lords Select Committee, Artificial Intelligence Commit-tee – publications, http://www.parliament.uk/business/committees/committees-a-z/lords-select/ai-committee/publications/. See also Dom Galeon, 'An Inside Look at the First Nation With a State Minister for Artificial Intelligence: "The future is not going to be a black or white"', 11 Dec. 2017, Artificial Intelligence, Futurism, https://futurism.com/uae-minister-artificial-intelligence/.

373 Max Opray, 'Artificial intelligence has arrived, but Australian businesses are not ready for it', *The Guardian*, International Edition, 24 Jan. 2017, https://www.theguardian.com/sustain-able-business/2017/jan/25/artificial-intelligence-has-arrived-but-australian-businesses-dont-know-how-to-use-it.

374 James Riley, 'On AI and strategic policy', InnovationAus.com Public Policy and Business Innovation, 5 Apr. 2018, http://www.innovationaus.com/2018/04/On-AI-and-strategic-policy.

375 Tim Dutton, 'An overview of National AI Strategies' (provides a link to every analysis of every available national strategy), Medium, 28 Jun. 2018, https://medium.com/politics-ai/an-overview-of-national-ai-strategies-2a70ec6edfd.

376 Opray, 'Artificial intelligence has arrived but Australian businesses are not ready for it'.

377 'Transforming Cybersecurity: New approaches for an evolving threat landscape', Deloitte U.S. Center for Financial Services, https://www2.deloitte.com/us/en/pages/financial-servic-es/articles/dcfs-transforming-cybersecurity.html.

378 Tim O'Reilly, 'Government as a Platform' in *Open Government: Collaboration, Transparency, and Participation in Practice*, Daniel Lathrop & Laurel Ruma (eds), O'Reilly Media, 2010, reprinted in *innovations/Data Democracy*, vol. 6, no. 1, 2010, https://www.mitpressjournals.org/doi/pdf/10.1162/INOV_a_00056. See also http://radar.oreilly.com/2009/07/itunes-app-store-incubation-period-increases.html.

379 O'Reilly, 'Government as a Platform'.

380 O'Reilly, 'Government as a Platform'.

381 Government of Estonia (2018), Interoperability services: X-Road', e-Estonia, https://e-esto-nia.com/solutions/interoperability-services/x-road/.

382 Kattel & Mergel, 'Is Estonia the Silicon Valley of digital government?'.

383 O'Reilly, 'Government as a Platform'.

384 John Mant, 'Place Management As a Core Role in Government', *The Journal of Place Management and Development*, vol. 1, no. 1, Mar. 2008, available at http://www.johnmant.com/gallery/pdf_125464085040680.pdf.

385 Tom Loosemore, 'Making government as a platform real', Public Digital, 25 Sep. 2018, https://public.digital/2018/09/25/making-government-as-a-platform-real/.

386 Government of Australia, Digital Transformation Agency, Digital Service Platforms Strategy, 2018, https://www.dta.gov.au/our-projects/digital-service-platforms-strategy.

387 Eaves & McGuire, 'Proposing A Maturity Model for Digital Services'.

388 Pia Waugh, (2018) 'Exploring change and how to scale it', Pipka, 22 Apr. 2018, http://pipka.org/2018/04/22/exploring-change-and-how-to-scale-it/ .

389 Waugh, 'Exploring change and how to scale it'.

390 NSW Government, 'What is public digital infrastructure?' in Public Digital Infrastructure, https://www.digital.nsw.gov.au/digital-transformation/public-digital-infrastructure.

391 NSW Government, 7 March 2019, 'What is public digital infrastructure?'

392 Mike Bracken, 'Remixing my Christmas interview on Radio 4' (Today Programme), Public Digital, 14 Jan. 2019, https://public.digital/2019/01/14/remixing-my-christmas-interview-on-radio-4/.

393 Janet Hughes, quoted in Hillary Hartley's chapter, 'On Openness', in Alex Benay, *Government Digital: The Quest to Regain Public Trust*.

394 Interview, May 2018, with Leisa Reichelt, former head of user research for the DTA and the GDS, and now Head of User Insights, Atlassian, with Martin Stewart-Weeks and Simon Cooper.

395 Hill, 'Strategic design for public purpose'.

396 One of the authors (Simon) had to go through a variety of clearance levels to publish blogs such as this one on how he worked with policy teams in the development of a new digital service in the UK; see https://hodigital.blog.gov.uk/author/simon-cooper/.

397 NSW Government, Blog: Read all about the initiatives, strategies and projects within the digital space across the whole of NSW Government, https://www.digital.nsw.gov.au/blog.

398 Greg Wells, 'How might we … Change the Digital Funding Game?', 27 Feb. 2019, NSW Government, https://www.digital.nsw.gov.au/article/how-might-we-change-digital-funding-game.

399 Janet Hughes, 'What a digital organisation looks like', 6 Jun. 2017, Doteveryone, Medium, https://medium.com/doteveryone/what-a-digital-organisation-looks-like-82426a210ab8.

400 Eggers, *Delivering on Digital*.

401 Interview with Paul Shetler, July 2018.

402 'Coined by former Australian Foreign Minister Gareth Evans in a press interview shortly after his retirement, Relevance Deprivation Syndrome is the term given to a feeling of impotence often experienced by someone who has left or been evicted from a position of power and influence and sometimes, their efforts to remain or seem relevant to ongoing events.' See Relevance Deprivation Syndrome, Everything2 Media, https://www.everything2.com/title/Relevance+Deprivation+Syndrome.

403 Martin Stewart-Weeks, 'More on the Talent Question: Skills for the Future Public Service', Government and Public Sector Reform, Innovation/Social Innovation, Blog, 5 Nov. 2017, https://publicpurpose.com.au/talent-question-skills-future-public-service/.

404 Interview, March 2019, with the Hon. Victor Dominello, MP, Minister for Customer Service, NSW Government.

405   The Hon. Victor Dominello, MP, '...my "Ten Digital Commandments"', 7 Jun. 2018, Twitter, https://twitter.com/VictorDominello/status/1004884200128835585

406   Gerald C. Kane, Doug Palmer, Anh Nguyen Phillips, David Kiron & Natasha Buckley, 'Achieving Digital Maturity: Adapting Your Company to a Changing World', MIT Sloan Management Review, Findings from the 2017 Digital Business Report, Global Executive Study and Research Project, in collaboration with Deloitte Digital, https://sloanreview.mit.edu/projects/achieving-digital-maturity/.

407   Hughes, 'What a digital organisation looks like'.

408   'The rise (and fall?) of the CDO', Deloitte Digital, https://www2.deloitte.com/content/dam/Deloitte/uk/Documents/consultancy/deloitte-uk-the-rise-and-fal-of-cdo.pdf.

409   Terry Moran, 'Digital transformation in the fourth age of public administration', 26 Oct. 2016, The Mandarin, https://www.themandarin.com.au/71901-terry-moran-digital-transformation-public-sector-readiness/.

410   See @ClareMoriarty, Twitter.com.

411   'Core Skills for Public Sector Innovation: A beta model of skills to promote and enable innovation in public sector organisations', OECD, Apr. 2017, https://www.oecd.org/media/oecdorg/satellitesites/opsi/contents/files/OECD_OPSI-core_skills_for_public_sector_innovation-201704.pdf. See also 'When Tomorrow Comes: The future of local public services', Policy Commission report, University of Birmingham, in collaboration with Demos, https://www.birmingham.ac.uk/Documents/research/SocialSciences/FullPolicyCommissionreport1507.pdf. See also 'Civil service capabilities plan: How civil servants' skills will be improved in the 4 priority areas of digital, commercial, project management and leadership of change', UK Government, 18 Apr. 2013, https://www.gov.uk/government/publications/civil-service-capabilities-plan. See also Lisbeth Schorr, Common Purpose: Strengthening Families and Neighbourhoods to Rebuild America, Anchor Publishing, 1998. See also Chris Eccles, 'The Way Forward: Making it happen...', Director General's Speech, 2012 IIPAA Conference, http://cdn.nsw.ipaa.org.au/docs/IPAA-NSW-2012-State-Conference/Chris%20Eccles%20Speech%20IPAA%20Conference%202012%20-%20The%20Way%20Forward.pdf.

412   'Digital delivery of government services' report, Commonwealth of Australia, Senate Finance and Public Administration Committee, Parliament of Australia, 27 Jun. 2018, https://www.aph.gov.au/Parliamentary_Business/Committees/Senate/Finance_and_Public_Administration/digitaldelivery/Report/c01.

413   Andrew Greenway, Ben Terrett, Mike Bracken & Tom Loosemore, Digital transformation at scale: why the strategy is delivery, London Publishing Partnership, 2018.

414   E.g., Jordan Hatch, currently Deputy Chief Digital Officer at the Australian Trade and Investment Commission (Austrade).

415   PGPA Act 2013, Government of Australia, Resource Management, 25 Oct. 2017, https://www.finance.gov.au/resource-management/pgpa-act/.

416   Natasha Nasir, 'Smart Nation and Digital Government Group Office to be formed under PMO', 20 Mar. 2017, Singapore Government, https://www.gov.sg/news/content/smart-nation-and-digital-government-group-office-to-be-formed-under-pmo.

417   'Creating a more digital Danish public sector', Agency for Digitisation, Ministry of Finance, Government of Denmark (2019), https://en.digst.dk/.

418   Department of the Prime Minister and Cabinet, 'Terms of Reference – Australian Digital Council', 1 Apr. 2019, Government of Australia, https://www.pmc.gov.au/resource-centre/public-data/terms-reference-australian-digital-council

419   Ry Crozier, 'Woolworths boosts $100m WooliesX investment', 22 Nov. 2018, iTnews, https://www.itnews.com.au/news/woolworths-boosts-100m-wooliesx-investment-515870; see also Ry Crozier, 'WooliesX predicts ways to connect with customers' 15 Apr. 2019, iTnews, https://www.itnews.com.au/news/wooliesx-predicts-ways-to-connect-with-customers-52368.

420 'NHSX: new joint organisation for digital, data and technology', 19 Feb. 2019, Department of Health and Social Care, UK Government, https://www.gov.uk/government/news/nhsx-new-joint-organisation-for-digital-data-and-technology.

421 'NHSX', UK Government.

Chapter 5

422 OECD Legal Instruments, Declaration on Public Sector Innovation, Section D iii, adopted 22 May 2019, https://legalinstruments.oecd.org/en/instruments/OECD-LEGAL-0450.

423 The Cluetrain Manifesto, Cluetrain, http://cluetrain.com/. See also Wikipedia, 'The Cluetrain Manifesto', https://en.wikipedia.org/wiki/The_Cluetrain_Manifesto. See also Wikipedia, 'Ninety-five Theses', https://en.wikipedia.org/wiki/Ninety-five_Theses.

424 The Cluetrain Manifesto.

425 The Cluetrain Manifesto.

426 David Weinberger & Doc Searls, 'New Clues', Cluetrain 8 Jan. 2015, http://newclues.cluetrain.com/.

427 Shoshona Zuboff, *The Age of Surveillance Capitalism: The Fight for a Human Future at the New Frontier of Power*, Public Affairs, Jan. 2019, as discussed in Sam Biddle's '"A Fundamentally Illegitimate Choice": Shoshana Zuboff on the Age of Surveillance Capitalism', *The Intercept_*, 2 Feb. 2019, https://theintercept.com/2019/02/02/shoshana-zuboff-age-of-surveillance-capitalism/.

428 Weinberger & Searls, 'New Clues'.

429 Thomas Madsen-Mygdal et al., 'The Copenhagen Catalog: 150 principles for a new direction in tech', 2017, https://www.copenhagencatalog.org/pdfs/thecopenhagencatalog-ebook.pdf.

430 The Copenhagen Letter, 2017, https://copenhagenletter.org/.

431 New Zealand Government, Digital government, International partnerships, 'The Digital 9', Digital.govt.nz, https://www.digital.govt.nz/digital-government/international-partnerships/the-digital-9/. See also New Zealand Government, 'D7 Charter', https://www.digital.govt.nz/dmsdocument/28-d7-charter/html.